International Politics

States, Power and Conflict since 1945

G. R. Berridge

Professor of International Politics and Director of the Centre for the Study of Diplomacy, University of Leicester

Third Edition

PRENTICE HALL
HARVESTER WHEATSHEAF

NEW YORK   LONDON   TORONTO   SYDNEY   TOKYO
SINGAPORE   MADRID   MEXICO CITY   MUNICH

First published 1997 by
Harvester Wheatsheaf
Campus 400, Maylands Avenue
Hemel Hempstead
Hertfordshire, HP2 7EZ
A division of
Simon & Schuster International Group

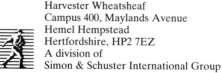

Typeset in 10/12pt Times
by Dorwyn Ltd, Rowlands Castle, Hants.

Printed and bound in Great Britain by Redwood Books,
Trowbridge, Wiltshire.

Library of Congress Cataloging-in-Publication Data

Berridge, Geoff.
    International politics : states, power, and conflict since 1945 /
G.R. Berridge. — 3rd ed.
      p. cm.
    Includes bibliographical references and index.
    ISBN 0-13-230327-2 (pbk.)
    1. World politics—1945–   I. Title.
D840.B44   1996
327'.0904—dc20   96-14149
                                        CIP

British Library Cataloguing in Publication Data

A catalogue record for this book is available from
the British Library

ISBN 0–13–230327–2 (pbk)

---

1 2 3 4 5   01 00 99 98 97

For my wife, Sheila

Contents

Preface to the first edition

This is a textbook of international relations. It is designed to introduce students to the subject, provide a critical sweep over the conventional wisdom, and point them in the direction of further reading. It has grown out of the undergraduate survey course for which I have been responsible at the University of Leicester since 1978. Because the book was conceived as a textbook, its style and tone are self-consciously didactic and references have been kept to a minimum. The greater part of it is obviously derivative and, despite the lack of footnoted references (except for quotations), the sources on which I have drawn especially heavily – for example, Inis Claude's *Power and International Relations* at the beginning of Chapter 9 [now 10] – will be clear to those who may be concerned about this. I freely acknowledge my debt to all those scholars on whose works I have leaned, and which are listed under the heading of 'Further Reading' at the end of each chapter.

I am grateful to the following friends and colleagues who have helped me by criticising sections of the manuscript: Chris Andrew, Brian Bond, Edward Elgar, Alan James, Maurice Keens-Soper, Peter Savigear, Jack Spence, Robin White, and John Young. Derek Heater has done me the great service of reading all of it. None of them bears responsibility for any remaining errors of fact or weaknesses of interpretation.

I should add that the section dealing with the great powers in Chapter 1 will be appearing in elaborated form – and co-authored with John Young – in *Political Studies* at the end of 1987.

I am grateful to the Macmillan Press for permission to reproduce in Chapter 10 [now 11], in slightly amended form, material from my contribution to *Diplomacy at the UN* (Macmillan: London, 1985), which, together with A. Jennings, I also edited.

G. R. B., Leicester, 1986

Preface to the second edition

In response to critics, as well as events, I have made some substantial changes to this edition, though the structure of the book remains the same. Apart from attempting to improve the style, stiffen the arguments, reorganise some chapters (especially Chapter 5) to make the arguments more clear, and generally bring the work up to date (at mid-1991), I have included a considerable amount of new material. The most important addition is an entirely new chapter on the world economy, but there is also a little more both on alternative approaches and international political theory in the Introduction, a lot more on nationalism in Chapter 4, a new section on foreign aid in Chapter 7 (restyled 'Economic Statecraft'), a new section on the problem of intervention in Chapter 9, and much more on unconventional diplomacy in Chapter 11. I have also added a short conclusion, and there are more entries in the 'Notes on Reference Books' (Appendix 1). Finally, I have added many illustrations (tables and maps) and boxes. As well as providing more detail, I hope that these improve the presentation of the book.

In an attempt to keep the price of the book as low as possible, I have tried to make some space for this new material by pruning back the old wherever possible. In particular, I have cut back the chapter on secret intelligence and removed the section on sanctions against South Africa, in any case now somewhat redundant. I have also shaved the footnotes, not least by giving only abbreviated references to works which are given in full under 'Further Reading'.

For valuable criticism of sections of the manuscript of this edition, I would like to express my warmest thanks to Ian Harris and Roger Tooze. My greatest debts, however, are to Margaret Doxey, for detailed advice on the second edition, and to Cedric Rawlings, who cheerfully assumed the burden of going through the whole manuscript with the greatest care. I would like to extend similar thanks to Rashid Siddiqui and Sue Smith of Leicester University Library for expert assistance in researching materials. For general guidance and encouragement, I would like equally to thank Clare Grist and Bridget Johnson of Harvester Wheatsheaf. I hardly need say that none of these individuals bears the slightest responsibility for the book's remaining deficiencies.

G. R. B., Leicester, September 1991

International Politics

Previous books by the author:

Economic Power in Anglo-South African Diplomacy: Simonstown, Sharpeville and after (Macmillan: London, 1981)

Diplomacy at the UN, (ed.) with A. Jennings (Macmillan: London and St Martin's Press: New York, 1985)

The Politics of the South Africa Run: European shipping and Pretoria (The Clarendon Press: Oxford, 1987)

Return to the UN: UN diplomacy in regional conflicts (Macmillan: London, 1991)

South Africa, the Colonial Powers and 'African Defence': The rise and fall of the white entente, 1948–60 (Macmillan: London, 1992)

Introduction to International Politics, with Derek Heater (Harvester Wheatsheaf: Hemel Hempstead, 1993)

Talking to the Enemy: How states without 'diplomatic relations' communicate (Macmillan: London, 1994)

Diplomacy: Theory and practice (Prentice Hall/Harvester Wheatsheaf: Hemel Hempstead, 1995)

Preface to the third edition

In this edition I have concentrated on updating the text and illustrations. Having said this, the word 'race' is retained in Chapter 4 despite the fact that for good reasons it is now out of vogue; I have done this because it was the common currency of the literature of the 1960s and 1970s which I attack. I am grateful to Nicola James for her assistance, and to Richard Aldrich, Alan James, Jan Melissen, Gary Rawnsley, Rashid Siddiqui and Sue Smith for their advice. I also wish to thank Ruth Pratten, my new editor at Prentice Hall, for technical assistance, and especially the two anonymous readers, who picked up some embarrassing errors and lapses.

G. R. B., Leicester, October 1995

Acknowledgements

The author and publisher wish to thank the following who have kindly given permissions for the use of copyright material:

Penguin Books Ltd for the maps from *Strategic Atlas: World Geopolitics* by Gerald Chaliand and Jean-Pierre Rageau, Penguin Books, 1986.

The *Financial Times* for the map of Bosnia–Hercegovina on the eve of 'Deliberate Force', *Financial Times*, 31 August 1995.

The Independent Newspaper Publishing plc for the illustration on American television propaganda and Cuba originally published in the *Independent on Sunday*, 11 February 1990.

CIRCA Research and Reference Information Ltd for the illustration on the 100-hour battle for Kuwait originally published in *Keesing's Record of World Events*, February 1991.

While every effort has been made where appropriate to trace the copyright holders of illustrative material included in this volume, the author and publishers would be pleased to hear from any interested parties.

Introduction

International politics (or international relations) is a subject rather than a discipline, a field rather than a form of knowledge. In contrast to a discipline, which is distinguished chiefly by the application of a singular form of testing to its propositions,[1] a subject derives its identity simply from its focus of analysis (or 'subject matter'); its tests of truth are borrowed from the disciplines. In this regard international relations is no different from, say, geography or sociology. What, then, is the subject matter of international politics and which of the disciplines – science, history, mathematics, religion, philosophy, literature and the fine arts, and ethics – has it pillaged most successfully for its methods?

At its broadest, the *subject matter* includes the following: first, the activities of classes of states (great powers, capitalist states, liberal democracies, and so on) and other international 'actors', such as multinational corporations; secondly, the means which they commonly employ in pursuit of their policies, such as propaganda; and thirdly, the rules and institutions of the 'states-system' within which these states and other agents more or less willingly operate.

As for the *disciplines* which have been most fruitfully employed in the study of these subjects, something should first of all be said about science, for it is commonly argued that international relations is a subdivision of the discipline of science – that it is, indeed, a 'social science'. Of course, the questions raised by this contention are the same as those raised by a claim for scientific status made on behalf of any social science. They are also major issues in the philosophy of knowledge and I do not, as a result, propose to dwell on them.[2] Suffice it to say here that while it may *in principle* be possible to apply the characteristic proposition-test of science, namely controlled experimentation, to the subject matter of international relations the practical obstacles to it remain enormous. Not surprisingly, therefore, the enterprise has so far proved entirely barren. Some maintain that religion, in which the test of truth is consistency with divine revelation, plays an important role in our understanding of some subjects in international relations.[3] However, one's judgement of this claim will naturally be coloured by one's attitude to religious thought in general as well as to the beliefs of particular churches. Certainly, some theologians, such as Reinhold Niebuhr, and scholars of strong religious conviction, such as Herbert Butterfield and Martin Wight, have achieved prominence in the field, though whether this is because or in spite of their religious thought is another matter. No doubt, too, there are extreme behaviouralists who believe that there is still a slot in international relations for mathematics. And war and diplomacy can probably be judged by aesthetic standards, though who would want to do this and to what end is hard to say.

There is little doubt, however, that the most important contributions in international relations have been made by history (the explanation of events by reference to evidence of thought and action contained principally in documents and artefacts), ethics (the elaboration of the distinction between right and wrong) and philosophy (the clarification of concepts and the unpicking of incoherent arguments).

In practice, the application of these three disciplines to the subjects studied in international politics has produced a two-fold division of the field which corresponds to that found in the study of politics within the state ('government' and 'political theory'). On the one hand are *historical studies* of the foreign policies of classes of states ('comparative foreign policy analysis'), transnational actors, instruments of policy, and states-systems; this corresponds roughly to the study of 'government'. On the other there is *international political theory*, which is not to be confused with 'predictive theory',[4] though it may contain it; this corresponds to 'political theory'. International political theory employs history, philosophy, and ethics, though it is from its moral component that its real flavour derives. For this reason it is sometimes referred to as 'normative' theory.

Though international political theory was little more than a footnote to political theory until the twentieth century (Machiavelli, Rousseau, Locke, Kant, Hobbes, and others had something to say on it but not a great deal), it is now at least a lengthy appendix if not a large chapter in its own right. This is in great part because world politics is now much more dangerous and it is imperative to devote attention to the sources of conflict between states and especially to ways of preventing their disputes from escalating into war; and also because the states-system has developed features which have perennially attracted the attention of political theorists, such as law, rights, and power dressed in claims to authority – most notably in the case of the UN Security Council. Moreover, most contemporary students of international politics, even if principally historians rather than theorists and even if preoccupied with a special problem which might invite a special label (see Box I.1), are located more or less squarely in one or other of the three great – and, of course, contending – traditions of international political theory. According to Wight, the first of these is the Hobbesian or, latterly, 'realist' tradition, which holds that international politics is an unmediated clash of sovereign wills in which, therefore, morality is irrelevant and power decisive. The second is the Grotian tradition. This admits the international anarchy but insists on its compatibility with effective international rules. The third is the Kantian tradition, which declares that individuals rather than states are the ultimate reality and that single-minded attention should be directed to securing, whether by peaceful means or holy war, the victory of the elect over the damned.[5] Nevertheless, however great the temptation,

Box I.1   Contending approaches to the field

It is the convention in the present study of international relations to identify three main approaches. Between these approaches the rivalry is great.*

Realism
This school was born in reaction against the progressivist 'idealism' of the Anglo-American scholarship prominent after the First World War, which was believed to hold an excessively generous view of human nature and place unwarranted faith in the League of Nations. According to realism, the main actors remained states and – human nature 'in reality' being irredeemably selfish – their main preoccupation would continue to be the aggrandisement of their power. Only the 'balance of power' (see Chapter 10), rather than shallow-rooted international institutions, could prevent a condition of permanent war or the eclipse of the system of states altogether. At one time it was common to find this view described as the 'billiard-ball' model. E. H. Carr's *The Twenty Years' Crisis, 1919–1939* (1939) gave realism its name. After the war, Hans J. Morgenthau made another famous statement in this tradition: *Politics Among Nations* (1948), which subsequently ran to five editions.

'Neo-realism' has accommodated international economics to this line of thought, and also lays greater emphasis on the explanatory power of the character of an international system, especially on the number of major powers. Here Kenneth Waltz's *Theory of International Politics* (1979) is the main work.

Pluralism
Exasperated by the blinkered emphasis of realists on the state (the residual potency of which they nevertheless do not deny), pluralists dwell on the enormous number of other agencies actively operating across national frontiers. Sinn Fein, the UN, and the computer software company, Microsoft, each illustrate a different kind of such agency, account of whose activities must be taken by a comprehensive explanation of world politics. For pluralists (known alternatively as 'globalists'), world politics represents more the density and sheer intricacy of the cobweb than the simple cannoning of a small number of balls on a billiard table. In this cobweb of 'interdependent' relations the state is just another fly (there is no spider). Names with which to conjure here are Keohane, Nye and Morse.

Structuralism
This school is much influenced by Marxist thought and reflects especially the preoccupation of scholars in the 'underdeveloped' world. Structuralists see the world as dominated by the institutions of international capitalism (enter the spider), which employ their power both directly and

via home states in order to exploit the poorer countries. It is sometimes said that, rather than seeing the world as a billiard table or cobweb, they see it instead as a 'layer-cake'. Students of this school speak the language of 'centre-periphery' relations and generally direct their thoughts to means of overturning the various regimes which have an interest in perpetuating this state of affairs. Exemplary contributions to this tradition have been made by Johan Galtung and Immanuel Wallerstein.

*An excellent treatment of these approaches, as well as of those on the fringe, is provided by M. Hollis and S. Smith in *Explaining and Understanding International Relations* (1990), ch. 2.

the student should perhaps not rush straight into this part of the field. International political theorists tend to assume a historical knowledge and clear conceptual grasp of the various kinds of player on the international scene, the instruments which they employ and the institutions – if not the rules – through which they usually work. An introduction to international relations should thus start here. Though it will not duck normative questions as they crop up, an introductory grounding in these essential preliminaries is principally what this textbook will try to achieve. As a glance at the contents list will confirm, it is also an unapologetic defence of the tradition which takes its name from the great seventeenth-century Dutch jurist, Hugo Grotius.

Notes

1. P. H. Hirst, 'Liberal education and the nature of knowledge', in R. F. Dearden, P. H. Hirst and R. S. Peters (eds), *Education and Reason: Part 3 of education and the development of reason* (Routledge & Kegan Paul: London and Boston, 1975), p. 16.
2. For discussion of these questions, see E. Nagel, *The Structure of Science* (Routledge & Kegan Paul: London, 1968); C. Reynolds, *Theory and Explanation in International Politics* (Martin Robertson: London, 1973).
3. For example, N. A. Sims (ed.), *Explorations in Ethics and International Relations* (Croom Helm: London, 1981).
4. By this I mean 'a form of explanation that explains by subsuming a class of phenomena within the framework of a set of propositions organized in a deductive argument, from which are deduced general statements that assert that, given specific conditions and relationships, specific conclusions will follow', C. Reynolds, *Modes of Imperialism* (Martin Robertson: Oxford, 1981), p. 110.
5. Wight, *International Theory*.

Further reading

Banks, M., 'The evolution of International Relations theory', in M. Banks (ed.), *Conflict in World Society* (Wheatsheaf: Brighton, 1984).

Bull, H., 'Martin Wight and the theory of international relations', *British Journal of International Studies*, vol. 2, no. 2, 1976.

Butterfield, H. and M. Wight (eds), *Diplomatic Investigations* (Allen & Unwin: London, 1966).

Carr, E. H., *The Twenty Years' Crisis, 1919–1939: An introduction to the study of international relations*, 2nd edn (Macmillan: London, 1946).

Cutler, A. C., 'The "Grotian tradition" in international relations', *Review of International Studies*, vol. 17, no. 1, 1991.

Donelan, M., *Elements of International Political Theory* (The Clarendon Press: Oxford, 1990).

Galtung, J. 'A structural theory of imperialism', *Journal of Peace Research*, vol. 8, no. 1, 1971.

Groom, A. J. R. and M. Light (eds), *Contemporary International Relations: A guide to theory* (Pinter: London and New York, 1994).

Hill, C. and P. Beshoff (eds), *Two Worlds of International Relations: Academics, practitioners and the trade in ideas* (Routledge: London and New York, 1994).

Hoffman, M., 'Critical theory and the inter-paradigm debate', *Millenium*, vol. 16, no. 2, 1987.

Hoffmann, S., 'An American social science: international relations', *Daedalus*, vol. 106, no. 3, 1977.

Hollis, M. and S. Smith, *Explaining and Understanding International Relations* (The Clarendon Press: Oxford, 1990), ch. 2.

Holsti, K. J., *The Dividing Discipline: Hegemony and diversity in international relations* (Unwin Hyman: London, 1985).

Keohane, R. (ed.), *Neorealism and its Critics* (Columbia University Press: New York, 1986).

Keohane, R. and J. Nye, *Power and Interdependence: World politics in transition* (Little, Brown: Boston, 1977).

Little, R., 'International relations and the methodological turn', *Political Studies*, vol. 39, no. 3, 1991.

Morgenthau, H. J., *Politics Among Nations: The struggle for power and peace*, 5th edn (Knopf: New York, 1973).

Morse, E., *Modernization and the Transformation of International Relations* (Free Press: New York, 1976).

Smith, S. (ed.), *International Relations: British and American perspectives* (Blackwell: Oxford and New York, 1985).

Vasquez, J. A. (ed.), *Classics of International Relations*, 2nd edn (Prentice Hall: Englewood Cliffs, NJ, 1990).

Wallerstein, I., *The Capitalist World Economy* (Cambridge University Press: Cambridge, 1979).

Waltz, K., *Theory of International Politics* (Addison-Wesley: Reading, MA, 1979).

Wight, M., *International Theory: The three traditions* (Leicester University Press: Leicester, 1991).

PART A
States and their setting

1

Great powers and lesser states

The 'sovereign state', which is a set of institutions possessing the authority (however derived) to make and enforce laws over a geographically bounded territory, remains the main agent in world politics. Supporters of the view that 'transnational actors' such as the multinational corporation have latterly increased in importance concede this much. Moreover, the Islamic fundamentalists who are now such a force in the Middle East and North Africa, though rejecting the legitimacy of the state in favour of the 'community of believers' (like the Bolsheviks before them), still find the practical focus of this community located in a state – Iran. However, despite the legal equality entailed in the doctrine of sovereignty, states vary enormously and it is important to understand the differences between them because these affect expectations of proper behaviour as well as assumptions concerning likely behaviour. Though various features of states are held by scholars to be significant for the kinds of foreign policy they pursue (capitalist or socialist, liberal/democratic or authoritarian, homogeneous or heterogeneous, developed or underdeveloped, insular or continental, merchant or warrior, and so on), the characteristic which has traditionally been held the most important by scholars and statesmen alike has been *the extent of a state's power*. Hence the principal distinctions are between great powers (or 'superpowers'), middle powers, small states and micro-states.

Though it is true that the number of infantrymen possessed by a state was a clear and widely accepted index of power in nineteenth-century Europe, the general ranking of states has never been entirely a simple arithmetical exercise. This is partly because only war itself can prove the real power of a state and partly because the rank assigned to states by other states is rarely the product of impartial assessment. Furthermore, several developments since the Second World War have rendered these perennial problems even more difficult.

To begin with, the strategic implications of nuclear weapons have been the subject of great controversy. On the one hand it is argued that, since nuclear weapons are the most potent of all weapons, a 'lesser power' which acquires an invulnerable nuclear strike force is thereby elevated into the ranks of the 'great powers' – a position certainly favoured by the British and the French. But against this it is maintained that nuclear weapons are 'unusable' and therefore altogether fail to provide any increment of power to their possessors, perhaps even hobbling their activity through fear of provoking nuclear war. Second, there is the disjunction which has developed between military and economic power, with Japan and Germany enjoying more and more of the latter but constrained by postwar agreements to humble – and specifically non-nuclear – ambitions in regard to the former. This has led some to conclude that one can no longer talk of 'great powers' but only of 'great military powers' and 'great economic powers'.

In view of all of these difficulties, it is not surprising that considerable confusion surrounds the subject of the ranking of states in the contemporary world, and this is no more evident than in the case of the great powers themselves. Until the end of the 1980s there was a consensus that the United States and the Soviet Union were unambiguous members of this class, though others added China, Japan and reunited Germany. What, then, is a 'great power'? What, that is to say, are the attributes and typical relationships of those powers which have historically been regarded by *statesmen* as 'great powers'? This is an important issue because the class of great powers has asserted a special right to interest itself in all matters which threaten international tranquillity and is widely expected to assume special international obligations as well. It was, of course, as 'great powers' that the United States, Britain, the Soviet Union, France and China alone obtained permanent seats on the Security Council of the United Nations.

Great powers

Though as an index of great power standing this has to be treated with caution, the principal mechanism whereby recognition as a great power is conferred is inclusion in the inner councils of important diplomatic conferences, characteristically those convened to draw up peace treaties following the termination of major conflicts. The first occasion on which this happened in European diplomacy was at the Congress of Vienna in 1814–15, when Austria, Russia, Prussia, Britain and France were thereby identified as the current great powers. These five maintained their position for a century, though by 1914 Austria (by then Austria-Hungary) had declined enormously, while the standing of Prussia (by then Germany) had been further consolidated. The main change by the eve of the First World War was that three new powers were now in contention. One of these, Italy, had claimed great power status since its unification in 1860, though others were doubtful about this (especially after its defeat by Ethiopian tribesmen at Adowa in 1896) and if it was included in great power councils it was largely as a 'courtesy'.[1] The other two claimants lay outside Europe: the United States, which had become a formidable industrial power after resolving its internal conflicts with the civil war in 1865; and Japan, which had been modernising rapidly and in the war of 1904–5 had created a considerable upset by inflicting defeat on Russia.

The First World War inevitably affected membership of the great power club, though less perhaps than one would have expected. Austria-Hungary literally disintegrated in 1918, while America's position as a great power was confirmed. The positions of Italy (though it was included among the Allied 'Big Four' at Versailles and obtained a permanent seat on the Council of the new League of Nations) and Japan (though it also obtained a permanent seat on the Council) remained somewhat uncertain. Nevertheless, by the 1930s they had managed to secure their status as great powers. Germany and Russia, of course, were both temporarily eclipsed by defeat in 1918 but they, too, had re-emerged by 1939 to be included among the 'great'. There is wide agreement that on the eve of the Second World War the great powers were Germany, Russia, Britain, France, Italy, Japan and the United States.

By 1945 only the 'Big Three' – the United States, the Soviet Union and Britain – were left. However, by virtue of their inclusion as permanent members of the new UN Security Council, the rank of 'great power' was also granted to France at the insistence of the British and to China under pressure from the Americans. (Britain was anxious to restore French power after the war in order that France might assist with the occupation of Germany and act as a counter to the Soviet Union after the withdrawal of American forces from Europe, while the United States wanted to strengthen the position of China so that it would have a useful lieutenant in the Pacific.) Not long after the war Britain, too, was acknowledged by everyone – except, of course, the British – to have lost its standing as a great power or, as such a power was now known, a 'superpower'. Until the end of 1991, when the USSR ceased to exist as both a political and juridical entity, America and the Soviet Union remained the only unambiguous great powers, or superpowers. What, then, have all those powers had in common which, in their various periods, have entitled them to be placed *unambiguously* in the category of 'great power'?

It is sometimes said that a great power must possess general or universal interests; by contrast, smaller powers have only local or, at most, regional interests. But, apart from being vague on the important question of interests which are general *relative to what* (the essentially Europe-centred states-system prior to the Second World War or the global states-system thereafter), this view confuses a cause of membership of the great power club with one of its probable consequences. In fact, at least three powers have lacked general interests during periods in which they were nevertheless regarded as unambiguous great powers: Prussia until 1860, with interests which were largely confined to Germany; Japan, with interests which were always chiefly restricted to the Far East; and Austria-Hungary, whose interests were arguably limited to south-eastern Europe by 1914. If a great power can be regarded as indubitably a great power in the absence of general interests, it remains true, of course, that great powers usually do have such interests. The point is, though, that great powers usually have general interests because they are already great powers.

A second criterion which must also be rejected is suggested by Hedley Bull: 'Great powers', he says, 'are powers recognized by others to have, and conceived by their own leaders and people to have, certain special rights and duties.'[2] In addition to having the right to a pre-eminent role in the great conferences which affect the fate of the world, great powers must assume a special responsibility for enforcing international law, preserving the balance of power, and so on. In this light, as Bull states, powers such as Napoleon's France and Hitler's Germany 'are not *properly speaking* great powers'.[3] The mistake here is obvious: a question of concept is being confused with a question of normative theory. It may well be true that great powers *should* behave in this way but in a consideration of the characteristics possessed by the historical great powers this is neither here nor there. A criterion which excludes revisionist great powers such as Napoleon's France, Hitler's Germany and Mussolini's Italy, as well as irresponsible status quo great powers such as post-World War I America (which refused to join the League of Nations), is not one which can be taken seriously.

If the possession of general interests and 'responsible' behaviour is unnecessary, what does a state require to be a great power? The historical record suggests that the answer is *a reputation for existing or latent military strength which may be equalled but not significantly surpassed by that of any other power.* A great power, in other words, is a power of the first rank in terms of reputation for military strength or military 'prestige'.[4] The reputations of great powers are generally built on the successful employment of military strength in a major war, but it is also possible for great power standing to be achieved by a state which manifestly develops an abundance of those characteristics in which military strength is conventionally assumed to repose – as did America before 1914 and as would a hypothetical power which achieved a large nuclear arsenal in the contemporary era. As great powers may become great powers merely by the demonstration of potential power, so great powers which have triumphed in great wars must be able to demonstrate a continuation of great potential if they are to retain their standing, while great powers which suffer defeats may either shrug them off or quickly regain their standing provided they can still demonstrate such potential. This is why Britain ceased to be a great power during the late 1940s despite victory in the Second World War, and why the United States remained a great power despite its humiliation in Vietnam in the late 1960s and early 1970s.

Which are the great powers today? In fact, according to the notion of a great power advanced above, only the United States obviously qualifies for the designation at the moment, and it is the only state to have done so throughout the post-1945 period. Here, the demonstrable quality and size of nuclear forces has been vital. Of course, until at least 1991 the Soviet Union was also a clear member of this class. However, at the end of that year this state ceased to exist and was replaced by the loosely bonded and politically fractious Commonwealth of Independent States (CIS). While the Russian Federation, the political fulcrum of the new CIS, effectively inherited control of most of the former Soviet Union's nuclear forces, together with its permanent seat on the Security Council, there is now nevertheless a question mark over Russia's claim to superpower status. Its active armed forces are less than half the size of those of the former Soviet Union; half of these are conscripts; and professionals and conscripts alike are transparently in a condition of serious demoralisation. The alliance system presided over by Moscow – the Warsaw Pact – has also been dissolved (see Box 10.2) and its former members are courting the North Atlantic Treaty Organization (NATO). The Russian economy has been moved from an ordinary ward into intensive care and is being kept alive in part by a drip-feed of aid supplied by the West. Internal strains within the Russian Federation itself are now severe, and Russia's worldwide interests are but a pale reflection of those of the former Soviet Union. Not surprisingly, the performance of Russia's armed forces in battle, most recently in Chechnya, has been lamentable. If this is the description of a superpower, it is the description of a superpower in apparently terminal decline.

As for the United States itself, while certainly suffering from the 'imperial overstretch', military inefficiency and acute economic problems described in Paul Kennedy's blockbusting *The Rise and Fall of the Great Powers*, it is inconceivable that a country of its size, natural resources and passionate commitment to entrepreneurialism could – barring catastrophe – cease to be a great power. (The great reduction in the Russian threat has also reduced the burden of the nuclear arms race on its economy.) That America will not remain 'number one' forever is, of course, more likely, though its sweeping victory over Iraq in early 1991 seems certain to have set back that time.

What of future great powers? China, despite the huge size of its territory, population and armed forces (see Table 1.1) and the nuclear status which it achieved in 1964, still lacks a reputation for first-class military strength. Damaging to China's reputation are its relative poverty, its poor showing in conventional military engagements with the Vietnamese in 1979, the inferior equipment of its armed forces, its lack of a 'blue water' navy and the evidence of internal disunity provided by events culminating in the massacre of students in Tienanmen Square in 1989. It must be admitted, however, that the new spirit of economic competition fostered in China by Deng Xiaoping, together with the steps now being taken to modernise the doctrines, organisation and equipment of the armed forces (including intercontinental ballistic missiles), suggest that China has the potential to become a superpower in the foreseeable future. Jonathan Pollack has said that already 'China must be judged as a candidate superpower in its own right'.[5]

The other potential superpowers are, of course, the great economic powers, Germany and Japan, though the difficulty (moral, ideological and diplomatic) of throwing off postwar constraints on the building of nuclear weapons, among other reasons, seems likely to delay their elevation for some years yet. The extreme military diffidence of Germany and Japan was demonstrated once more during the Gulf crisis in 1990–1, though there were hints of change on that occasion and there have been a few more since. A particular

Table 1.1   The population and the total active armed forces of the major powers, 1990 and 1994 (millions)

	Population		Total active armed forces	
	1990	1994	1990	1994
Russia[1]	288.6	148.9	4.00	1.70
China	1,115.6	1,201.2	3.00	2.90
United States	248.9	259.6	2.10	1.60
Germany[2]	60.4	81.0	0.47	0.37
France	56.4	57.8	0.46	0.41
United Kingdom	56.6	58.1	0.31	0.25
Japan	123.6	125.3	0.25	0.24

Notes
1. Soviet Union in 1990.
2. West Germany in 1990.

Source
Adapted from *The Military Balance 1990–1991* and *The Military Balance 1994–1995* (IISS: London, 1990, 1994).

complication for Germany is the distraction of the problems of integrating East Germany into the Federal Republic. The European Union (see Box 2.5), of which Germany is, of course, a member, is sometimes described as a future superpower as well, though its acquisition of that status will first require it to become a state. That, too, is not an imminent development.

The 'Permanent Five'

The great powers in most eras have usually insisted that they have special rights in the affairs of the world and acknowledged, albeit with somewhat less enthusiasm, that they have special obligations as well. The special rights are mainly a disproportionate say in the deliberations of peace conferences and international organisations; the special obligations are mainly a disproportionate contribution to the stability of the world economy and the maintenance of the balance of power. (These questions are discussed at greater length in Chapters 2 and 10, respectively.) Special rights are justified mainly by the worldwide interests that great powers usually possess and the bigger contributions which they make to world order. Special obligations are justified by their power. In a world of nuclear-armed sovereign states, there is no alternative to such a regime.

The special role of the great powers in the field of 'international peace and security' is legally confirmed in the Charter of the United Nations, which was drawn up in the later stages of the Second World War. This vests 'primary responsibility' for the maintenance of international peace and security in the Security Council, and provides that only the United States, the Soviet Union (now Russia), France, Britain and China shall be *permanent* members. Until recently known as the 'Big Five', it is now more common to see them referred to as the 'Permanent Five' or 'P5', which is certainly more accurate. These powers are not only permanent members of the Security Council but the only ones with the coveted right of veto over questions of substance which come before it. (This means that the UN cannot bless a defensive action by its members – a 'collective security' operation – against any aggressive move by one of the P5, since the latter would obviously veto any resolution put before the Council for this purpose. The UN's security role is thus largely confined to what are now referred to as 'regional conflicts'.) The UN Charter also provides for a Military Staff Committee, composed of the chiefs of staff of the permanent members, which has the task of supervising military action by the United Nations. It should be noted, however, that the P5 cannot legally impose their own solutions, since Security Council action requires nine affirmative votes, while for propaganda reasons (as the Gulf crisis of 1990–1 demonstrated) there is a premium attached to unanimity. Nevertheless, the legal role of the P5 clearly remains central.

For the greater part of the postwar period, of course, the cold war ensured that great power collaboration, either inside or outside the Security Council, was of limited significance. Since the middle of the 1980s, however, great improvements in relations between Moscow and Washington, together with some improvements in relations between Moscow and Beijing as well, have dramatically transformed this position. The P5, now regularly caucusing in secret, are playing an increasingly important role in arm-twisting belligerents in regional conflicts to the negotiating table. This was particularly notable in the events leading up to the ceasefire in the Iran–Iraq war (accepted by Iraq in July 1987, and by Iran a year later), in the subsequent attempt to bring peace to Cambodia and, above all, in the operation to drive Saddam Hussein's forces out of Kuwait.

The considerable increase in the importance of the Security Council has naturally revived the issue of membership, for the possession of permanent seats reflects the distribution of power in 1944 rather than in the mid-1990s. In consequence, the legitimacy of Security Council decisions is significantly weaker than it ought to be, as the present Secretary-General has frequently pointed out. The trick, of course, is to make the Council more representative without compromising its ability to make good decisions quickly. Box 1.1 summarises the main options for reform and notes some of the advantages and disadvantages of each. However, with the present arrangement working better than it has ever worked (assisted by informal collaboration with the Germans and the Japanese), the British and the French disinclined to surrender their own seats, and the absence of any consensus on reform, there seems no immediate prospect of radical change.

Middle powers

The status of middle power was implicitly recognised by the creation of semi-permanent seats on the Council of the League of Nations in 1926, though the

---

Box 1.1   New permanent members for the UN Security Council?

The Security Council currently has fifteen members, five of whom are both permanent and veto-wielding:

The 'Permanent 5'
$\begin{cases} \text{France} \\ \text{China} \\ \text{Russia} \\ \text{United Kingdom} \\ \text{United States} \end{cases}$

The ten non-permanent members (sometimes referred to ironically as the 'Temporary 10') are elected by the General Assembly for two-year terms in the light of the need for 'equitable geographical distribution'.

A working group of the General Assembly is currently considering proposals for reform of the composition of the Security Council. Among the dozens which have been put forward, most are a variation on one or other of the following ideas:

1. Change the Permanent 5 (P5), for example by replacing France and Britain with the European Union (EU) and adding Japan. This keeps the core decision-making unit small and efficient, and makes the Council more representative by diluting the 'whiteness' of the P5 and bringing in Germany via the EU. However, this proposal is probably too optimistic about the ability of the EU to produce a coordinated foreign policy (though it would intensify the pressure for this) and does not really address Third World aspirations.
2. Leave the P5 untouched but add a small category of permanent but non-veto-wielding states. Common suggestions for inclusion here are Germany, Japan, India, Indonesia, Brazil, Mexico, Nigeria, Egypt and South Africa. This adds more legitimacy to the Security Council without compromising its efficiency, and circumvents opposition from Britain and France. However, it fails to address the demands of Germany and Japan for equal status with the existing P5.
3. Expand the P5 and the Temporary 10, for example by adding Brazil, Germany and Japan to the existing P5 (thereafter P8) and increasing the Temporary 10 to, say, 15 in order to reflect the great increase in the number of UN member states in recent years, now standing at 185. This is the least bruising option to implement, but it maximises legitimacy at the expense of efficiency.

---

subsequent efforts of Canada and Australia (sometimes described as 'the original middle powers') to have priority given to this class of states in elections to non-permanent seats on the UN Security Council did not prove successful. Nevertheless, it remained obvious that there were enormous differences within the ranks of the lesser states and it is now common for scholars, at any rate, to identify small states and micro-states[6] as well as middle (or medium) powers.

In his *Power Politics*, Wight suggests that a middle power 'is a power with such military strength, resources and strategic position that in peacetime the great powers bid for its support, and in wartime, while it has no hope of winning a war against a great power, it can hope to inflict costs on a great power out of proportion to what the great power can hope to gain by attacking it'.[7] This definition certainly gives us a feel for the weight of middle powers, though it perhaps overlooks other characteristics of states which might lead great powers to bid for their support in peacetime, for example ideological reputation and quality of leadership.

Defining the upper limit of middle powers is easy enough: middle powers are powers which are regarded as the next most powerful to the great powers themselves. Sometimes referred to as 'powers of the second rank', they typically have large populations, considerable national wealth and substantial armed forces – possibly with a small nuclear component. They have interests in many parts of the world and are therefore widely represented by their diplomatic services. It is also usual for them to possess influence within one or more regions of the world which is comparable to the influence that the great powers have in the world as a whole (though the extent of this will tend to be dictated by their own relationship with the great powers, and by the extent to which the great powers take an interest in their region – as Mexico has found in Central America). This is why it is often appropriate to refer to them as 'regional great powers'. France (with its nuclear *force de frappe* and substantial influence in West Africa, the Indian Ocean and the South Pacific as well as Europe), Britain (with its own nuclear force, European position, and lingering influence within the Commonwealth), China, Japan and Germany are widely regarded as the most obvious middle powers. In the only full-length study of such powers, Holbraad describes them as the 'upper middle powers'.[8] Indeed, these powers are often linked with the great powers and referred to collectively as 'the big powers' or 'the major powers'.

The difficulty with middle powers, of course, is defining their lower limit. Relying heavily on the crude indices of gross national product (GNP) at market prices in 1975 and population in the same year, Holbraad identifies eighteen of them, adding the following to the five already mentioned: Canada, Italy, Brazil, Spain, Poland, India, Australia, Mexico, Iran, Argentina, South Africa, Indonesia and Nigeria. This list will no doubt continue to produce endless arguments! Notable *exclusions* are Israel (the ability of which to siphon off American wealth Holbraad quite overlooks, and the military reputation of which he unwisely minimises); Egypt (which greatly improved its own military reputation after the Yom Kippur War in 1973 and obviously remains a 'great power' in the world's most explosive region); Syria (which has great influence in the Middle East under Assad's leadership, has flexed its muscles to some effect in the Lebanon and has been treated very gingerly by the United States); Turkey (with its large army, continuing importance to NATO and expansion into northern Cyprus); Iraq (which fought the Iranian revolutionary regime to a stalemate, then took on the American-led coalition after invading Kuwait, and still survives with the same regime despite sanctions); Pakistan (which also has a strong and frequently exercised army); Vietnam (following its successful encounters with the Americans and the Chinese, widely regarded as the 'Prussia' of South-East Asia, though profound economic weakness and withdrawal from Cambodia dented its image); and possibly South Korea, Taiwan, and Malaysia as well.

The Canadian statesman, Lester Pearson, advanced the interesting notion that middle powers were always likely to exhibit an unusual degree of international civic virtue. This is because they have *insufficient* power to generate the worldwide interests and client regimes which make great powers partisan for one side or another in regional conflicts; and, he might have added, insufficient power to foster arrogance. At the same time, however, middle powers have *sufficient* power to enable them to make a worthwhile contribution to the implementation of policies determined by global consensus through such bodies as the UN. Relatively detached from world quarrels and yet by no means puny, middle powers are more likely than any other class of state to have a 'sense of responsibility'.[9] There is some force to this argument, which no doubt helps to explain the strong representation of middle powers in UN peacekeeping operations, their significant contribution to international mediation, and their unusually strong preference for promoting policy by means of diplomacy – especially multilateral diplomacy – rather than by the instruments of conflict described in Part B of this book. Middle powers, unable to be active on every item on the international agenda, tend to find appropriate 'niches' and specialise in these, as in the case of the Netherlands and development assistance. On the other hand, it is not difficult to find middle powers in the list recorded earlier which have exhibited spectacular irresponsibility, not least, perhaps, because ideological zeal can lead the weakest state to take a strong public stand on a conflict even on the other side of the world.

Micro-states

After the middle powers come the 'small states' such as Morocco and Paraguay (which as such have generated no debate), and after them the 'micro-states'. The distinction between these two is usually made on the basis of population, both the United Nations and the Commonwealth now defining a micro-state as a state with under one million inhabitants.

'Statelets' of this sort multiplied after the dismantling of the greater part of the European colonial empires in the decades following the Second World War, and first attracted attention with the admission to the United Nations of the Republic of Maldives (population 143,000) and the Gambia (population 592,000) in 1965. According to the population definition, thirty-nine of the 184 states members of the United Nations in February 1994 were micro-states.

Micro-states have always been a cause of concern to some of the bigger states, though this is partly misplaced. First, micro-states were said to be too small to be economically 'viable'. Secondly, it was said that granting them full rights in the United Nations and its related agencies devalued the significance of votes within these organisations and eroded the support of their main financial backers, such as the United States. And, thirdly, it was alleged that their physical and economic vulnerability, together with the fact that they are often strategically located in the Caribbean, Indian (see Figure 1.1) and Pacific Oceans, was a standing invitation to outside intervention and thus a threat to 'global security'. The last allegation came to dominate discussion of micro-states following the American invasion of Grenada (population 110,000) in October 1983 against the background of rising tension in the 'new cold war'.

It is patronising to tell micro-states that they are not economically 'viable'. As Faber says, this implies 'some additional *external* judgement about what is an acceptable standard of living'.[8] Whether or not these states are

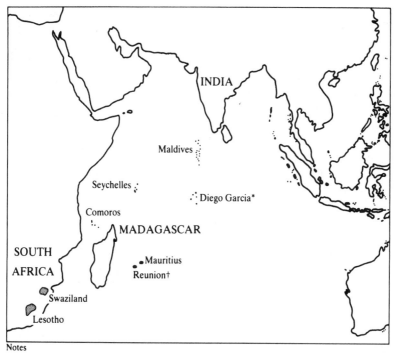

Notes
* British (leased to the United States for base facilities).
† French.

Figure 1.1 The micro-states of the Indian Ocean

economically 'viable', therefore, is something their own inhabitants might be left to decide for themselves. Moreover, by Western standards, it is by no means self-evident that – following the international economic disorders of the 1970s and 1980s – micro-states are any less economically 'viable' than many small states and middle powers. Indeed, while there certainly are poverty-stricken micro-states (such as the Cape Verde Islands, population 350,000), right now a citizen of Russia itself might well prefer life in the Republic of the Seychelles (population 70,000, per capita income in 1991 in excess of US$5,000) to life at home. So would I.

The claim that the vulnerability of micro-states might generate international conflict is also extremely dubious, and this is not only because of the now much-reduced scale of the competition between Russia and the United States. It might be accepted that micro-state vulnerability invites military intervention by bigger powers – there is sufficient evidence of this; it is quite another thing to agree that intervention by a bigger power is likely to provoke *counter-intervention* by a second. But it is precisely this which is needed to sustain the argument that micro-states are a threat to world stability. And the simple fact is that, as far as I am aware, no military intervention in a micro-state has provoked a military counter-intervention.

What are the reasons for this? One is that many micro-states find themselves located squarely within the 'sphere of influence' of a great power, 'regional great power', or alliance of bigger powers. This means that interventions are most likely to come from these quarters and are unlikely to be opposed by extraregional powers partly because their intraregional capabilities will be weaker and partly because they will be breaking the unwritten rules of the game (see Chapter 9). (For the same reasons, of course, extraregional powers are also highly unlikely to make initial interventions.) Since the Caribbean island state of Grenada was firmly within the United States sphere of influence, it was never remotely conceivable that the American intervention in 1983 would provoke a counter-intervention by the Soviet Union. Equally remote was the possibility of counter-intervention after the South African intervention in Lesotho in January 1986, or following the Indian intervention in the Maldives (see Figure 1.1) in November 1988.

Even when a micro-state finds itself in an international free-fire zone – which has certainly been the case for some in the Indian Ocean – the stakes are usually insufficiently high for an intervention by one power to provoke a counter-intervention by another. This was the hard lesson learned by the Seychelles leader, Jimmy Mancham, as he cast around fruitlessly for friends following the Tanzanian-supported coup which overthrew his government in June 1977. (Kuwait, where the stakes were far higher, did not have the same problem.) It is not unknown, moreover, for regional rivals to intervene *jointly* in the affairs of an unstable micro-state, prompted by the belief that the risks of competitive interventions far outweigh any likely gains. This happened in December 1989 when the French and the South Africans collaborated to get rid of the mercenaries who were controlling the government of the Comoro Islands (Figure 1.1). In sum, the charge that *Small is Dangerous* (see 'Further Reading') is a considerable exaggeration.

Having said all this, there seems little doubt that many micro-states would benefit from assistance in strengthening their defences, as well as from an increase in the peacekeeping capacity of the United Nations, and that regional cooperation between neighbouring micro-states should be assisted if this is the desire of their citizens. The Caribbean Community (Caricom), which closely resembles the former European Community (now European Union) and was created in the early 1970s, now embraces ten Caribbean micro-states and one tiny British island colony (two others have associate status), as well as Jamaica and Trinidad and Tobago.

As to whether or not micro-states should have full rights in the United Nations and other international organisations, here the grounds for concern were more justified. It is simply unrealistic to expect major powers, which are required to accept disproportionate obligations to international organisations (including financial ones), to endure indefinitely a position in which they can be regularly outvoted by coalitions boosted by large numbers of micro-states. In the event, however, the mood of the UN General Assembly became far less anti-Western in the second half of the 1980s and the UN's budgetary system was reformed to give more effective influence to the bigger powers. Hence the steam has substantially been taken out of the criticism of micro-states on grounds of their equal representation in international organisations.

Notes

1. Wight, *Power Politics*, p. 46.
2. *The Anarchical Society*, p. 202.
3. *ibid.*, emphasis added.
4. For a view that the hierarchy of power will in future be based less on military reputation and more on such things as technology, education and economic growth, see Nye, 'Soft power'.
5. Quoted in Kennedy, *The Rise and Fall of the Great Powers*, p. 590.
6. The term 'small state' sometimes subsumes micro-states.
7. *Power Politics*, p. 65.
8. *Middle Powers in International Politics*, p. 91.
9. *Memoirs 1948–1957*, vol. 2, p. 121.

Further reading

General

Clark, I., *The Hierarchy of States: Reform and resistance in the international order* (Cambridge University Press: Cambridge and New York, 1989).

Gilpin, R., *War and Change in World Politics* (Cambridge University Press: Cambridge and New York, 1981), pp. 27–34.

Hall, J. A. and G. J. Ikenberry, *The State* (Open University Press: Milton Keynes, 1989).

Nye, J. S., Jr, 'Soft power', *Foreign Policy*, no. 80, Autumn 1990.

Singer, J. D. and M. Small, 'The composition and status ordering of the international system: 1815–1940', *World Politics*, vol. 18, January 1966.

Small, M. and J. D. Singer, 'The diplomatic importance of states, 1816–1970', *World Politics*, vol. 25, July 1973.

Spiegel, S., *Dominance and Diversity: The international hierarchy* (Little, Brown: Boston, 1972).

Great powers

Adomeit, H., 'Russia as a "great power" in world affairs: images and reality', *International Affairs*, vol. 71, no. 1, January 1995.

Berridge, G. R. and J. W. Young, 'What is a "great power"?', *Political Studies*, vol. 36, June 1988, pp. 224–34.

Bull, H., *The Anarchical Society* (Macmillan: London, and Columbia University Press: New York, 1977), ch. 9.

Carr, E. H., *The Twenty Years' Crisis, 1919–1939: An introduction to the study of international relations*, 2nd edn (Macmillan: London, 1946), ch. 8.

Ciechanski, J., 'Restructuring of the UN Security Council', *International Peacekeeping*, vol. 1, no. 4, Winter 1994, pp. 413–39.

Commission on Global Governance, *Our Global Neighbourhood: The report of the Commission on Global Governance* (Oxford University Press: Oxford, 1995).

Huntington, S. P., 'The US – decline or renewal?', *Foreign Affairs*, vol. 67, no. 2, 1988/9.

Jönsson, C., *Superpowers* (Pinter: London, and St Martin's Press: New York, 1984).

Kennedy, P., *The Rise and Fall of the Great Powers: Economic change and military conflict from 1500 to 2000* (Random House: New York, 1987, and Fontana: London, 1989).

Krauthammer, C., 'The unipolar moment', *Foreign Affairs*, vol. 70, no. 1, 1991, pp. 23–33.

Maull, H. W., 'Germany and Japan: the new civilian powers', *Foreign Affairs*, vol. 69, no. 5, 1990, pp. 91–106.

Nau, H., *The Myth of American Decline: Leading the World Economy into the 1990s* (Oxford University Press: New York, 1990).

Nye, J. S., Jr, 'Soft power', *Foreign Policy*, no. 80, Autumn 1990.

Nye, J. S., Jr, *Bound to Lead: The changing nature of American power* (Basic Books: New York, 1990).

Nye, J. S., Jr, 'What new world order?', *Foreign Affairs*, vol. 71, no. 2, 1992, pp. 83–96.

Roberts, A. and B. Kingsbury (eds), *United Nations, Divided World: The UN's roles in international relations*, 2nd edn (Clarendon Press: Oxford, 1993), pp. 39–43, 441–4.

Rostow, W. W., 'Beware of historians bearing false analogies' [review of Kennedy's *The Rise and Fall of the Great Powers*], *Foreign Affairs*, vol. 66, no. 4, 1988.

Segal, G., *Defending China* (Oxford University Press: Oxford, 1985).

Waltz, K. N., *Theory of International Politics* (Addison-Wesley: Reading, MA, 1979).

Wight, M., *Power Politics*, H. Bull and C. Holbraad (eds) (Leicester University Press: Leicester, and Holmes and Meier: New York, 1978).

Wolf, J. B., *The Emergence of the Great Powers, 1685–1715* (Harper & Row: New York, 1951).

Wortzel, L. M., 'China pursues great-power status', *Orbis*, vol. 38, no. 2, Spring 1994.

Zhan, J., 'China goes to the blue waters', *Journal of Strategic Studies*, vol. 17, no. 3, September 1994.

Middle powers

Cooper, A. F., *Niche Diplomacy: Middle powers after the cold war* (Macmillan: London, forthcoming).

Cooper, A. F., R. A. Higgot and K. R. Nossal, *Relocating Middle Powers: Australia and Canada in a changing world order* (University of British Columbia Press: Vancouver, 1993).

Cox, R., 'Middlepowermanship, Japan, and the future world order', *International Journal*, vol. 44, no. 4, 1989.

Holbraad, C., *Middle Powers in International Politics* (Macmillan: London, and St Martin's Press: New York, 1984).

Holmes, J. W., *The Shaping of Peace: Canada and the search for world order, 1943–1957*, vol. 1 (University of Toronto Press: Toronto, 1979).

Mares, D. R., 'Mexico's foreign policy as a middle power: the Nicaragua connection, 1884–1986', *Latin American Research Review*, vol. 23, no. 3, 1988.

Mares, D. R., 'Middle powers under regional hegemony: to challenge or acquiesce in hegemonic enforcement', *International Studies Quarterly*, vol. 32, 1988.

Neumann, I., *Regional Great Powers in International Politics* (St Martin's Press: New York, 1992).

Pearson, L., *Memoirs 1948–1957, The International Years, Volume 2* (Gollancz: London, 1974), ch. 6; first published in Canada under the title *Mike Volume II* (University of Toronto Press, 1973).

Wight, M., *Power Politics*, ch. 5.

Micro-states

Alford, J., 'Security dilemmas of small states', *The Round Table*, vol. 292, 1984.

Bowman, L. W., *Mauritius: Democracy and development in the Indian Ocean* (Westview Press: Boulder, CO, 1991).

Clarke, C. and T. Payne (eds), *Politics, Security and Development in Small States* (Allen & Unwin: London, 1987).

Dorrance, J. C., 'The Pacific islands and US security interests', *Asian Survey*, July 1989.

Faber, M., 'Island microstates: problems of viability ', *The Round Table*, vol. 292, 1984.

Handel, M., *Weak States in the International System* (Cass: London, 1981).

Harden, S. (ed.), *Small is Dangerous: Micro states in a macro world* (Pinter: London, 1985).

Payne, A., P. Sutton and T. Thorndike, *Grenada: Revolution and invasion* (Croom Helm: London, 1984).

Reid, G. L., *The Impact of Very Small Size on the International Behaviour of Micro-states* (Sage: Beverly Hills, CA, 1974).

2

The world economy

The years since the Second World War have witnessed a huge growth both in the absolute levels of international trade and financial transactions and in their levels relative to world output. In 1956 total world exports were worth $98.8 billion; by 1994 they had risen to $4,269 billion, by no means most of which was explained by currency inflation. Indeed, in the last seven years (1988–94) the *volume* of world trade has continued to grow, at an average rate of 5.6 per cent each year. Moreover, while exports were equivalent to 9.4 per cent of world gross domestic product in 1956, by 1980 they had reached 17.7 per cent; and, despite the slump of the early 1980s, they remained at 14.9 per cent in 1987.

What these figures signify, therefore, is that the principles and institutions of the world economy are of unprecedented importance to the economies of the member states of the international system. What is more, some states do less well than others out of this system (to put it mildly) and there is widespread resentment over the behaviour of the system's managers. This combination of circumstances means that international economic transactions, and the world economic regime through which they are mediated, are of enormous *political* significance: they contribute to the conflicts between states out of which international politics arises (see Chapter 4); and they are fashioned into instruments of foreign policy (see Chapter 7).

The world economic regime was naturally shaped by the most powerful states of the nineteenth and early twentieth centuries, that is to say, the advanced capitalist states of Western Europe (especially Britain) and the United States. They had the power and they constructed the system to suit their interests, although, of course, except in the period between the two world wars, they also provided international 'public goods' (see Box 2.1). During the final stages of the Second World War, this regime was overhauled during negotiations between America and Britain which culminated in a wider conference at Bretton Woods in the United States. The 'Bretton Woods system' made provisions for both international monetary and international trade arrangements. The new monetary regime lasted until the beginning of the 1970s and has even now by no means entirely disappeared. As for the international trade regime created at Bretton Woods, this has recently been re-created more in the manner of the original plan.

The Soviet-dominated economic system of the Communist world, which was organised from 1949 through the Council of Mutual Economic Assistance (CMEA or COMECON), had only limited dealings with the Bretton Woods system. This was partly because of the 'cold war' between the Soviet Union

---

Box 2.1   International public goods

'A public good', according to the leading American international economist, Charles P. Kindleberger, 'is one the consumption of which by an
individual, household or firm does not reduce the amount available for
other potential consumers. The classic example of the pure public good
is the lighthouse.' Unfortunately, because the consumer's benefit from
the good is virtually automatic, he or she has no incentive to incur costs
in order to ensure its continued availability – 'free riders' abound. Because of lack of support, together with resentment at the free riders,
public goods are 'typically underproduced'. If this is true of states, where
governments have varying degrees of commitment to the production
and maintenance of public goods, it is even more true of the states-
system, which is devoid of government.

Kindleberger believes that among the most important *international*
public goods (apart from peace) are open markets in glut, a steady if not
counter-cyclical flow of capital, a mechanism for providing the international money needed to finance trade, foreign exchange stability, and a
degree of coordination of domestic monetary policies.

See Kindleberger, *The International Economic Order*, especially chs 9
and 14.

---

and the NATO powers, and partly because of the inherent difficulties of
promoting economic transactions between free market and state-controlled
economies. There was some increase in trade between the two systems in the
late 1950s and a significant spurt during the *détente* of the early 1970s. (This
was prompted mainly by political motives on the American side and economic
ones on the part of the Soviet Union.) With the collapse of Communism in the
Soviet Union and Eastern Europe during the second half of the 1980s, the
CMEA has disappeared and those of its members who have not already done
so are negotiating the terms of their entry into the Western-dominated global
markets. For this and other reasons, not the least of which are 'globalisation'
and the continuing fall in the costs of computing power and telecommunications, these markets, though climbing out of the recession of the early 1990s,
are still themselves experiencing a period of deep uncertainty.

The international monetary system

The Bretton Woods regime

The United Nations Monetary and Financial Conference which was held at
Bretton Woods in July 1944, while the war was still raging in Europe and the

Pacific, was attended by forty-four states. Among these, important roles were played by Canada and Britain. The significance of the British contribution was a result not only of Britain's traditional leading role in the world economy and its intimate relationship to America in the war, but also of the fact that its delegation was led by John Maynard Keynes. Keynes was the greatest economist of his era and the economists on the American delegation, including its leader, Harry White, had been brought up on his writings. Nevertheless, Bretton Woods was dominated by the United States. (The Soviet Union attended the conference and eventually contributed to its success but it could not compete with the power of the United States and in any case only understood 'what was afoot with the utmost difficulty'.)[1]

The war had left America sharing the status of military superpower with the Soviet Union but in the economic sphere it was quite without rivals. With much of continental Europe devastated and Britain virtually bankrupted by the war effort, only the United States economy had the productive capacity to provide the machines and materials required for postwar reconstruction. As a result, the dollars needed to purchase these goods were in huge demand, and the dollar – because of what it alone could buy – was thought by central bankers to be 'as good as gold' (the traditional token of value and backing for national currencies). It was also technically 'as good as gold' since the American government promised that dollars would be converted into gold on demand at the rate of $35 per troy ounce. Moreover, since at this time the US Federal Reserve held 70 per cent of the world's reserves of monetary gold (see Figure 2.1), few were inclined to regard this promise as a hollow one. As well as being the world's provisioner, the United States had also become the world's banker.

Two important things happened at Bretton Woods. First, a new world monetary regime was endorsed; this was based on plans originally produced by the Americans and modified in the course of negotiations between Keynes and White, which had started ten months earlier. Second, agreements on the varying financial rights and obligations of the forty-four states under this new regime were negotiated. What was this new regime? What principles governed the distribution of rights and obligations within it?

The main concern at Bretton Woods regarding monetary policy, with the Great Depression of the 1930s still a fresh memory, was to create a system which would avoid wild fluctuations in exchange rates (the price of one currency in terms of another). This, it was thought, would make the earnings from exports and the costs of imports *more predictable* and, by thus making business planning which hinged on international transactions less of a gamble, encourage trade. This, in turn, would make everyone better off in the long run as each state was able to specialise in what it could produce most efficiently (the principle of 'comparative advantage'). Thus, it was agreed that each state would maintain 'par values' for its currency expressed in terms of the US dollar, which was in turn tied in value to gold. If a state should run into

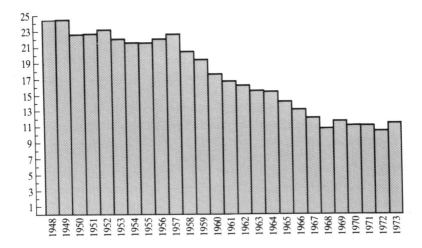

Figure 2.1   US gold reserves, 1948–73 ($bn, at end of period) (Source: *International Financial Statistics, Supplement 1972* and *Supplement 1973*, IMF: Washington, DC)

balance-of-payments difficulties (earning less from exports than it was paying out for imports), it would be expected to correct them by internal measures such as improving productive efficiency; it could no longer make its exports more price-attractive to foreigners and imports more costly to its citizens by allowing its currency to float downwards on foreign exchange markets. Since the adjustment could be painful (and thus politically fatal to the system), it was also agreed at Bretton Woods that, while a state in payments difficulties was taking the necessary corrective measures at home, it would be helped by 'loans' from a new institution, the International Monetary Fund (IMF), which was formally established in December 1945. (Though usually described as 'loans', technically these were sales of useful currencies in exchange for the useless national currency of the applicant; some sales were more or less conditional.)

Since the IMF was not to be allowed to print its own money to lend to countries in payments difficulties (which had in fact been the more radical preference of Keynes), the new regime also contained rules governing contributions to the Fund, as well as ones prescribing 'drawing rights'. Members would contribute according to the level of their national income, the value and character of their trade, and the level of their holdings of gold and convertible currencies, largely dollars. (Until 1973 these contributions had to be paid partly in gold.) As for drawing rights, the general principle was that the more hard currency members sought to purchase from the Fund the tougher became the conditions attached.

The Bretton Woods conference also recognised, however, that a system of rigidly fixed exchange rates – even with IMF loans – made no market sense and was thus unlikely to endure. Such a system would have been fatally tied to the balance of international economic forces which obtained at the time of their fixing, which was hardly likely to remain unchanged. No amount of 'internal adjustment' – if only for reason of domestic political resistance – would be likely to compensate for this. In addition to allowing a measure of short-term flexibility by permitting currencies to fluctuate within 1 per cent either side of par, therefore, Bretton Woods also made provision for the development of a 'fundamental disequilibrium' in a member country's payments position. In this vaguely defined event, a member would normally be allowed to 'devalue' or, contrariwise, 'revalue' its currency.[2]

The IMF was provided with a board of governors, on which each member government would be represented, usually by its minister of finance or central bank governor. This would meet annually. Below this would be executive directors, who, as their title implies, would be responsible for the day-to-day work of the Fund. *Voting power in the IMF would reflect the size of a member's contribution to its stabilisation fund.* Here, the key provisions were that the five members with the largest quotas each automatically appointed an executive director, whose voting power was proportionate to the quota of the government represented. The remaining directors (in 1994, nineteen) would be elected by groups of countries on the basis of their own quotas. As with the appointed directors, the elected ones would wield voting power equivalent to the quotas of the members they represented. This realistic arrangement confirmed the huge influence of the advanced capitalist states within the IMF, and of the United States in particular. As can be seen from Table 2.1, in 1946 the appointed director of the United States alone controlled 33.52 per cent of the votes. With the votes of Britain and France added, this mounted to 55.25 per cent. Even in 1994 America retained not far short of one-fifth of all votes, while each remaining member of the 'Big Five' was a friend. (In the same year Russia had an elected director with 2.91 per cent of the total votes.) Inevitably, the executive directors were set up in Washington, and have remained there ever since. However, no doubt in order to assuage the national pride of the allies of the United States, the managing director, who is selected by the executive directors for a five-year term, has never been an American. Instead, he or she has always been a European or Scandinavian – the last two have both been French.

The IMF did not complete the Bretton Woods monetary regime, which is just as well since the liquidity which it injected into the system was meagre. Another institution was also created which was initially styled the International Bank for Reconstruction and Development but is now better known as the World Bank. This was set up, as its original name suggests, in order to raise and disburse the funds needed for the 'reconstruction' of war-devastated Europe and, if there was any left over, for 'development' in other parts of the world. Unlike the IMF, the Bank was conceived as a genuine lending agency, extending loans (and guarantees) – at a price – for productive purposes and

Table 2.1 The voting power of *appointed* executive directors of the IMF as a percentage of total votes in selected years

	1946	1950	1960	1970	1980	1990	1994
United States	33.52	30.51	25.98	22.63	19.83	19.10	17.81
United Kingdom	16.00	14.57	12.36	10.76	6.94	6.62	4.99
China	6.95	6.32	—	—	—	—	—[1]
France	5.73	6.05	5.09	4.41	4.57	4.80	4.99
India	5.13	4.67	3.91	3.38	—	—	—[2]
Germany	—	—	5.09	5.35	5.13	5.78	5.54
Japan	—	—	—	—	3.96	4.52	5.54
Saudi Arabia	—	—	—	—	1.47	3.44	—
Italy	—	—	—	2.84	—	—	—
Total	67.33	62.12	52.43	49.37	41.90	44.26	38.87

Notes
1. In 1994 the People's Republic of China possessed 2.29 per cent of the Fund's voting power and had an *elected* director.
2. In 1994 India wielded 2.59 per cent of the Fund's voting power and had a director elected by the votes of Bangladesh, Bhutan and Sri Lanka in addition to its own.

Source
Adapted from IMF, *Annual Report*.

not tying them in any way to the contributions of members to its funds. However, in other regards it was very similar to its 'sister' institution, especially in regard to its decision-making structures and voting procedures.

More important in the medium term to the relaunching of world trade after the Second World War than either IMF or World Bank resources, however, were the dollars which the United States injected by way of *bilateral aid* into Western Europe. It was the $20 billion of the European Recovery Programme (or 'Marshall' Aid, after the US Secretary of State at the time) which really completed the 'Bretton Woods system', according to the broad definition of that term. It was this which really closed the 'dollar gap' during the 1950s. And it was this which confirmed the true importance of Bretton Woods; that, as Keynes reported on his return, lay not in the letter of the agreements but in the fact that America now took responsibility if things went wrong. 'That remark', as Fred Hirsch observed, 'summed up the next fifteen years of world financial history.'[3]

The collapse of Bretton Woods

During the 1960s the international monetary system which emerged from Bretton Woods was periodically modified in an attempt to provide international trade with more liquidity. In 1962 the 'General Arrangement to Borrow' was introduced, whereby the 'Group of Ten' (G-10) countries (see Box 2.2) plus Switzerland undertook to provide the IMF with additional convertible currencies should the need for them arise. And in 1969, following further

---

Box 2.2   The Group of Ten (G-10)

Belgium	Canada
France	Germany
Italy	Japan
Netherlands	Sweden
Switzerland	United Kingdom
United States	

The 'Group of Ten' consists of the countries which agreed to the General Arrangement to Borrow (GAB) at a meeting of their finance ministers in Paris on 13 December 1961. Thereafter it was intermittently an important informal forum for policy coordination by the major Western industrialised nations but did not achieve prominence again until 1983 when, against the background of the debt crisis, it agreed to enlarge the GAB. In the following year Switzerland became the eleventh member but the Group retained its original name. It generally meets twice a year. In order to be able to deal with financial crises such as that recently suffered by Mexico, the GAB was once more enlarged at the Halifax summit in June 1995; in fact, it was doubled – to $55bn.

---

tinkering with the system by central bankers, a more radical step to increase international liquidity was taken on G-10 initiative when 'special drawing rights' (SDRs) were introduced. These were in effect a kind of IMF bank note, and were allocated for the first time in the following year. But, despite all of these efforts at improvement, in 1971 the Bretton Woods system of fixed exchange rates collapsed.

The reasons for this dramatic development were many and various. The flood of dollars into their reserves had certainly enabled Europe and Japan to make handsome economic recoveries from the war, and the corollary of this (the absence of a United States need to balance its own payments) had facilitated America's extravagant foreign policy. But the Bretton Woods system had inherent weaknesses which became more and more obvious as the 1960s progressed. For example, speculation against weak currencies was encouraged by the fact that everyone knew that they would have to be devalued sooner or later and – because of the inflexibility of the system – by large amounts. More fundamentally, confidence in the dollar itself began to wane as the US balance of payments deteriorated. As Graham Bird has pointed out, this demonstrated the 'basic dilemma' of any system using a *national* currency as its main international reserve currency in a prolonged period of world economic expansion:

> In order to be widely acceptable as an international reserve a national currency must be strong in the sense that devaluation cannot be contemplated. But at the same time, in order to make a contribution to the stock of reserves owned by

other countries, the currency must be weak in the sense that the reserve centre country must run balance of payments deficits.[4]

Because international trade was expanding dramatically, as noted at the beginning of this chapter, and because US gold stocks were falling independently (see Figure 2.1), the size of America's liquid external debt relative to the gold held by the Federal Reserve at Fort Knox was eleven times larger in 1970 compared to 1950. And added to the economic anxiety about the diminishing strength of the dollar were political arguments (especially between the French and the Americans) over the distribution of costs and benefits within the system. These were not helped either by strains in the Western alliance caused by disagreements over United States policy in Vietnam.

It was against this background that in August 1971 the United States unilaterally suspended the convertibility of the dollar into gold, and in February 1973 devalued the dollar once more. The anchor of the system had come adrift, and thereafter most major currencies were allowed to float to their 'natural' level on the world's foreign exchange markets. (Floating was legalised by an amendment to the IMF's Articles of Agreement at Jamaica in 1976.) The IMF was further marginalised when the Organisation of Petroleum Exporting Countries (OPEC) introduced the first of its big hikes in the oil price following the Middle East war in October 1973, and privately 'recycled' surpluses from the OPEC countries replaced IMF drawing rights as the main means for oil-importing countries to finance their inflated deficits. By the early 1980s there was a real risk that even the institutional remnants of the Bretton Woods monetary system (the World Bank as well as the IMF) would be abandoned.

The ghost of monetary order

Bretton Woods may be dead but its ghost is still a lingering presence. This is because, while floating rates had some important advantages (they probably coped better with the economic shocks of the 1970s and 1980s than the fixed-rate system could have done), they also had serious drawbacks. In fact, by 1985 even in Washington and London small signs of doubt concerning the rightness of unqualified *laissez-faire* policies – 'benign neglect' – began to appear. This helped to preserve some remnants of the old order, while simultaneously energising the search for a new one.

The main problem with floating exchange rates was that they permitted large and sometimes puzzling fluctuations in the level of rates, especially in the short term. This was no less true of the United States dollar which, despite the growing importance of the German Deutschmark and the Japanese yen, in 1988 remained by far the most important reserve currency held by the world's central banks (see Table 2.2). Perhaps the main reason why exchange

Table 2.2 The share of national currencies in total identified official holdings of foreign exchange of all countries, end of year, 1973–93, selected years (percentage)

	1973	1980	1984	1988	1991	1993
US dollar	76.1	68.6	69.4	63.3	58.4	61.4
Pound sterling	5.6	2.9	3.0	3.1	3.6	3.4
Deutschmark	7.1	14.9	12.3	16.2	16.5	16.1
French franc	1.1	1.7	1.0	1.7	2.8	2.2
Swiss franc	1.4	3.2	2.1	1.5	1.4	1.5
Dutch guilder	0.5	1.3	0.8	1.1	1.1	0.6
Japanese yen	0.1	4.3	5.6	7.2	9.4	9.0
Other	8.1	3.1	5.8	6.0	7.0	5.8

Source
IMF, *Annual Report 1983*, p. 68; *Annual Report 1989*, p. 55; and *Annual Report 1994*, p. 158.

rates became so volatile was the huge increase in the size of global financial markets in the 1980s. This was fostered by the relaxation of controls on foreign entry into the domestic markets of most developed countries, and the great strides made in telecommunications and computer technology. Added to this, financial specialists became more and more adept at working the new global markets. As Joan Spero notes: 'The emergence of a highly integrated world capital market facilitated enormous international funds flows that respond as much to political risk and interest rate differentials as to trade balances.'[5]

Though damaging to international trade, volatile foreign exchange markets might have been regarded as tolerable had the floating rates 'system' which permitted them been successful in ironing out the huge current account surpluses of some countries and the equally large deficits of others – as supporters of floating rates had claimed it would. Unfortunately, this had not occurred. Huge surpluses continued to be accumulated by the traditionally strong countries of Germany and Japan, while newly industrialised countries such as Taiwan and South Korea also began to acquire seriously large balances. By contrast, during the 1980s the trade deficit of the United States assumed unprecedented proportions. Finally, there was the emergence of the debt crisis in the early 1980s, which was sparked by the announcement by Mexico in 1982 that it could no longer make regular repayments to its creditors. This provoked fears of a wave of Third World defaults which would plunge the world into even deeper recession via a crisis of confidence in financial institutions and markets. (In the 1970s, developing countries had borrowed heavily abroad to finance oil imports and development programmes, and as a result found themselves acutely embarrassed when oil prices soared again in 1979, interest rates in creditor countries reached record heights, and export earnings diminished as demand for commodities dropped along with the general level of economic activity.) The seriousness and the complexity of the debt problem clearly demanded some kind of coordinated international action if long-term solutions, as well as 'rescheduling agreements', were to be achieved.

The world had managed to muddle through, it is true. The creditor countries, chiefly the rich free-market economies, concerted their policies to a degree through permanent intergovernmental bodies such as the Organisation of Economic Cooperation and Development (OECD) and – since November 1975, in the aftermath of the first oil price crisis – at annual summit meetings (see Box 2.3). Debtor countries tried to do likewise through bodies such as the Group of Twenty-four and the Latin American 'Cartagena Group'. And they came together in forums such as 'the Paris Club', where *official* debt was restructured. Debtor countries normally renegotiated their debts to *commercial* banks through liaison committees created to represent the many banks involved. Moreover, the IMF continued to play a role in these and other international monetary matters as 'part credit union, part referee and part economic adviser'.[6] And inside the European Community at any rate, exchange rate stability had been achieved via the Exchange Rate Mechanism (ERM).

Box 2.3   The Western economic summits

Year	Location	Year	Location
1975	Rambouillet	1986	Tokyo
1976	Puerto Rico	1987	Venice
1977	London	1988	Toronto
1978	Bonn	1989	Paris
1979	Tokyo	1990	Houston
1980	Venice	1991	London
1981	Ottawa	1992	Munich
1982	Versailles	1993	Tokyo
1983	Williamsburg	1994	Naples
1984	London	1995	Halifax, Nova Scotia
1985	Bonn		

The original proposal for the convening of an economic summit of the major Western industrialised nations was made in a press interview in July 1975 by President Giscard d'Estaing of France. The first summit, at Rambouillet near Paris, was attended by the leaders of France, West Germany, Japan, the United Kingdom, the United States and Italy. Canada was not invited to this meeting but participated from the second summit onwards. The President of the European Commission (presently Jacques Santer) was permitted to participate for part of the deliberations from the third meeting onwards.

In contrast to the generally more technical (and frequent) discussions of finance ministers and central bankers within the context of the 'Group of Seven' and 'Group of Ten', the summits tend to concentrate on broad policy questions.

Nevertheless, against the background of the debt crisis, a US trade deficit of alarming proportions, and topsy-turvy conditions in the foreign exchange markets, in September 1985 at a secret meeting in New York the United States, Japan, West Germany, France and Britain agreed to cooperate more closely in international monetary management. This meant not only coordinated intervention in the foreign exchange markets but also, more radically, *domestic* economic management conducted with a view to its impact on the health of international financial relations. Following this watershed development, more frequent meetings of the finance ministers and central bankers of the 'Group of Seven' (G-7) (Canada and Italy were added in 1986; see Box 2.4) became the institutional vehicle of the new policy of multilateral monetary management. Since February 1987 the main currencies have been linked loosely under the Louvre Accord.

Box 2.4   The Group of Seven (G-7)

The Group of Seven leading industrialised countries grew from the 'Group of Five' (G-5) which itself was a subgroup of the most powerful members of the 'Group of Ten' (see Box 2.2). The *finance ministers and central bankers* of the G-5 countries – the United States, Japan, West Germany, France and Britain – began to meet intermittently at informal gatherings in 1973 and later more regularly. Their leaders also began to hold annual summits in 1975 (see Box 2.3). Following the Versailles summit of 1982, the managing director of the IMF was also normally invited to attend for part of the agenda. At a meeting at the Plaza Hotel, New York, in September 1985 the G-5 states agreed to cooperate more closely in monetary management. The Five became Seven with the addition of Canada and Italy at the economic summit in Tokyo in May 1986. The Group has its internal squabbles but possesses a pronounced esprit de corps and usually presents a united front once decisions are taken.

In addition to cooperating in the world's currency markets, the G-7 collaborates in areas such as economic support to Russia and combating drug trafficking and money laundering. One of its most important meetings is that held immediately prior to the gatherings of the IMF and the World Bank each September. This amounts to a pre-meeting caucus, and – since the G-7 countries control the largest slice of votes in both institutions – is where the key decisions are usually taken. The G-7 is not now, however, as omnipotent as it used to be, since the developing countries as a group have grown faster over the last twenty years, and the G-7 countries now produce less than half the world's economic output. In the IMF's annual meeting in autumn 1994 the G-7, whose self-appointed role as global monetary manager many other countries now find irksome, failed to win the support of other members for a limited increase in global liquidity.

It is a widely noted fact that international monetary management has been much more difficult since the early 1960s because the world economy is no longer dominated by one power – the United States. Whereas at Bretton Woods America could lay down the law and, over the next two decades, enforce it, since then it has had to share power more and more, as well as endure with rising frustration the 'free riders' in the international community who have benefited from the 'public good' of stability without making any commensurate contribution towards it. The dispersal of financial power, with Japan and Germany now particularly important players as well, means much more difficulty in agreeing and enforcing the rules. This fact, together with the predictable political obstacles encountered by the new system in the legislatures of the Group of Seven, meant that international monetary management did not work especially well at first.

However, the fright of the stock exchange crash of October 1987 made the Group of Seven redouble its efforts and since then – despite having to abandon the dream of coordinating domestic economic policies – it has achieved more success, at least in keeping currencies reasonably stable. The G-7/IMF–World Bank set-up has also gained in authority (though it has also obviously inherited more problems) with the remaining ex-Communist states of Eastern Europe, together with the successor states to the former Soviet Union, finally joining the fold in the early 1970s. In a states-system (see Chapter 9), leadership by one state or small group of states is as necessary in world economic management as in world security management, even though it may degenerate into exploitation or collapse under resentment at an unequal distribution of burdens.

There is, therefore, leadership in international monetary affairs once more. But, having said this, crisis management rather than crisis prevention is still its style, and will remain so until real inroads are made into the US trade (and budget) deficits and the debt problems of the Third World and Eastern Europe. Europe's ERM had to endure a severe crisis in August 1993, and at the end of 1994 the international monetary order was rocked by another financial debacle in Mexico. This required a rescue package of $20bn from the United States and $17.8bn from the IMF.

The international trade system

The GATT regime

In the same way that the United States was the main architect of the new international monetary system, so it was the chief mover behind the new system of international trade created after the Second World War. Convinced that the rampant protectionism ('economic nationalism') of the 1930s had not only reduced world output but also contributed to the atmosphere of malevolent rivalry which had spawned the aggression of the Axis powers, US Secretary of State Cordell Hull was determined to create a world free of barriers to trade, an 'open' or 'liberal' trading system. In the process, trade discrimination such as that embodied in Britain's scheme of 'Imperial Preference' would be gradually eliminated. The desire that trade should be at once freer and less discriminatory was expressed notably in the 'most-favoured nation' (MFN) principle which stated that tariff preferences granted to one state must be granted to all others.

To encourage the liberalisation of international trade, the Havana Charter of 1948 not only elaborated the rules of the new regime but also proposed a commercial equivalent to the IMF to oversee it. This was to be called the International Trade Organisation (ITO). But, because trade policy normally has more immediate effects on sectional interests, the commercial negotiations had been far more difficult than the monetary ones and the Havana Charter was an uncomfortable compromise. Moreover, in a manner reminiscent of the fate which befell the Treaty of Versailles in the United States after the First World War, a mixed coalition of Congressional interests prevented American ratification of the Havana Charter despite the leading role played by Washington in its difficult birth. This finished the ITO, and what emerged instead was the General Agreement on Tariffs and Trade (GATT).

Designed in 1947 as merely an interim measure, the GATT certainly placed great emphasis on non-discrimination and the removal of both tariff and non-tariff barriers to trade. However, there were important exceptions. This was especially true of the agricultural field, where lobbies were well organised and powerful. The code was also silent or vague on many contentious issues, and GATT's dispute settlement machinery was inevitably cumbersome and non-binding. With the exception of Czechoslovakia, the socialist state-trading countries remained outside. Nevertheless, GATT provided guidelines for commercial negotiations on a multilateral basis, and the result was that, as Joan Spero notes: 'From a temporary treaty, GATT became not only an established commercial code but also an international organization with a secretariat and a director general to oversee the implementation of its rules, manage dispute settlement, and provide a forum and support for multilateral trade negotiations.'[7]

Largely on United States initiative, GATT subsequently provided the framework for six 'rounds' of multilateral trade negotiations between the foundation of the organisation and the mid-1960s. The last of this series, the so-called Kennedy Round (1964–7), was probably the high-point of GATT's achievements. Here, tariffs on non-agricultural products in the industrialised countries were reduced by about one-third, bringing them down on average to roughly 10 per cent. Not surprisingly, international trade grew dramatically during this period and prosperity, at least in the developed world, grew with it.

The weakening of the GATT regime

With the relative decline in America's economic power during the 1960s, the liberal trading ideals on which the GATT regime was founded were doomed to much harder times. But the weakening of American leadership was by no means the only reason for this prospect. Even before the Kennedy Round, the United States had countenanced the compromising of GATT ideals by endorsing – even encouraging – Western European regional protectionism in the interests of strengthening and stabilising a key area in the confrontation with the Soviet Union. In 1957 the European Economic Community (EEC) was created by the Treaty of Rome (see Box 2.5). This provided not only for a gradual elimination of tariffs among members but also for a common external tariff. The EEC, in other words, was a 'customs union'. The European Free Trade Association (EFTA), which was the British-led response to this, also permitted discrimination against non-members even though it had no *common* external tariff. For political reasons, Japanese protectionism had also been accepted. Meanwhile, pressures had been mounting for more and more trade discrimination in favour of the newly emerging developing countries.

The Kennedy Round itself had not attempted to deal with tariff barriers in the politically intractable area of agricultural products which became even more difficult with the EEC's introduction of its Common Agricultural Policy (CAP) in 1962. This was designed to protect high-priced EEC farm products (especially in West Germany and France) against cheaper foreign imports. Partly because these included those from the United States, protectionist sentiment in Congress began to strengthen: the economic challenge of a revitalised Western Europe was seen as an increasing threat. The multilateral free trade regime was further weakened by the EEC's granting of non-reciprocal preferential trade terms to many countries in the developing world (the Lomé Convention, 1975), the expansion in full membership of the Community (see Box 2.5), and the extension of associate status to others.

If the GATT regime was being undermined by the entrenchment of regional exceptions which the United States, largely for cold war reasons, had initially encouraged, it was also weakened by other developments. For one thing, GATT was a victim of its own success. As international trade had increased under its more liberal regime, so trade affected more sectors – and thus more jobs. This increased the number and strength of protectionist lobbies, while simultaneously making trade negotiations more extensive and complex. In addition, the economic disorders of the 1970s and 1980s (and especially the massive rise in unemployment associated with them) played a major role in encouraging protectionism, not least because in such circumstances the sectional sacrifices required to obtain the more generalised benefits of a free trade regime seemed much more painful. Moreover, with the strengthening of the incentive to circumvent GATT rules, new 'non-tariff' methods of distorting trade were invented and old ones were used with

Box 2.5   The European Union (EU)

The European Union grew out of the belief that Europe would be a safer and more prosperous region if a sense of common European interests could be forged which would gradually override the entrenched conception of national interests. This would be achieved by promoting cooperation between European nation-states in initially limited spheres where a common interest was most evident. The hope was that success in such (mainly economic) areas would encourage cooperation in more difficult ones and thus lay the foundations for 'political unity', that is, a European state.

In 1951 six West European states formed a European Coal and Steel Community (ECSC), and in 1957 'the Six' created two further communities in the Treaties of Rome. These were the European Economic Community (EEC) – generally known as the 'Common Market' – and the European Atomic Energy Agency (Euratom). There were thus strictly three 'European Communities', though in 1967 they came to be served by common institutions and were increasingly regarded as a single entity, the 'European Community' (EC). Subsequently, other European states joined the EC, either as full or associate members. In December 1985 the founding treaties were amended by the Single European Act which provided, among other things, for stronger Community institutions and a single market by 1992. They were amended again at the Maastricht summit in December 1991, which was notable for limited moves towards political union and a common currency.

On 1 November 1993, following ratification of Maastricht (which was a close call), the *European Union* came into being. Dealing with foreign and security policy ('Pillar Two'), judicial and police affairs ('Pillar Three'), EU matters were placed under the Council of Ministers (see below) rather than under the supranational institutions of the EC ('Pillar One'), which was a major concession to those members, notably the UK, hostile to genuine political union. Despite this important technicality, the 'EU' is widely assumed to subsume the 'EC'.

Membership (with year of entry)

1957	Belgium	1981	Greece
	France	1986	Portugal
	Germany (West)		Spain
	Italy	1995	Austria
	Luxembourg		Finland
	Netherlands		Sweden
1973	Denmark		
	Ireland		
	United Kingdom		

Further enlargement of the EU/EC is also high on the Brussels agenda, with former Communist states in central and eastern Europe particularly anxious to join.

Main institutions

The main EU/EC institutions are the following:

- The European Council – the regular meeting (usually three times a year) of EU heads of state and government, which started in 1974 and was formalised by the Single European Act in 1985; it attempts, among other things, to resolve deadlocks at lower levels.
- The Council of Ministers – foreign ministers of the member governments; main decision-making body (on foreign and security policy, too, since Maastricht); it operates by trying to harmonise national interests, though majority voting increased following the Single Act; the Presidency (an influential role) is held by individual member states for six months in rotation.
- The European Commission – guardian of the European flame, the Commission is charged with acting in the interests of the Community as a whole; it initiates proposals consistent with the Treaties and executes decisions of the Council.
- The European Parliament – the directly elected assembly, which is largely consultative but also has important budgetary and legislative powers.
- The European Court of Justice – adjudicates on disputes arising out of the application of the Treaties.

greater sophistication. Among the new ones were unilaterally imposed import quotas, negotiated 'voluntary' export restrictions, bans on the importation of products which did not meet national safety or environmental protection standards, and government subsidies and favourable tax regimes to sectors producing for export markets (including shipping companies).

Against this unpropitious background, the seventh set of multilateral trade negotiations organised by GATT, the Tokyo Round, dragged on from 1973 until 1979. Some progress was made, for example on further reductions in tariffs on manufactured goods and the introduction of codes of practice on certain non-tariff barriers. But no agreement was reached on a code for 'voluntary export restraints' (which were by now very important), and the Tokyo Round's unprecedented attempt to grapple with agriculture achieved little.

The Uruguay Round and the birth of the WTO

The impetus for the latest round of multilateral trade negotiations under GATT auspices came from the United States, Japan and the GATT

Secretariat. Launched at a GATT meeting at Punta del Este in Uruguay in September 1986, the negotiations began in the following year and were due to be completed in 1990. They represented the most ambitious attempt ever made to liberalise world trade, seeking not only to strengthen GATT rules in traditional areas but also to reform GATT mechanisms and bring into its orbit long-standing exceptions such as agriculture and new sectors such as services. (By the 1980s, services accounted for more than half of the gross domestic product of the advanced industrial states.)

The Americans and the 'Cairns Group' (see Box 2.6) argued that a substantial reduction in trade-distorting agricultural subsidies was the essential basis for the creation of a new international trade order because without large concessions here (and a freer market in textiles, clothing and tropical goods), developing countries would have had little incentive to make the concessions sought by the EC and others elsewhere on the agenda. The EC wanted liberalisation in services (for example, telecommunications, aviation and shipping) and intellectual property.

Not surprisingly, these negotiations were no easier than earlier rounds. Indeed, they were punctuated by recurrent threats of imminent collapse and even dire warnings of the formal disintegration of the GATT regime into warring regional trade blocs. Nevertheless, in December 1993 agreement was finally reached – even on the critical issue of agriculture – and accords were formally signed at a ministerial meeting in Marrakesh in the following April. In return for concessions on services and other things, substantial reductions in farm support were agreed, together with greater transparency for that which was permitted to remain, and it was also agreed that negotiations for further reductions would take place before the end of the decade. The GATT secretariat estimated that the total trade liberalisation package would boost global economic output by at least $235bn by the year 2002. GATT itself, 'provisional' to the end, was to be replaced by a properly constituted World

---

Box 2.6   The Cairns Group

Argentina	Hungary
Australia	Indonesia
Brazil	Malaysia
Canada	New Zealand
Chile	Philippines
Colombia	Thailand
Fiji	Uruguay

An informal alliance of agricultural exporting countries, this group was created at a meeting in Cairns (Queensland, Australia) in August 1986 in order to make common cause against protectionism in agriculture (especially by the EC) during the Uruguay Round of GATT negotiations.

Trade Organisation (WTO), which would have a wider remit, provide a permanent forum for trade negotiations, and stronger mechanisms for settling international trade disputes. However, apart from an operating budget, it would still – unlike the IMF and the World Bank – have no resources of its own and no powers to enforce rulings. It is also open to doubt that a permanent forum, in contrast to periodic 'rounds', will be able 'to generate the complex linkages [on 'linkage', see Chapter 11] and sense of urgency needed to achieve substantial breakthroughs'.[8] In any event, the WTO came into existence in 1995, with a membership of over 120 states but excluding Russia and China.

Box 2.7   Regional trade groups

Despite the strengthening of multilateral trade rules by the successful completion of GATT's Uruguay Round, at least a hundred regional trade groups had been formed by the end of 1994, nearly a third of them in the previous five years. Most have overlapping memberships and the United States is one of their most active enthusiasts. Among the more important of the new groups is the *North American Free Trade Area* (Nafta), which was created in December 1992 and embraces the United States, Canada and Mexico. Another is the Singapore-based *Asia-Pacific Economic Co-operation forum* (Apec), which was established in November 1989 and has eighteen members: Canada, Chile, Mexico, United States; Brunei, China, Hong Kong, Indonesia, Japan, South Korea, Malaysia, Philippines, Singapore, Taiwan, Thailand; Australia, New Zealand, Papua New Guinea. Agreement on farming permitting, Apec plans to achieve free movement of capital and goods among developed countries in the region by the year 2010 and to have drawn in the developing countries by 2020, by which time it will represent the world's biggest free trade zone. A third important regional grouping is the Latin American *Mercosur* trade area, which came into existence at the beginning of 1995. Short for 'Mercado Común del Sur', Mercosur includes Argentina, Brazil, Paraguay and Uruguay. The year 1995 also saw a renewal of interest in Europe and the United States in a *North Atlantic Free Trade Area.*

Regional economic groups are often inspired by political motives (as in the case of the EU, see Box 2.5), despair over the achievement of genuine multilateralism and, among other things, by a desire to obtain more leverage in global economic negotiations. Their supporters counter the charge that they distort the world trade system by claiming that trade groupings promote liberalisation among their members and thus – albeit in patchwork fashion – free trade in the world as a whole. In general, the WTO, which vets regional groups for conformity with multilateral rules, endorses this argument, though it is nervous that any North Atlantic Free Trade Area could prove particularly divisive.

Like the international monetary system, the international trade regime has suffered from a loss of leadership with the diffusion of economic and political power at the top – a situation compounded by lack of strong central authority to determine commercial policy in both the EU (which is *not* a state) and the United States (where the separation of powers between White House and Congress is invariably troublesome). The weakening of leadership has been the more serious in this sphere in light of the greater political sensitivity of foreign commercial policy, and was witnessed in cameo in the very bruising and protracted struggle over the appointment of the first director of the new WTO.[9] Nevertheless, despite periods of serious recession in the world economy over recent decades, the continuing entrenchment of protectionist sentiment in some countries, and the fashion for regional groupings (see Boxes 2.5 and 2.7), what remains impressive is that the economic great powers have once more re-affirmed their faith in commercial multilateralism: to corrupt only slightly an observation of Joan Spero's, offered before the Uruguay Round was finally completed, the postwar political consensus supporting a liberal trade regime remains 'alive, if not well'.[10] That this should be so is partly a result of the continuing influence of two lessons: first, the lesson of the interwar period that an illiberal trade regime helped to plunge the world into super-recession; and second, the lesson of the 1950s and 1960s that a liberal regime helped to produce unprecedented wealth. The GATT Secretariat (now the WTO) and other international and intergovernmental bodies have helped to keep these memories alive. In addition, while powerful commercial interests in major states are threatened by free trade, others stand to gain from it. This is the best guarantee of the system.

Notes

1. Keynes, quoted in Harrod, *The Life of John Maynard Keynes*, p. 581.
2. Members of the IMF also agreed, in principle, to dispense with exchange restrictions on the current account of the balance of payments, while allowing destabilising ('hot money') capital flows to be discouraged by exchange controls. However, 'free convertibility' had to wait upon European reconstruction, and was not achieved until 1958.
3. *Money International* (Penguin: Harmondsworth, 1969), p. 101.
4. Bird, *World Finance and Adjustment*, p. 57.
5. *The Politics of International Economic Relations*, pp. 50–1.
6. J. de Larosière, quoted in Barston, *Modern Diplomacy*, p. 152.
7. *The Politics of International Economic Relations*, p. 71.
8. Guy de Jonquières in *Financial Times*, 5 Jan. 1995.
9. The eventual victor was the former Italian trade minister, Renato Ruggiero, but his appointment was resisted until almost the end by the Clinton administration, which believed him to be too protectionist and likely to favour the EU, where he had previously worked as a senior Commission official.
10. *The Politics of International Economic Relations*, p. 93.

Further reading

General

Avery, W. P. and D. P. Rapkin (eds), *Markets, Politics and Change in the Global Political Economy* (Lynne Rienner: Boulder, CO. 1989).

Block, F. L., *The Origins of International Economic Disorder* (University of California Press: Berkeley and Los Angeles, 1977).

Bromley, S., *American Hegemony and World Oil* (Penn State University Press: University Park, PA, 1991).

Gilpin, R., *The Political Economy of International Relations* (Princeton University Press: Princeton, NJ, 1987).

IMF, *World Economic Outlook* (IMF: Washington DC, annually).

Isaak, R. A., *International Political Economy: Managing world economic change* (Prentice Hall: Englewood Cliffs, NJ, 1991).

Keohane, R. O., *After Hegemony: Cooperation and discord in the world political economy* (Princeton University Press: Princeton, 1984).

Kindleberger, C. P., *The International Economic Order: Essays on financial crisis and international public goods* (Harvester Wheatsheaf: Hemel Hempstead, 1988).

Krasner, S. D., *International Regimes* (Cornell University Press: Ithaca, NY, 1983).

Marris, S., *Deficits and the Dollar: The world economy at risk*, 2nd edn (Institute for International Economics: Washington, DC, 1987).

Olson, M., *The Rise and Decline of Nations: Economic growth, stagflation, and social rigidities* (Yale University Press: New Haven, 1982).

Porter, G. and J. W. Brown, *Global Environmental Politics* (Westview: Boulder, CO, 1991).

Spero, J. E., *The Politics of International Economic Relations*, 4th edn (St Martin's Press: New York, 1990).

Strange, S., *Paths to International Political Economy* (Allen & Unwin: London, 1984).

Strange, S., *States and Markets: An introduction to international political economy*, 2nd edn (Pinter: London; and St Martin's Press: New York, 1994).

Thurow, L. C., *Head to Head: Coming economic battles among Japan, Europe, and America* (Morrow: New York, 1992).

Walters, R. R. and D. H. Blake, *The Politics of Global Economic Relations*, 4th edn (Prentice Hall: Englewood Cliffs, NJ, 1992).

World Resources Institute, *World Resources 1992–93* (Oxford University Press: New York, 1992).

International finance

Barston, R., *Modern Diplomacy* (Longman: London and New York, 1988), ch. 7.

Bird, G., *World Finance and Adjustment: An agenda for reform* (Macmillan: London, 1985).

De Vries, M. G., *The International Monetary Fund, 1966–71*, 2 vols (IMF: Washington, DC, 1976).

De Vries, M. G., *The International Monetary Fund, 1972–78*, 3 vols (IMF: Washington, DC, 1985).

De Vries, M. G., *The International Monetary Fund in a Changing World, 1945–85* (IMF: Washington, DC, 1986).

Harrod, R. F., *The Life of John Maynard Keynes* (Macmillan: London, and St Martin's Press: New York, 1966), ch. 13.

Hormats, R. D., *Reforming the International Monetary System: From Roosevelt to Reagan* (Foreign Policy Association: New York, 1987).

Horsefield, J. K., *The International Monetary Fund, 1945–65, Volume 1* (IMF: Washington, DC, 1969).

Horsefield, J. K. and De Vries, M. G., *The International Monetary Fund, 1945–65, Volume 2* (IMF: Washington, DC, 1969).

Strange, S., 'The politics of international currencies', *World Politics*, vol. 23, January 1971, pp. 215–31.

Tew, B., *International Monetary Cooperation 1945–67*, 9th rev. edn (Hutchinson, London, 1967).

International trade

Bhagwati, J., *The World Trading System at Risk* (Princeton University Press: Princeton, NJ, 1991).

Barston, R., *Modern Diplomacy*, ch. 8.

Cline, W. R. (ed.), *Trade Policy in the 1980s* (Institute for International Economics: Washington, DC, 1983).

Fletcher, L. B. (ed.), *World Food in the 1990s: Production, trade, and aid* (Westview: Boulder, CO, 1992).

Graham, T. R., 'Revolution in trade politics', *Foreign Policy*, no. 26, 1979, pp. 49–63.

Gray, H. P., *Free Trade or Protection?* (St Martin's Press: New York, 1985).

International Financial Statistics, Supplement on Trade Statistics, Supplement Series no. 15 (IMF: Washington, DC, 1988).

Krasner, S. D., 'The Tokyo Round', *International Studies Quarterly*, vol. 23, December 1979, pp. 491–531.

Lloyd, P. J., 'Regionalisation and world trade', *OECD Economic Studies*, no. 18, Spring 1992.

3

States and multinational corporations

The general focus of this book is interstate relations. However, there is a prominent school of thought which holds that since the Second World War the power of the state has been steadily eroded by the increasing weight in international politics of 'transnational' or 'non-state' actors. If the focus on interstate relations is to be justified, it needs to be demonstrated that this argument is exaggerated.

A transnational actor is usually understood as a non-governmental organisation which operates internationally. This comprehensive category embraces many religious movements, political parties, trade unions, sporting associations, scientific societies, charities, and so on. Most especially, however, it includes the multinational corporation. (It excludes organisations such as the World Bank and the IMF, discussed in the previous chapter, since these are made up of the representatives of states; these are '*inter*governmental' organisations.)

The multinational corporation is the transnational actor which, above all others, is held to be the most potent source of challenge to the state in the realm of international, as indeed in domestic, politics. This view is associated particularly with the 'dependency theory' school of neo-Marxist thought, but it is by no means exclusive to thinkers of the far left. It received a remarkable shot in the arm when the aspirations of the International Telephone and Telegraph Corporation (ITT) to a role in the opposition to the Popular Unity coalition of Salvador Allende in Chile in the early 1970s were confirmed by the investigations of various US Congressional committees.

What is a 'multinational corporation'? It is certainly not a firm which operates equal-opportunity employment policies between many nationalities at senior management level. (It is to avoid this connotation of the term that some, including the UN, prefer the designation 'transnational corporation' – TNCs.) On the contrary, and despite a limited tendency in recent years to transfer to selected foreign units *global responsibility* for particular products or even whole business divisions, it is well known that multinationals are still generally dominated by personnel selected from their country of origin, whether it be Americans in the case of IBM, Japanese in the case of Nissan, or Italians in the case of Fiat. What does distinguish a multinational, then, is simply that its operations – be they in the manufacturing, extractive, agricultural, service or transport sectors – are carried out in more than one country. A multinational, in other words, is a company which engages to a significant degree in 'foreign *direct* investment', as opposed to indirect or portfolio investment.

Cross-border investment flows are nothing new. Indeed, relative to world output, they have only recently approached the level reached before the First

World War, 9 per cent of the total. Nevertheless, the character of modern TNCs is such that, according to the UN's *World Investment Report*, they now directly control as much as a third of world output. American-based firms still account for far more of this 'international production' than firms of any other nationality, though the American proportion of total world stocks of foreign direct investment had shrunk from almost a half in 1960 to barely a quarter by the early 1990s. In the late 1960s multinationals based in other parts of the developed world, especially West Germany and Japan, began to play an increasingly important role. Even more strikingly, by the late 1980s multinationals with origins in the developing countries were estimated to hold foreign direct investments worth $110bn, which amounted to between 8 and 10 per cent of the world total compared to under 1 per cent in 1960. It should be stressed, though, that only a handful of countries account for most investment activity by 'Third World' multinationals (see Table 3.1).

In contrast to the state, with its territorial base and wide range of functions, the multinational is exclusively an economic institution with no remit beyond showing a healthy balance sheet to its shareholders. As a result, and despite Anthony Sampson's sensationalist description of ITT as a 'sovereign state',[1] its resemblance to the state is at most superficial. Even the widely remarked parallel between the diplomacies which both conduct through far-flung envoys is inexact since corporate diplomats do not enjoy the extensive privileges accorded to accredited diplomats of the state under international law, though it is true that the businessmen are sometimes able to compensate for this in other ways.

Table 3.1 The top ten home countries for developing-world multinationals: outward stock of direct foreign investment

Rank	Country	Investment (US$bn)
1	Hong Kong (1990)	18.9
2	Kuwait (1987)	5.4
3	Taiwan (1991)	4.7
4	South Korea (1991)	3.4
5	Brazil (1990)	2.4
6	Saudi Arabia (1990)	2.2
7	Singapore (1989)	1.6
8	Malaysia (1988)	1.5
9	Iran (1990)	1.2
10	Argentina (1990)	1.0

Note
For comparison, the figures for 1990 for a selection of developed countries were as follows: USA, $408bn; UK, $226bn; France, $110bn; Denmark, $8.7bn.

Source
Adapted from UNCTAD, *Transnational Corporations from Developing Countries* (UN: New York, 1993), Table II.3.

The role of the multinational corporation in international politics is sometimes vaguely formulated, so it is important to clarify precisely what this means. The multinational may be *politically* significant in the international sphere in the following ways: first, through influence, or even control, over both the foreign and domestic policies of its *host* states, at least in matters where its interests are affected; second, through its employment as an instrument of the foreign and domestic policies of its *host* states; third, through influence, or even control, over the policies of its *home* state towards its host, or potential host, states; and fourth, through its employment as an instrument of the policies of its *home* state towards, among others, its host states, irrespective of whether or not it has also contributed to shaping these policies.

It is hardly surprising that the multinational should be seen by so many as a powerful influence on the policies of both home and host states[2] and by the more imaginative as a replacement for the state which has already taken over. It is, after all, an axiom of political science that wealth generates influence, and the wealth of the multinationals is certainly enormous. It is often pointed out that the annual turnovers of the biggest of them even exceed the GNPs of countries the size of Switzerland, South Africa and Saudi Arabia (see Table 3.2), and there is no doubt that in practice this wealth translates into real influence with the state. There are three main reasons for this: first, host states need the knowledge, skills, marketing networks and, above all, investment capital which the wealth of the multinationals represents; second, this wealth can be used directly in both home and host states to undermine political enemies and support political friends, for example by financing election campaigns, subsidising newspapers, and so on; and third, this wealth can be used in both kinds of state to corrupt ministers and officials.

However, it is one thing to concede that multinationals have influence with the state, even, on occasions, great influence; it is quite another to accept that they exercise uninterrupted control over even micro-states and small states, let alone middle or major powers. Only sleight of hand has allowed this *impression*, and it is no more than that, to become established. In order to create such an impression, the resources and activities of multinationals are repeatedly described as 'global' and 'extraordinary'[3] (significantly, a favourite adjective of the fiction writer Robert Ludlum), metaphors such as 'the Octopus' are invoked,[4] resort is had to illustration rather than comprehensive evidence, and the convenient assumption is made that *because* multinationals sometimes 'exploit' the people of a host state they must also *control* its government. Quite apart from the fact that what constitutes 'exploitation' is the subject of controversy, some governments (for example, that of the late President Marcos in the Philippines) are so autocratic and corrupt that they would not need to be 'dominated' in order to permit their citizens to be 'exploited'.

Besides the consideration that some multinationals are actually owned by states (this is now particularly true in the oil industry), the reason why the remainder do not exercise a steady domination over either home or host

Table 3.2   The top twenty transnational corporations ranked by foreign assets, 1992

Rank	Corporation	Home country	Foreign assets as % total assets	Foreign employees as % total employees
1	Royal Dutch Shell	UK/Neth.	69	72
2	Exxon	USA	57	62
3	IBM	USA	53	48
4	General Motors	USA	22	36
5	Hitachi	Japan	—	—
6	Matsushita Electric	Japan	—	38
7	Nestlé	Switzerland	92	97
8	Ford	USA	16	51
9	Alcatel Alsthom	France	—	52
10	General Electric	USA	13	25
11	Philips Electronics	Neth.	80	88
12	Mobil	USA	56	44
13	Asea Brown Boveri	Switzerland	86	93
14	Elf Acquitaine	France	—	—
15	Volkswagen	Germany	—	40
16	Toyota Motor Co.	Japan	30	15
17	Siemens	Germany	—	39
18	Daimler-Benz	Germany	—	20
19	British Petroleum	UK	—	73
20	Unilever	UK/Neth.	80	88

Source
Adapted from UNCTAD, *World Investment Report 1994: Transnational Corporations, Employment and the Workplace* (UN: New York, 1994), Table I.2.

states is that the state has in its gift things to trade for the economic benefits which the multinational is able to confer in return. In the case of home states, these characteristically include more or less generous treatment in the areas of tax and antitrust policy, the provision of insurance for certain kinds of foreign direct investment (in the United States through OPIC, the Overseas Private Investment Corporation), and diplomatic support in the event of moves to expropriate the assets of multinationals in host states. The latter can themselves offer, among other things, access to their territory, security, guarantees (in some well-known instances in East Asia) of trade union docility, protected local markets, tax and other financial privileges, and – not least – government contracts. When it is also remembered that the state as host is politically buttressed against the multinational by nationalism, the most vigorous ideology of the twentieth century, it will be clear that its countervailing power is considerable.

The relationship with host states

In view of the fact that both the multinational and the state possess things which the other wants, it is not surprising that the essence of their relationship is not domination by the former of the latter but a constant process of *bargaining*, in which sometimes the one and sometimes the other has the upper hand. As far as the general relationship between multinationals and host countries is concerned, the balance of power swung from the companies to their hosts between the 1960s and 1970s. This was mainly because of the reduced fear of the protecting power of home governments (particularly that of the United States), the growth in competition between multinationals, the appearance of alternatives to foreign direct investment for host countries (such as technology under licensing), the considerable growth in the competence of host states to negotiate with the multinationals (assisted, in the case of developing countries, by the UN's Centre on Transnational Corporations created in 1975), and the appearance of producers' cartels, most famously the Organisation of Petroleum Exporting Countries (OPEC).

The results of this swing in the balance of power from multinationals to host states were easily seen. Rather than suffering from the domination of multinationals, host states nationalised their subsidiaries by the drove (see Table 3.3). In the case of raw materials, virtually all multinational operations had been nationalised by the middle of the 1970s. Moreover, many host states were able to insist that the branches and affiliates of multinationals which remained should tailor their activities to local needs. Thus, employment prospects were improved by the writing of local content regulations into contracts, external accounts were strengthened by the stipulation of export targets, and national sentiment was appeased by an infusion of indigenous management and, where practical, compulsory sale of stock on national exchanges.

An early illustration of the manner in which a major multinational was made to dance to the tune of national sentiment is provided by the experience of a Unilever subsidiary which was the largest single enterprise in Sukarno's Indonesia. During the dispute between Indonesia and The Netherlands over Western New Guinea (West Irian) in 1957–8, Unilever found that it had no option but to replace all of its Dutch personnel in Indonesia with Britons, Indonesians, Germans and Scandinavians, and transfer the subsidiary's shares from Rotterdam to London. However, in 1964, following the start of what Sukarno dubbed 'Confrontation' with Britain provoked by the latter's support for the Malaysian Federation, the whole process had to be put into reverse: the Dutch returned, the British departed, and the shares had to travel back across the North Sea!

Sometimes the vulnerability of multinationals to the pressure of host states is such that they can even be employed as instruments of the latter's foreign policies. For example, following the Middle East war in October 1973, the OPEC states were able to insist that the oil multinationals should help to enforce the oil embargo on the Western states 'supporting' Israel, that is to say, on their own home states. In the second half of the 1960s and during the 1970s the South African government forced the Europe/South Africa shipping conference – albeit with some difficulty – to adopt a friendlier attitude to

Table 3.3 Nationalisations of multinationals' foreign affiliates or branches by developing countries, 1960–85

	Number of acts	Percentage of total	Number of countries expropriating
1960	6	1.0	5
1961	8	1.4	5
1962	8	1.4	5
1963	11	1.9	7
1964	22	3.8	10
1965	14	2.4	11
1966	5	0.9	3
1967	25	4.4	8
1968	13	2.3	8
1969	24	4.2	14
1970	48	8.4	18
1971	51	8.9	20
1972	56	9.8	30
1973	30	5.2	20
1974	68	11.8	29
1975	83	14.5	28
1976	40	7.0	14
1977	15	2.6	13
1978	15	2.6	8
1979	17	2.9	13
1980	5	0.9	5
1981	4	0.7	2
1982	1	0.2	1
1983	3	0.5	3
1984	1	0.2	1
1985	1	0.2	1
Total	574	100.0	

Source
Adapted from UNCTAD, *Transnational Corporations in World Development* (UN: New York, 1988), Table XIX.1.

Italian, Spanish and Greek companies, as well as to the new Marxist government in Mozambique, in the interests of South African foreign policy. And, fearful of the growing anti-American sentiment in Argentina following President Reagan's decision to side with Britain in the Falklands crisis in 1982, many of the 500 American multinationals with operations in Argentina put their names to an open telegram to the president condemning British policy; Ford also donated sixty lorries to help Argentina's military effort, while Union Carbide offered $30,000-worth of torches and batteries. Many such examples could be given.

It should also be added that, in order to strengthen even further the hand of the host states against the multinationals, some limited steps have been taken since the 1970s, both regionally and globally, towards their *collective regulation*. The European Community and the Andean Common Market, for example, both introduced regulatory regimes within their own regions, while in 1974 – in the context of the Third World demand for a 'New International Economic Order' (NIEO) – a serious agitation for legally binding instruments directed at TNCs was also started at the UN by the developing countries, backed by Western trade unions. Though the attempt to obtain a mandatory UN code was subsequently abandoned and negotiations even for a voluntary code became permanently deadlocked in the 1980s and were formally terminated in July 1992, the UN agitation did produce some results. This was not least because, in order to take the steam out of it, the OECD Council (the principal grouping of the rich, free-market economies) approved its own voluntary code of conduct for multinationals as early as June 1976 (see Box 3.1). Having been subsequently referred to in court cases and in some instances actually incorporated into state law, the OECD 'guidelines' do not seem to have been entirely inconsequential. In the 1990s developments in international environmental law have also placed restrictions on the activities of TNCs, especially in the Third World.

If the balance of power swung in favour of host states (including those in the Third World) between the late 1960s and the mid-1970s, it seems clear that it began to tilt back to the multinationals during the 1980s. This was chiefly a result of two related developments, the first of which was the economic stagnation, indebtedness and currency instability in most developing countries during the decade, which made it more difficult for them to attract new investment from multinational corporations. As can be seen from Table 3.4, during the 1980s multinationals tended to concentrate on strengthening their position in their home markets and in other developed market economies, with the result that in an average year in the late 1980s only 16 per cent of new foreign direct investment was going into developing countries compared to almost double this proportion in 1975. Second, the decade witnessed the political rebirth of market economics, which reduced the ideological hostility to multinationals in much of the Third World. The upshot of these twin developments was that many poorer host countries liberalised their policies towards the multinationals, and bilateral investment treaties designed chiefly to protect the multinationals proliferated. In September 1992 the World Bank even announced its own voluntary guidelines prescribing a code of good behaviour for host governments towards the TNCs,[5] while the Uruguay Round of GATT accords in December 1993 (see Chapter 2) contained an agreement providing for the progressive elimination of trade-distorting restrictions on multinationals, albeit that the poorest countries were to be given the longest to phase them out. Already five years earlier Peter Hansen, executive director of the UN Centre on Transnational Corporations, had written: 'The era of confrontation has receded and been replaced by a practical search for a meaningful and mutually beneficial accommodation of interests.'[6] It was against this background that the early 1990s witnessed a dramatic resumption of a significant proportion of foreign direct investment going to the developing world. These years also witnessed a new trend towards investment in the emergent market economies of Central and Eastern Europe (see Table 3.4).

Box 3.1 OECD guidelines for multinational enterprises

Following a year and a half of intensive negotiations, the guidelines were agreed by the OECD Council at ministerial level in June 1976. Incorporated in a communiqué entitled 'Declaration on International Investment and Multinational Enterprises', the new guidelines were described as a response to the fact that 'advances made by multinational enterprises in organising their operations beyond the national framework may lead to abuse of concentrations of economic power and to conflicts with national policy objectives'. The communiqué stressed, however, that 'observance of the guidelines is voluntary and not legally enforceable', and ducked the issue of precise definition of a 'multinational enterprise'. The detailed guidelines covered disclosure of information, competition, finance, taxation, employment, industrial relations and science and technology, but were preceded by certain 'general policies'. The guidelines stated that enterprises should:

- take fully into account established general policy objectives of the Member countries in which they operate;
- in particular, give due consideration to those countries' aims and priorities with regard to economic and social progress, including industrial and regional development, the protection of the environment, the creation of employment opportunities, the promotion of innovation and the transfer of technology;
- while observing their legal obligations concerning information, supply their entities with supplementary information the latter may need in order to meet requests by the authorities of the countries in which those entities are located for information relevant to the activities of those entities, taking into account legitimate requirements of business confidentiality;
- favour close cooperation with the local community and business interests;
- allow their component entities freedom to develop their activities and to exploit their competitive advantage in domestic and foreign markets, consistent with the need for specialisation and sound commercial practice;
- when filling responsible posts in each country of operation, take due account of individual qualifications without discrimination as to nationality, subject to particular national requirements in this respect;
- not render – and they should not be solicited or expect to render – any bribe or other improper benefit, direct or indirect, to any public servant or holder of public office;
- unless legally permissible, not make contributions to candidates for public office or to political parties or other political organisations;
- abstain from any improper involvement in local political activities.

Source: *The OECD Observer*, no. 82, July/August 1976, where the guidelines are published in full.

Table 3.4 Inflows of foreign direct investment by type of country and in Central and Eastern Europe, 1975–93, selected years (percentage share in world total)

	1975[1]	1981–5	1986–90	1991	1992	1993
		Annual average				
Developed countries	71	74	84	74	65	56
Developing countries	29	26	16	24	32	41
Central and Eastern Europe	—	0.04	0.1	1	3	3
All countries	100	100	100	100	100	100

Note
1. Excludes the centrally planned economies of Europe.

Source
Adapted from UNCTAD, *Transnational Corporations in World Development* (UN: New York, 1988), Table V.1; and UNCTAD, *World Investment Report 1994: Transnational Corporations, Employment and the Workplace* (UN: New York, 1994), Table I.4.

Irrespective of the general balance of power, it also remains true, of course, that there always have been and always will be great variations in the distribution of power between different multinational–host state relationships within the same historical period. This is for the obvious reason that there are enormous variations in kinds of multinational corporation, kinds of host state and kinds of market condition. Common sense suggests that a large multinational will have a stronger hand in any dealings with a micro-state than a small multinational will have in bargaining with a major power, while the nature of the business concerned is also very significant. Such evidence as there is suggests that, other things being equal, multinationals in the extractive business (ores, gas and oil) are weaker relative to host states than those in manufacturing because their operations are much more geographically limited and their initial capital costs are extraordinarily high (the last also applies to liner shipping countries and airlines). Thus, mining companies faced with truculent host governments can threaten to leave with their equipment and skills but they cannot threaten to take away coal seams or diamond-bearing rocks as well, any more than oil companies can threaten to decamp with underground oil lakes. Moreover, if they do depart they will also lose a vast investment. In short, while such multinationals have a strong hand before their capital is irrevocably and literally 'sunk', they soon have a very weak one. This means that the good terms which they can initially win are likely to be overthrown in the course of *renegotiations* subsequently demanded by the host state. A well-known phenomenon in the natural resources industries, this is referred to as the 'obsolescing bargain'.[7]

Also important to the distribution of power between the multinational and the host state is the degree to which the corporation occupies a monopoly position in its market. Even in an era of competition between multinationals and between multinationals and alternatives to foreign direct investment, some corporations will have a stronger market position than others; market position also varies, of course, between different subsidiaries of the same multinational. Equally, a multinational subsidiary which produces largely for export will have a stronger bargaining position than one which produces almost exclusively for home consumption.

The relationship with home states

While there is no doubt that an era of considerable multinational influence over the poorer host states preceded the late 1960s, the evidence for the multinationals' manipulation of the foreign policies of their home states (as opposed to general foreign economic policy) has always existed more in the imagination than in the facts. Though he did not deny that influence was sometimes successfully exerted by investors, this was the conclusion arrived at in 1935 by Eugene Staley in *War and the Private Investor* – a work of formidable historical scholarship – and nothing has happened since to suggest that this judgement should be changed. There have simply been too many well-documented cases of home states resisting pressure from multinationals to adopt a particular course in foreign policy.

If multinationals had controlled the foreign policies of their home governments the United States would probably not have entered the Second World War, the cold war would have been less likely to have started (revisionist historiography notwithstanding) and, in any event, economic warfare would certainly not have been employed in it by the US government. Equally, Henry Kissinger, National Security Adviser to President Nixon and subsequently Secretary of State, would not have been allowed to get away with 'linking' trade and investment concessions to the Soviet Union with political and security concessions in return; the United States would have moved decisively to prevent the Marxist, Salvador Allende, from succeeding to the Chilean presidency in 1970, instead of doing too little too late; and it would have abandoned Israel for a pro-Arab posture years ago (though it may be said that this is unduly to minimise Jewish influence within the American multinationals). For its part, South Africa would not have introduced apartheid, nor adopted a contemptuous attitude towards the black states of Africa, and Britain would never have introduced a comprehensive arms embargo against it; nor, for that matter, would the United States have done so. In each of these cases, 'powerful' multinationals opposed the policy adopted.[8]

Stephen Krasner records additional evidence of the same sort as this in the context of the relationship between the United States government and American multinationals involved in raw materials. In addition, he shows that in the relatively small number of cases where Washington was directly or indirectly responsible for forcible intervention *in support of a foreign policy urged upon it by corporate interests* – either to open up a region to investment or, more commonly, to protect an established investment from the threat of expropriation – this only occurred because a broader foreign policy aim was at stake. Such was the case in Guatemala in 1954, Cuba and the Dominican Republic in the first half of the 1960s, and Chile in the early 1970s. Here, of course, the broader foreign policy aim was halting the spread of Communism in the Western hemisphere. Where corporate interests were taken over without prompt and adequate compensation but no American political interest was equally threatened, government support was confined to diplomatic and economic pressure on behalf of the multinationals concerned, as in the case of the nationalisation of the International Petroleum Company by the Peruvian government in the late 1960s; but 'even this policy instrument was tempered as it became increasingly clear that such action was counterproductive'.[9] When adequate compensation was paid for the expropriated assets of American multinationals and neither the security of supply of an important raw material nor a political interest was affected, Washington did not move at all and was in fact rarely asked to do so.

The significance of Krasner's analysis is considerable: first, because compared with the situation in other countries in the developed world the American state is weak relative to the other institutions of American society; and second, because the raw materials industries which he studied contain very large and wealthy companies, including the oil multinationals. If such companies cannot impose their wills on the American government, it is even less likely that other companies will impose theirs on other governments.

It will be clear, then, that the state in capitalist countries, contrary to all Marxist and much pluralist thinking, has a mind of its own. The content of this mind we call the 'national interest'. This more or less accurately reflects the general interests of a society and persists over time. It is penetrable by the historian. (In his brilliant and timely analysis, Krasner shows that the American national interest in the specific area of international raw materials policy in the twentieth century has consisted in the following: promoting broad foreign policy aims; insuring security of supply; and increasing competition to keep down prices – in that order.) Since the home state also has independent sources of power, as detailed earlier in this chapter, it is invariably able to resist pressure from the multinational corporation for a foreign policy which is inconsistent with the national interest.

This brings us to the final way in which multinationals may be politically significant in the international sphere: by their employment as *instruments* of the foreign policies of their home states. In fact, it was in this role that Staley found investor interests to be most commonly involved. This, however, was in an era when less odium attached to exerting political influence through private investor power and when, in addition, host countries had less power *vis-à-vis* foreign capitalists than has been the case for much of the time since the 1960s. The corollary of the swing in the distribution of power from multinationals to host countries in the 1970s, in other words, was that at any rate during that period corporate wealth was not available to the foreign policy of the home state to the extent that it used to be. In some cases, as already noted, it could actually be employed *against* the foreign policy of the home state.

Of course, it is not difficult to find examples in the recent past of foreign direct investment being manipulated by governments for political ends. As mentioned earlier, this was a Kissinger tactic used against the Soviet Union in the 1970s; and President Reagan later followed in his footsteps. Reagan also applied pressure to the Noriega regime in Panama later in the 1980s by forbidding the subsidiaries and branches of American multinationals to make any payments to it. American and EC codes of practice for their multinationals, together with restrictions on investment, were also used in the campaign against apartheid in South Africa. Once more, however, the complexity of the problem and, thus, the difficulty of making useful generalisations has to be emphasised. Despite the fact that multinationals from all states now come up against the same circumstance of host state power (in greater or lesser degree), some home states are in a stronger position than others to push their companies into a political role on their behalf. Furthermore, states which are usually strong in this regard will sometimes display weakness, while countries normally thought of as weak in this sense (such as the United States) will occasionally exhibit uncharacteristic strength.

The last case is well illustrated by the outcome of a tussle between the American government and Gulf Oil in late 1975. This was over the latter's tax and royalty payments to the Angolan authorities during the succession struggle between the American-backed forces of the National Front for the Liberation of Angola (FNLA) and National Union for the Total Liberation of Angola (UNITA) and the Communist-backed Peoples Movement for the Liberation of Angola (MPLA), which followed the independence of Angola from Portugal. By mid-November 1975 the MPLA had seized control of the Bank of Angola and taken possession of the dossier of contracts with Gulf; it also had physical control of the Cabindan oil fields. As for the American company, it had been obliged to suspend its operations and evacuate its personnel because of fears for their safety; it was not, however, under any threat of nationalisation from the MPLA. On the contrary, anxious to keep the revenues from oil flowing in, the MPLA urged Gulf to return and extended guarantees for its employees. According to John Stockwell, leader of the 'Angola task force' of the American Central Intelligence Agency (CIA), 'Gulf would gladly have taken the MPLA deal'. Had Gulf gone along with the MPLA, the Marxist party would have been paid $100 million on 11 December and a further $102 million on 15 January 1976. (In contrast, complained Stockwell, 'Our total budget was only $31.7m'.) As a result, both the CIA and the State Department brought pressure to bear on Gulf to divert their payments to the FNLA and UNITA. In this they failed, but Gulf was at least persuaded to deny the money to the MPLA for the time being. Instead, it placed all royalties and taxes in an interest-bearing escrow account until such time as a generally recognised government should emerge in Angola.[10]

Notes

1. *The Sovereign State: The secret history of ITT* (Coronet Books: London, 1974). Sampson himself concedes that 'the comparison of companies to countries can be misleading', p. 109.
2. These are not mutually exclusive categories. Many states, especially in the developed world, are both home and host to multinational corporations.
3. For example, by Barnet and Muller in *Global Reach*.
4. R. Jenkins, *Exploitation: The world power structure and the inequality of nations* (MacGibbon & Kee: London, 1970), p. 159.
5. A summary of these can be found in UNCTAD, Programme on Transnational Corporations, *World Investment Report 1993: Transnational corporations and integrated international production* (UN: New York, 1993), p. 29.
6. UN, *Transnational Corporations in World Development*, p. iii.
7. This phrase is attributable to Raymond Vernon.
8. It is true that not all of the American multinationals and banks with operations in Chile were as gung-ho as ITT and Anaconda. See US Senate, 'The International Telephone and Telegraph Company and Chile, 1970–1971', in Modelski's *Transnational Corporations and World Order*. There is also a dispute about the vigour with which the administration applied itself to stopping Allende in 1970.
9. Krasner, *Defending the National Interest*, p. 220.
10. This account is based on J. Stockwell's *In Search of Enemies: A CIA story* (Futura: London, 1979), pp. 211–12, and L. Turner's *Oil Companies in the International System*, 2nd edn (Allen & Unwin: London, 1980), pp. 77–9. Early in the following year the position of the MPLA regime was better consolidated and Gulf, with State Department approval, released the money to it. In 1978 Sonangol, the state-owned oil company formed in 1976, took a 51 per cent holding in the Gulf operation.

Further reading

Barnet, R. J. and R. E. Muller, *Global Reach: The power of the multinational corporations* (Simon & Schuster: New York, 1974; Cape: London, 1975).

Berridge, G. R., *The Politics of the South Africa Run: European shipping and Pretoria* (The Clarendon Press: Oxford, 1987).

Dunning, J., *The Globalisation of Business: The challenge of the 1990s* (Routledge: London and New York, 1993).

Dunning, J., *Multinational Enterprises and the Global Economy* (Addison-Wesley: London and New York, 1993).

Economist, 'Survey of Multinationals', 24 June 1995.

Fieldhouse, D. K., *Unilever Overseas: The anatomy of a multinational, 1895–1965* (Hoover Institution Press: Stanford, CA, and Croom Helm: London, 1978).

Frieden, J. A. and D. A. Lake, *Perspectives on Global Power and Wealth*, 3rd edn (Routledge: London, 1995).

Gilpin, R., *US Power and the Multinational Corporation: The political economy of direct investment* (Basic Books: New York, 1975).

Gilpin, R., *The Political Economy of International Relations* (Princeton University Press: Princeton, NJ, 1987), ch. 6.

Humes, S., *Managing the Multinational: Confronting the global–local dilemma* (Prentice Hall: Englewood Cliffs, NJ, 1993).

Jones, R. J. B., *Globalisation and Interdependence in the International Political Economy* (Pinter: London and New York, 1994).

Krasner, S. D., *Defending the National Interest: Raw materials investments and US foreign policy* (Princeton University Press: Princeton, NJ, 1978).

Krasner, S. D., *Structural Conflict: The Third World against global liberalism* (University of California Press: Berkeley, Los Angeles, and London, 1985), ch. 7.

Modelski, G. (ed.), *Transnational Corporations and World Order: Readings in international political economy* (Freeman: San Francisco, 1979).

OECD, *International Investment and Multinational Enterprises* (OECD: Paris, 1976).

Pinelo, A. J., *The Multinational Corporation as a Force in Latin American Politics: A case study of the International Petroleum Company in Peru* (Praeger: New York, 1973).

Reissinger, W. M., 'The MNC-developing state bargaining process: a review', *Michigan Journal of Political Science*, vol. 1, 1981.

Reynolds, C., *Modes of Imperialism* (Martin Robertson: Oxford, and St Martin's Press: New York, 1981).

Robinson, J., *Multinationals and Political Control* (Gower: Aldershot, 1983).

Spero, J. E., *The Politics of International Economic Relations*, 4th edn (St Martin's Press: New York, 1990), chs 4 and 8.

Staley, E., *War and the Private Investor* (University of Chicago Press: Chicago, 1935; repr. Howard Fertig: New York, 1967).

Stopford, J. M. and S. Strange, *Rival States, Rival Firms: Competition for world market shares* (Cambridge University Press: Cambridge, 1991).

UNCTAD, *Transnational Corporations in World Development: Trends and prospects* (UN: New York, 1988).

UNCTAD, *Transnational Corporations from Developing Countries* (UN: New York, 1993).

UNCTAD, *World Investment Report 1993: Transnational corporations and integrated international production* (UN: New York, 1993).

UNCTAD, *World Investment Report 1994: Transnational corporations, employment and the workplace* (UN: New York, 1994).

Walters, R. S. and D. H. Blake, *The Politics of Global Economic Relations*, 4th edn (Prentice Hall International: Englewood Cliffs, NJ, 1992), ch. 4.

4

States and conflict

International politics is the activity involved, peaceful or otherwise, in the working out of conflicts between states. Not surprisingly, the substance, the intensity and the scope of these conflicts fundamentally influence the character of international politics and no study of this field can ignore them or the theorising which they have provoked. However, understanding the full range of contemporary international conflicts, let alone their implications, is no easy matter, not least because the relatively clear (if cross-cutting) traditional fissures between East and West, and North and South, have lost their salience. All conflicts are now 'regional' conflicts.

In his influential work, *Man, the State and War*, Kenneth Waltz divides theories of conflict into those which attribute it to the nature of man (proud, power crazed, stupid and vicious), those which lay it at the door of the state (capitalist, dictatorial, and so on), and those which emphasise the malign influence of the anarchical states-system. The first of these 'images', as Waltz calls them, is unconvincing since, as he remarks, if human nature is *basically* evil, how can we explain acts of 'charity, love and self-sacrifice'.[1] The more plausible theories are those which emphasise either the economic, ideological or racial sources of conflict (the nature of the state), and those which lay stress on the power/security struggle (the structure of the states-system). This chapter will consider these theories in this order, and conclude by advancing the argument that the deepest conflicts occur when two or more of these sources of tension overlap.

Economic conflict

The view that international conflict is fundamentally rooted in economics, especially in the needs of advanced capitalism, has been extremely influential in the twentieth century and is, of course, a central aspect of Marxist-Leninist thought. It started its life as the theory of economic imperialism but in the 1970s mutated into 'dependency theory'.

The most influential figures in the development of the theory of economic imperialism were undoubtedly the British economist, J. A. Hobson, and the Bolshevik, V. I. Lenin. However, since the Second World War its elaboration, or at any rate its defence, has owed most to American Marxists, in particular Paul Sweezy, David Horowitz, Paul Baran, Gabriel Kolko and Harry Magdoff.[2] The essence of the theory[3] is that because of 'unequal exchange' capitalism in its monopoly stage produces a surplus of goods and capital which must find foreign outlets if a declining rate of profit at home is to be forestalled. The domestic habit of monopoly in turn leads to attempts to monopolise these outlets (*and* overseas sources of raw materials) at the expense of foreign rivals. Since the 'bourgeois class' entirely controls the government, the civil service and the military (the 'ruling class' theory of the state), the anxious monopoly capitalists have no difficulty in commanding political support for their foreign adventures. Finally, since there are a number of capitalist states in the mono-poly stage of development, international conflict is inevitable. Both the First and the Second World Wars are to be explained in these terms, as is the cold war, the Vietnam war, the simmering tension between the United States and Western Europe and between the United States and Japan, and so on.

The weakness – and the strength – of this theory is that it is not historically verifiable. That the theory of economic imperialism is neither provable *nor refutable* can be readily illustrated. In a famous article the economic historian, D. K. Fieldhouse, attempted to *refute* the theory by showing that by far the greater part of 'imperialist' investment did not go anywhere near the new colonies created by the European powers in the late nineteenth century.[4] But more than a decade earlier Paul Sweezy had anticipated this sort of argument by claiming that capitalist states 'had' to acquire colonies even where no immediate economic gain was in sight. This was either because colonies were a strategic requirement of their existing economic empires or because no monopolist could afford to overlook the possibility that they might develop economic value in the future.[5] Thus, he showed how the *fundamental* pur-poses which all capitalist foreign policy serves can still be held to remain economic in character, and so can attempts to refute the theory of economic imperialism on 'book-keeping' or 'balance-sheet' grounds be contemptuously dismissed.[6] Conversely, in the attempt to *prove* the theory of economic impe-rialism to be true its supporters draw attention, among other things, to the demonstrably close connections between the business and foreign policy com-munities in capitalist states. But this is easily countered, since such evidence could just as well be held to testify to the politicisation of the businessman as to the commercial enslavement of the politician, and such other evidence as exists does indeed tend to point to this, as argued in the previous chapter.

The theory of economic imperialism, then, rests essentially on *faith* – faith in the materialist claim that the mode of economic production is the indepen-dent variable in history, the great and original cause from which all else flows; it can be neither proved nor disproved. It is also instructive to recall, though this is admittedly an *ad hominem* argument (that is, one designed to slur rather than refute), that the theory of economic imperialism is a politician's theory, and that politicians are generally more interested in success than truth. Lenin had to show that advanced capitalism was 'responsible' for inter-national tension and war, as well as for all grave domestic evils, in order to make it the more reprehensible in the eyes of the Russian proletariat. The theory of economic imperialism is really an ideology.

Having said all this, it remains true that the period since 1945, as well as that going back to the late nineteenth century, has witnessed political clashes between capitalist states which have had clear economic undertones, even though these were muted by the premium placed on Western (or 'capitalist') solidarity during the cold war. For example, oil had a clear bearing on Anglo-American rivalry in the Middle East in the 1940s and 1950s, while the growth of US investment in Europe and the reserve currency status of the dollar were important elements in Franco-American tensions in the 1960s. It is notable, though, that, while there obviously has been competition between capitalists of different nationalities for markets and lucrative investment opportunities (increasingly on each other's territory rather than on that of states in the developing world), political tension during this period has normally only been associated with competition over valuable raw materials and energy sources, the pirating of intellectual property rights, and the threat of foreign control of 'strategic' industries. As the world population continues to grow, the limited availability of fresh water supplies has also emerged as a serious source of conflict between states with all manner of political-economic system. This is because three-quarters of the world's biggest river basins are shared between two states and a quarter of them between three to ten. Hot, dry areas such as the Middle East – where, for example, disputes over the waters of the Tigris and the Euphrates have poisoned relations between Turkey, Syria and Iraq – are particularly prone to conflict over this issue.

To return to the development of Marxist thinking, according to many latter-day members of this school, in a corruption of the theory of economic imperialism usually known as 'dependency theory', the smothering of conflicts between the capitalist states in the contemporary period did not have much to do with the need for solidarity in the face of competition with the Soviet bloc. Instead, it was a result of a change in the character of capitalism itself and a growth in its *collective* preoccupation with relations with the so-called under-developed world. According to this view, the change which has occurred within capitalism is the appearance and spread of multinational corporations, some developing into huge supermonopolies. Having thus broken through the shell of the state, this new vehicle of capitalist enterprise has rendered redundant the institution of rival 'national capitalisms', and replaced the capitalist state as the principal agency spearheading the struggle for markets, investment outlets and raw materials with *the world capitalist system as such*. As a result, as Reynolds says, 'contrary to Lenin, it [dependency theory] conceives of the capitalist *state* system as fundamentally non-competitive'.[7] The major political cleavage is thus held to be that between the giant multinational corporations (towing their governments in their wake) on the one hand, and the countries of the underdeveloped world (on which the former are parasitic) on the other. Loosely speaking, the main conflict is seen as that between the North and the South, and the dominant image that of a pervasive international 'class conflict'. What are we to make of this argument?

It is certainly true that a clash of economic interests between the rich and the poor countries is believed to exist, at any rate by the latter. This is demonstrated by the existence of two long-lived institutional expressions of a 'Third World Coalition' – the Group of Seventy-Seven (G-77) (see Box 4.1) and the Non-Aligned Movement (NAM) (see Box 4.2) – and the debates which they have stirred up with the richer states in the UN welfare network (see Chapter 13). These debates came to a head in the mid-1970s when the liberal (market-based) international economic regime was challenged head on by the Third World demand for a 'New International Economic Order' based on 'principles and norms that would legitimate more authoritative . . . modes of allocation'.[8] It is also true that this economic conflict has been a constant irritant in general relations between richer and poorer states, and coloured them in a particularly marked way in the 1970s.

Nevertheless, the claim that the North–South economic conflict is the master conflict of the states-system remains fundamentally flawed because it misunderstands the essentially *political* character of many of the Third World's demands (as well as the real relationship between the multinational and its home state, discussed in the previous chapter), and rashly minimises the corrosive effect on 'class solidarity' within the Third World of political conflicts between its members. As Krasner has so convincingly demonstrated, while the Third World Coalition has never been uninterested in economic

---

Box 4.1   The Group of Seventy-seven (G-77)

The G-77 is a highly institutionalised coalition of developing countries which was formed at the first UN Conference on Trade and Development (UNCTAD) in 1964. By 1988 the original membership had increased to 128. Based principally in Geneva, it is divided into three regional groups: Africa (52), Asia (43), and Latin America (the most structured of the three, with 33 member states). Attempts to negotiate common positions between the regional caucuses prior to the four-yearly UNCTAD conferences are made via a Preparatory Committee, a Senior Officials Meeting and a Ministerial Meeting.

The activities of the G-77 are not confined to UNCTAD but are seen in negotiations on the whole range of financial and commercial issues which affect the Third World, whether at the IMF and World Bank in Washington, the UN General Assembly, or elsewhere. (GATT, now the World Trade Organisation, does not officially recognise the G-77.) However, there is no formal method of coordination between the various sites of G-77 activity, or between them and the centre in Geneva. Nor does the G-77 have a permanent secretariat, partly because some secretariat functions are in effect performed for it by the UNCTAD Secretariat.

objectives, its predominant motives, dictated by the external and internal weakness of its members, have been concerned with fashioning an international economic order which would provide them with greater political stability: 'Vulnerability, not simply poverty, is the motivating force for the Third World's meta-power programme for transforming international regimes.'[9] As for 'class solidarity', this has been utterly compromised not only by regional political conflicts but also by deep hostility between those states within the Third World Coalition which have adopted 'radical' and those which have adopted 'moderate' attitudes towards relations with the richer states. Thus, Cuba's Marxist regime was not admitted to membership of the predominantly conservative Latin American group within the G-77 until 1971 and then was prevented from attending its all-important informal meetings; and within the African group there have always been profoundly different attitudes to cooperation with the ex-colonial metropolis between francophone and anglophone Africa. In any event, the voice of the moderates, or the 'pragmatists', became much stronger in the Third World Coalition in the 1980s (as noted in the discussion of multinational corporations in the previous chapter); in the changed conditions the campaign for a 'New International Economic Order' was effectively 'shelved' and one of its most important platforms, the UN Conference on Trade and Development (UNCTAD), was 'marginalised'.[10]

In sum, while there may well be a latent international class conflict there is not yet a great deal of evidence to support the actual existence of one. Furthermore, if one does exist it is certainly of no great significance compared to the other conflicts which divide states. It is not surprising that dependency theory should be so unilluminating. Like its parent, the Marxist-Leninist theory of imperialism, it is essentially an ideology rather than an historical explanation of international conflict: its priority is action not explanation, political success not truth.

Ideological conflict

It is common in discussions of the general elements in international conflict to find reference to 'ideologies', loosely conceived as all-embracing, universalistic political doctrines. They are alluring because they provide simple explanations of the human plight together with route maps designed to guide the chosen out of it. Chief among these ideologies are communism, liberalism (the theory of free-market capitalism and its political correlates), nationalism and – latterly – Islamic fundamentalism. The view that such doctrines are a principal source of conflict between states derives great strength from the turbulence which shook the Middle East following the Islamic Revolution in Iran in 1979, notably in the Iran–Iraq war. It was, however, already well established as a result of the cold war between the United States and the Soviet Union, for this was clearly the major conflict of the post-1945 era and coincided with an unbridgeable ideological gulf between communists and capitalists.

Any account of the origins of the cold war which failed to take serious account of the influence of ideology, not least over the attitudes of the United States, would indeed be utterly inadequate. Ideology was undoubtedly one of the primary factors which led President Truman to resist the extension of Soviet power beyond Eastern Europe, especially into Western Europe, northern Iran and Greece – the 'occasion' of the cold war. For the Soviet Union was seen as a 'world revolutionary power' in the State Department, which was newly influential following the death of President Roosevelt in April 1945 and the unexpected elevation of the inexperienced Truman. As a revolutionary power, the government in Moscow was viewed as a significant threat to the promotion of liberalism and representative democracy, which, by virtue of America's own revolutionary heritage and geographical isolation, had come to be regarded in Washington as the chief aims of a righteous foreign policy. Furthermore, by establishing a *closed* sphere of influence in Eastern Europe, Stalin's government was regarded as acting in a manner flagrantly inconsistent with the principles on which the new United Nations had been founded, and to which at that stage America attached so much importance. For his part, the Soviet leader, Stalin, undoubtedly saw the world through the prism of Marxism-Leninism which, with its emphasis on the rapacity and expansionist dynamic of capitalism, clearly intensified the fear of 'encirclement' by the 'imperialist' powers which he had acquired in the interwar period. This ideology also made Stalin believe that it was right, as well as prudent, to establish Communist regimes wherever it was in his power to do so.

The ideology of nationalism, the peculiarly modern notion that the boundaries of the state should coincide with the boundaries of the 'nation' (itself defined characteristically by language, according to the influential eighteenth-century German philosopher, Herder), is also an important source of conflict between states. This ideology flourished after the French Revolution of 1789, was the basis on which much of the map of Europe was redrawn after the First World War, and fired the 'national liberation struggles' against colonialism in Asia and Africa after the Second World War. For many years after 1945 stronger in the Third World than in Europe (where it tended to go under the euphemistic title of 'regionalism'), nationalism has recently resurfaced with great energy in the territories of the former Soviet Union (including Russia itself) and Eastern Europe, most notably, of course, in former Yugoslavia. According to Gellner, nationalism (or 'cultural chauvinism') is a feature of the modern era because modern industrialised societies cannot function in the absence of cultural homogeneity.

Nationalism is most commonly associated with conflict between states, as opposed to conflict within them, when it assumes the sort of virulent form which it did in Germany under Hitler and in Italy under Mussolini. Radical nationalisms of this sort, which deify the nation and assert its qualitative supremacy over all other nations, claim not only a right to territorial expansion but also a civilising duty to engage in it. This recipe for international disaster in a world of more or less established nation-states, which was used to serve up the Second World War, has fortunately been less popular since, at any rate in the West. However, the seeds of this kind of thinking are probably latent in all forms of cultural chauvinism.

On the face of it, however, there is no necessary connection between interstate conflict and the kind of liberal, 'normal' nationalism of which nineteenth-century Italian nationalism (the 'Risorgimento') is the prototype. If the principle of national self-determination was *in fact* universally accepted as the overriding basis for statehood, if there was *in fact* a consensus on the criteria of nationality, if there was *in fact* a consensus on which groups met these criteria, and if every nation thus identified was *in fact* precisely coexistent with one state, nationalism of this kind would lose its significance – its job would have been completed. However, this is hardly a description of the contemporary states-system or of reflection on its constitution, despite casual references to its members as 'nation-states'. It suffices to say that *in fact* the modern world is full of multinational states, such as Britain, Canada, Switzerland, Belgium, and Spain. It also includes 'nation-states', such as Somalia, Greece, and Serbia which have not completely swept up all of the territory inhabited by their 'nationals'. And it includes, too, nations which have no state of their own at all, for example the Kurds, the Tibetans, the Armenians and the Basques.

In this nationalistically messy world, nationalism provokes interstate conflict in two main ways. First, it may encourage attempts at secession in a multinational state and thus provide opportunities for varying degrees of outside intervention, as in the Nigerian civil war in the late 1960s. (Though the major powers have been extremely reluctant to encourage secessionist movements in established states, in part because of the fear of creating a precedent which may rebound on their own territories. Among recent examples of this are their coolness towards the idea of creating a Kurdistan or independent Chechnya.) Second, where a 'nation-state' fails to embrace all of the territory inhabited by its 'nationals' (or allegedly inhabited by its nationals in an earlier period), nationalism may inspire irredentism – that is, the attempt to extend the boundaries of the state in such a way that it absorbs the remaining territory – with serious consequences for relations between all concerned. For example, the campaign among Greeks and Greek Cypriots for *enosis* (union of Cyprus with Greece) has not only caused problems between Athens and Nicosia but periodically brought Greece and Turkey to the verge of war. This is partly because Cyprus contains a sizeable Turkish minority and partly because the island is only forty miles from the Turkish coast.

It should also be noted that nationalism may provoke particularly bitter and intractable dispute in the special case where, as during the long years of the conflict between Arabs and Jews which started in the mid-1930s and became intense following creation of the state of Israel in 1948, one nation claims the entire territory occupied by another. The passions which this conflict aroused and its fulcrum in the strategically significant and oil-rich Middle East meant that it was probably the most dangerous conflict in the world, producing six wars between 1948 and 1985 (see Box 6.1) and constantly threatening to pull in Moscow and Washington on opposing sides. Here Arab nationalism in general and Palestinian nationalism in particular were locked in deadly confrontation with Zionism. The Arabs who originated from the old British (League of Nations) mandate of Palestine (see Figure 4.1), together with their supporters in the Arab League, rested their title to the land of Palestine chiefly on the claim that they were the great majority until many were tricked or forced out of the territory by the Jews. Zionists, on the other hand, held that the experience of the Jewish diaspora – culminating in the Holocaust of the Second World War – had been so uniquely dreadful that they required the protection of a state of their own; and that, because it was their ancestral home, this state must be located in Palestine, embracing in its entirety the holy city of Jerusalem, Zion.

It is true that peace has now been made between Israel and two Arab states, Egypt and Jordan, as well as with the PLO itself.[11] It is also true that the end of the cold war has defused the globally explosive potential of the Arab–Israeli conflict. Nevertheless, the bulk of the Arab states, including Syria and Iraq, have still failed to make peace with Israel. It is also clear that the heavily qualified agreement with the PLO, to which there is less than meets the eye (it gives the PLO little more than certain devolved powers in the Gaza Strip and parts of the West Bank plus a commitment to future negotiations on a 'permanent settlement'), is experiencing serious difficulties.

Despite the cases noted above, ideological divisions between states are not always the main reasons for tensions between them. As Morgenthau claims, they sometimes serve chiefly as more palatable justifications or rationalisations for states' actions which have their real sources elsewhere.[12] This was the case with Britain's increased hostility towards South Africa at the beginning of the 1960s. Purportedly inspired by different ideologies of race relations – Commonwealth 'multiracialism' versus *apartheid* – British policy was influenced more deeply by horror at the diplomatic consequences of identification with South African racialism. (Though it is also true, of course, that the earlier determination of the National Party government itself to weaken relations with Britain had been inspired by ideology: the determination of Afrikaner nationalism to reverse the verdict of the Boer Wars of the turn of the century.)

However, even in ideologically garnished conflicts where it can be established that neither party was much influenced by ideological considerations 'at the beginning', as well as in those where it almost certainly was, ideology invariably remains significant in at least three ways. First, by providing justifications for disputes which might otherwise be unpalatable not only

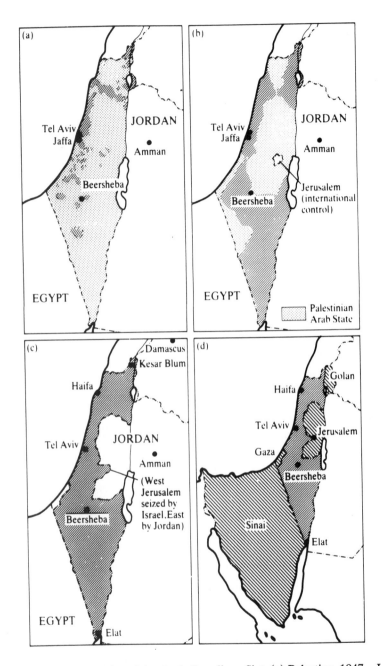

Figure 4.1 The geography of the Arab–Israeli conflict: (a) Palestine, 1947 – Jewish settlements; (b) Jewish state, 1947 – UN plan; (c) Israel, 1949; (d) Israel after 1967 and Occupied Territories (Source: Reproduced from G. Chaliand and J.-P. Rageau, *Strategic Atlas: World geopolitics*, Penguin: Harmondsworth, p. 128)

to important sections of domestic opinion but also to foreign friends and allies, ideologies *facilitate* conflict. Second, by casting a conflict in ideological terms, as a clash, that is to say, between believers and unbelievers, it is significantly *sharpened*: disagreements become 'struggles', wars become 'crusades', and dead soldiers become 'martyrs'. In short, restraint goes out of the window, and with it the laws of war. The Iran–Iraq war in the first half of the 1980s was particularly instructive in this regard. (A special case under this heading is the sharpening of conflicts by ideology where members of the same church or movement fall out, for in such instances – as in the Sino-Soviet dispute – to the charge of simply being an ideological enemy is added the highly emotive charge of being an ideological traitor.) Finally, by making compromise seem unthinkable and placing leaders who have come to have second thoughts at the mercy of the emotions they have themselves aroused, ideology *prolongs* international conflicts.

Racial conflict

It was in the 1960s that it became fashionable to draw attention to the factor of race in international conflict, that is, to the effect on international politics of the unfounded and pernicious view of influential people that biological differences – popularly known as racial differences – were behaviourally significant. The occasion of this was the entrance into the erstwhile white-dominated states-system of many new states in Black Africa, and the alliances (see Boxes 4.1 and 4.2) that they cemented with the new states in Asia which had obtained their independence a little earlier. The 'non-whites' were held to be obsessed by fresh memories of white domination and bitterly disillusioned to find that political independence had not generated its economic equivalent. For their part, the 'whites' were said to nurture feelings of contempt for the new states which were only thinly disguised by a rhetoric of racial equality. These feelings were purportedly inspired by the racist judgement that Asian and, especially, African regimes were congenitally incapable of efficient management, corruption-free administration, fair treatment of minorities, or any arrangement for changing the character of governments other than by military *coup d'état*. The white states were held to reveal their true 'colours' in the continuing support which they gave to two white regimes implanted in the Third World that had constitutions based on racial criteria: Israel (in reality founded on religion) and South Africa. As a result, writers such as Ronald Segal even claimed that the struggle between 'whites' and 'non-whites', dramatised by vitriolic exchanges in the UN General Assembly, was already 'the major preoccupation of mankind'.[13] South Africa itself was not an exception but a microcosm of the racial conflict endemic in the world as a whole, the front line of the 'race war'.

It is beyond doubt that belief in racial difference is a factor in some international conflicts and it would be surprising if it is not an element in some where

Box 4.2   The Non-Aligned Movement (NAM)

The NAM owes its more immediate origins to the resolve of twenty-nine Afro-Asian states, meeting at summit level in the Indonesian city of Bandung in April 1955, to resist superpower attempts to incorporate them into one or other of their alliances. This reflected the view of the Afro-Asian states that they were part of a distinctive 'Third World', as well as their fears that alliance membership would immediately compromise the freedom which they had only just won from European colonialism. The Indian leader, Jawaharlal Nehru, was the NAM's founding father. Since the 'neutralism' of the NAM was concerned only with remaining out of one conflict in particular (the cold war), it is necessary to distinguish it from the 'permanent neutrality' of a state such as Switzerland; the latter guarantees non-involvement in *any* war or peacetime alliance. Since the NAM also periodically aspired to diplomatic attempts to end the cold war, its doctrine was sometimes known as '*positive* neutralism'.

At a summit held in Belgrade in 1961, the NAM was formally launched. A much bigger meeting was held at Cairo in 1964, and following the Lusaka summit in 1970 summit meetings – preceded by foreign ministers' meetings – were held triennially. The last one was held in Cartagena in Colombia in October 1995. The NAM, which now has well over 100 members, has no secretariat, secretariat functions being discharged by the government of the country hosting the last summit. While the NAM includes most developing countries, there has always been a significant number of them which have not wished (or been able) to remain aloof from superpower alliances. As a result, the NAM was never identical in membership with the G-77. Moreover, it was not long after the movement's launch that leading members betrayed its cardinal principles by themselves leaning to one side or other in the cold war, Cuba's relationship with the Soviet Union being perhaps the most glaring example. The ending of the cold war has now rendered the NAM redundant, though it remains a church to be seen in on Sundays.

there is no conclusive evidence. The conflict between pre-Mandela South Africa and the 'Afro-Asian' states, especially those constituting the black 'Front Line States' in southern Africa, was certainly one which falls into the first of these categories. This conflict culminated in the vicious 'destabilisation' campaigns of the South African Defence Force in the late 1970s and early 1980s. It owed its origins not only to the affront to racial dignity caused by South Africa's domestic policy of *apartheid* but also to the increasingly visible extension of white racialism into the Republic's foreign policy in the 1950s and early 1960s. This policy included opposition to Africa's decolonisation, hostility to the presence of armed blacks in the local forces of the European colonial powers (which, not surprisingly, hindered cold war planning over defence between these powers and South Africa in the 1950s), resistance to further Asian immigration into British East Africa, and a refusal to treat 'non-white' visiting dignitaries (including cricketers) in the same way as their white counterparts. In the 1950s white racism also led South Africa to oppose a role for UN welfare agencies in the African continent and to become a leading member of an alternative scheme based on cooperation between the colonial powers.

In sum, the conflict between South Africa and the Front Line States had its origins chiefly in the attempts of the first National Party prime ministers (Malan, Strijdom and Verwoerd) to make Africa safe for 'European/Christian [that is, white] civilisation'. It is also important to note, however, that tensions between South Africa and administrations to the north (especially the self-governing colony of Southern Rhodesia – now Zimbabwe – and Portuguese-controlled Mozambique) predated decolonisation. These were rooted in conceptions of a 'Greater South Africa', as well as in economics, and would probably have endured even had there been no change in the racist character of the regimes concerned.

Into the second category, that is, the category of conflicts in which race is widely suspected to be an element but regarding which the evidence is more slender (and sometimes merely anecdotal), fall a number of serious clashes. One of these is the Sino-Soviet conflict (on hearing that Chinese troops had fired on Russian frontier guards on the Ussuri River in 1969, Yakov Malik, the long-serving Russian ambassador to the UN, is reported as referring to the Chinese as, among other things, 'squint-eyed bastards' and 'yellow sons of bitches').[14] Another such conflict is that between the United States and Japan in the Second World War, in the context of discussion of which it is often said that the Americans would not have dropped the atomic bomb on Europeans.

It is, however, one thing to concede the element of race – in effect, belief in biological superiority – in certain conflicts; it is quite another to accept that it has become the 'transcending' factor in international politics. In the first place, no state except South Africa has openly subscribed to a doctrine of racial supremacy since the Second World War, and even South Africa soon began to emphasise its own attachment to racial separation rather than to racial supremacy. Racial arrogance was in fact more in evidence in international relations in the nineteenth and early twentieth centuries, in Europe's attitude towards 'the unspeakable Turk', in the mutual and open contempt of the Orient and the Occident, in the near-genocidal policy of the United States towards the American Indians, and in the ferocious hatred of the Nazis for the Jewish and Slavic *Untermenschen* ('subhumans') of Eastern Europe. In the second place, racial differences (as with the 'class' differences discussed earlier with which to some extent they coincide) invariably recede into the background when ideology, economic assistance or the balance of power, for example, require extension of the hand of friendship. Here, the Sino-American *rapprochement* in the 1970s and the exchange of ambassadors between South Africa and Malawi in 1967 are instructive illustrations.

Conversely, racial similarities between states are hardly any guarantee that conflicts will not engulf them. If they were there would have been no cold war, while India and Pakistan would not have been at loggerheads since partition, and the Arab world would stand united, instead of hopelessly divided, against Israel – even had there been, given the common 'Semitic' bond, any 'Arab–Israeli conflict' to begin with! Evidently, the theory of impending race war, like the theory of economic imperialism, is in effect nothing more than an ideological vision. We know this for certain when one of its supporters attempts to cope with the sort of contrary evidence mentioned above (specifically, the Sino-American *rapprochement*) by asserting simply that, 'of course history does not unfold on completely clear-cut lines. Fundamental divisions', he continues, 'can become blurred by secondary considerations.'[15] The Chinese would probably not be impressed by the claim that their security from a Soviet nuclear attack was a 'secondary consideration'.

In the contemporary period, then, while race – like ideology – may exacerbate conflicts, it would seem to be only rarely a decisive reason for sparking them off. This is partly because the imperatives of international trade and finance have required 'colour-blindness', partly because Third World states have continued to need the skills of native as well as expatriate whites, and partly because the major Western powers have been made more sensitive to foreign policy issues with racial overtones by the presence in their midst of growing minorities of blacks, Asians and (especially in the case of France) Arabs from the Maghreb. It is salutary to remember, in particular, that 'One out of every five black men lives outside Africa'.[16] Many of these live in the United States, and there is little doubt that their influence contributed to the decision of the US Congress to pass the Comprehensive Anti-Apartheid Act (over President Reagan's veto) in 1985. Current projections of the Census Bureau of the United States, which over recent decades has witnessed a massive increase in immigration, suggest that by the middle of the twenty-first century almost half of the total American population will be non-white, though hispanics will have overtaken blacks as the largest component of this group.[17] Above all, however, race has probably been less significant as a source of international conflict than some suppose because of the deep and widespread revulsion caused by the appalling consequences of Hitler's racially influenced policies during the Second World War. It is true that much is now made of 'ethnic' conflict in the territories of the former Soviet bloc and Yugoslavia, but the conflicts here would seem to be more ones of nationality and religion than of race narrowly conceived.

Structural conflict

The last of the main general theories of conflict is associated with the 'neorealist' school. It rests on the view that states find themselves so often locked in struggles not because of the dynamics of their economies or because of ideological or racial differences but because of the anarchical *structure* of the states-system itself. This is Waltz's 'third image'. With no world government possessing the power to curb the violence of its more aggressive members, the states-system is pervaded by insecurity. In this distracting situation, states have no alternative but to give top priority to reducing their insecurity and defending their other 'national interests' by reliance on military means. (This tendency is strongly encouraged by the career instincts of professional soldiers and the greed of arms manufacturers, the 'merchants of death' of an early rhetoric and the 'military/industrial complex' of a later one.) But, as states strive to improve their security by strengthening their armed forces, expanding their alliances and tightening their grip on 'strategic' assets abroad (bases, lines of communication, vital fuels and raw materials), some will be more successful in these regards than others. This is a function of their unequal assets and skills.

Having deduced the pre-eminence of security policy from the international anarchy and established the 'law of uneven growth',[18] realism proceeds to what is probably its key claim: the more powerful will appear threatening to the less powerful, even if the intentions of the former are entirely pacific. This is partly because the more powerful will be busying themselves reshaping the political and economic features of the states-system to their special interests, and partly because they have acquired the *capacity* to offer mortal threats to the weaker without being able to offer any guarantees that a more bellicose national regime may not one day come to power. In other words, as the realist saying goes, one state's security is another state's insecurity. Consequently, prudence dictates that states which have been slow off the mark should strive hard to catch up. Arms build-ups thus generate arms races, alliances provoke counter-alliances, and bids on the part of a state to expand its influence into regions hitherto ignored lead its rivals to do the same. In short, insecurity leads to a *power struggle*, the logical outcome of which is war, since a time will arrive when one state or alliance will feel that it has an edge and decide to strike at its rivals in order to end its insecurity once and for all. (Neo-realists argue among themselves about whether this is more likely to occur in a bipolar or multipolar world. This issue is taken up in Chapter 10.)

The structural theory of international conflict is the most persuasive of all such theories and is now possibly the most widely accepted. Most historians regard it as pointing at least to the 'permissive' causes of the majority of international conflicts, including the two world wars of this century. It is also the theory on which the idea of 'collective security' is predicated. (The fact that collective security was a failure under both the League of Nations and – until Kuwait – the UN, does not necessarily cast doubt on the diagnosis of conflict which it assumes; this merely testifies to the difficulty of doing anything about it.)

Like all of the general theories, however, the structural theory soon looks rather threadbare when held up to the light of history. In the first place, it cannot explain why hostility develops between some states and not others in situations where the military capacity of each state to threaten all others is roughly similar – why did Hitler attack France but sign a non-aggression pact with the Soviet Union? In the second place, the structural theory is distinctly uncomfortable with those conflicts provoked by states under no obvious security threat from the targets of their hostility. Three examples here are provided by the conflict between the post-Mao leadership of China and distant Albania, which started in 1977; that between Britain and even more remote Argentina in 1982 ('the Falklands war'); and that between Iraq and Kuwait in August 1990. In the last case it was hardly Kuwait's military capacity to threaten Iraq which led to the Iraqi invasion. On the contrary, it was its very weakness, plus the desirability of its assets.

When sources of conflict overlap

While all general theories of international conflict should thus be treated with great caution, it remains true that one or more of the factors to which they seek to attribute pre-eminent significance – power/security rivalry, economic competition, ideological antipathy and even racial prejudice – have indeed been predominant influences on the most important conflicts of the contemporary era. Not surprisingly, however, the deepest conflicts are those where two or more of these factors overlap, as in the Arab–Israeli conflict (land – the ultimate economic resource – and ideology). Two further important illustrations of this point are provided by the cold war and the Sino-Soviet dispute, conflicts which emerged – the first more quickly than the second – after the end of the Second World War and endured until the Soviet Union fell apart at the end of the 1980s.

A variety of secondary considerations had a bearing on the origins of the cold war: the paranoia of the Soviet leader, Stalin, which was fed by Western intervention against the Bolsheviks during the Russian civil war and the delay in opening the second front against Germany in the Second World War; the pugnacious style of the American president, Harry Truman, and his need to demonstrate presidential calibre (he had not been elected to office and was relatively unknown); the assertiveness injected into American attitudes by unrivalled wealth and exclusive possession of the A-bomb; the traditional antipathy of both the Soviet Union and the United States, for different reasons, to diplomacy; apprehension in Washington at the effect on the 'ethnic vote' of a sell-out on Poland; and so on. However, there is little doubt that the chief reason for the start of the cold war was a potent *coincidence*. This was the conjunction, on the one hand, of profound ideological differences with, on the other, the fact that by 1945 the humiliation of France, the destruction of Japanese and Axis power, and the terminal weakening of Britain had left only America with the military capacity to threaten Soviet security and only the Soviet Union with the potential to threaten the United States.

As in the cold war, so in the Sino-Soviet conflict a variety of secondary considerations were of significance in its origins: the resentment of the scholarly Mao at the refusal of the 'rumbustious political boss',[19] Khrushchev, to treat him as the senior figure in the world Communist movement following the death of Stalin in 1953; the memory of how little the Russians had helped the Chinese in making their own revolution; the refusal of the Soviet Union to share its full nuclear secrets with Peking; and so on. But there is little doubt that the length and bitterness of the Sino-Soviet dispute was a result of a series of *coincidences*: the coincidence of a traditional power struggle involving disputed territory along the longest common land frontier in the world with mutual racial prejudice and serious ideological disagreements, including the dispute over the Soviet policy of 'peaceful coexistence' with the West.

Notes

1. p. 28.
2. See 'Further Reading' at the end of this chapter.
3. The following is, of course, an idealisation of the 'theory'. Each of its supporters has a different version and the bitterness of the arguments between them is notorious. See, for example, Kemp, *Theories of Imperialism*.
4. ' "Imperialism": an historiographical revision', *The Economic History Review*, 2nd ser., vol. 14, no. 2, 1961.
5. *The Theory of Capitalist Development*, p. 303.
6. Magdoff, *The Age of Imperialism*, p. 14.
7. *Modes of Imperialism*, p. 81.
8. Krasner, *Structural Conflict*, p. 5.
9. *Ibid.*, p. 27.
10. Williams, *Third World Cooperation*, p. 167.
11. Peace treaties were concluded with Egypt in 1979 and Jordan in 1994, while a 'Declaration of Principles on Interim Self-Government Arrangements' was signed between Israel and the PLO in Washington on 13 September 1993.
12. Morgenthau, *Politics Among Nations*, p. 92.
13. Segal, *The Race War*, p. 13.
14. A. N. Schevchenko, *Breaking with Moscow* (Cape: London, 1985), p. 164.
15. Tinker, *Race, Conflict and International Order*, p. 119.
16. Mazrui and Tidy, *Nationalism and New States in Africa*, p. 361.
17. S. A. Taylor, 'The foreign policy implications of recent developments in immigration, ethnicity, and assimilation', unpubl. paper, British International Studies Association Annual Conference, York, Dec. 1994, p. 16.
18. Gilpin, *War and Change in World Politics*, p. 94.
19. P. Calvocoressi, *World Politics since 1945* (Longmans: New York, 1982), p. 64.

Further reading

Economic conflict

Baran, P. A. and P. M. Sweezy, *Monopoly Capital: An essay on the American economic and social order* (Monthly Review Press: New York, 1966; Penguin: Harmondsworth, 1968).

Bhagwati, J. N. and J. G. Ruggie (eds), *Power, Passions and Purpose: Prospects for North–South negotiations* (MIT Press: Cambridge, MA, 1984).

Fieldhouse, D. K., *The Theory of Capitalist Development* (Longman: London, 1967).

Hansen, R. D., 'North–South policy – what is the problem?', *Foreign Affairs*, vol. 58, Summer 1980.

Hobson, J. A., *Imperialism: A study*, 3rd edn (Allen & Unwin: London, 1938; first pub. 1902).

Horowitz, D., *Empire and Revolution: A radical interpretation of contemporary history* (Random House: New York, 1969); published in the UK as *Imperialism and Revolution* (Allen Lane: London, 1969).

Iida, K., 'Third World solidarity: the Group of 77 in the UN General Assembly', *International Organization*, Spring 1988.

Kemp, T., *Theories of Imperialism* (Dobson Books: London, 1967).

Knorr, K., *Power and Wealth: The political economy of international power* (Basic Books: New York, and Macmillan: London, 1973).

Kolko, G., *The Roots of American Foreign Policy* (Beacon Press: Boston, 1969).

Krasner, S. D., *Structural Conflict: The Third World against global liberalism* (University of California Press: Berkeley, Los Angeles and London, 1985).

Lenin, V. I., *Imperialism: The highest stage of capitalism* (Progress Publishers: Moscow, 1966; first pub. 1917).

Magdoff, H., *The Age of Imperialism* (Monthly Review Press: New York, 1969).

Mortimer, R. A., *The Third World Coalition in International Politics* (Westview Press: Boulder, CO, 1984).

Naff, T. and R. T. Matson, *Water in the Middle East: Cooperation or conflict?* (Westview: Boulder, CO, 1984).

Reynolds, C., *Modes of Imperialism* (Martin Robertson: Oxford, and St Martin's Press: New York, 1981), ch. 3.

Rothstein, R. L., *The Weak in the World of the Strong: The developing countries in the international system* (Columbia University Press: New York, 1977).

Rothstein, R. L., *Global Bargaining: UNCTAD and the quest for a new international economic order* (Princeton University Press: Princeton, NJ, 1979).

Rothstein, R. L., *The Third World and US Foreign Policy: Cooperation and conflict in the 1980s* (Westview Press: Boulder, CO, 1981).

Sauvant, K. P., *The Group of 77* (Oceana: New York, 1971).

Sklair, L., *Sociology of the Global System* (Johns Hopkins University Press: Baltimore, 1991).

Sweezy, P. M., *The Theory of Capitalist Development* (Dobson: London, 1946).

Wallerstein, I., *The Capitalist World-Economy* (Cambridge University Press: Cambridge and New York, 1979).

Williams, M., *Third World Cooperation: The Group of 77 in UNCTAD* (Pinter: London, and St Martin's Press: New York, 1991).

Wriggins, W. H. and G. Adler-Karlsson, *Reducing Global Inequities* (McGraw-Hill: New York, 1979).

Ideological conflict

Crick, B., *In Defence of Politics*, 2nd edn (Penguin: Harmondsworth, 1982).

Crockatt, R., *The United States and the Cold War 1941–53*, BAAS Pamphlets in American Studies 18 (British Association for American Studies: 1989).

Dawisha, K. H., 'The roles of ideology in the decision making of the Soviet Union', *International Relations*, vol. 4, no. 2, 1972.

Gaddis, J. L., *The United States and the Origins of the Cold War, 1941–1947* (Columbia University Press: New York, 1972).
Gaddis, J. L., *Long Peace: Inquiries into the history of the cold war* (Oxford University Press: Oxford and New York, 1989).
Morgenthau, H. J., *Politics Among Nations*, 5th edn rev. (Knopf: New York, 1978).
O'Brien, C. C., *The Siege: The saga of Israel and Zionism* (Weidenfeld & Nicolson: London, 1986).
Paterson, T. A., *Meeting the Communist Threat: Truman to Reagan* (Oxford University Press: New York, 1987).
Quandt, W. B., *Camp David: Peacemaking and politics* (The Brookings Institution: Washington DC, 1986).
Quandt, W. B. (ed.), *The Middle East: Ten years after Camp David* (The Brookings Institution: Washington DC, 1988).
Reynolds, C., *Modes of Imperialism* (Martin Robertson: Oxford, and St Martin's Press: New York, 1981), ch. 4.
Rosecrance, R. N., *Action and Reaction in World Politics: International systems in perspective* (Little, Brown: Boston, 1963; repr. Greenwood: Westport, 1977).
Rosecrance, R. N., *International Relations: Peace or war?* (McGraw-Hill: New York, 1973).
Taylor, T. and S. Sato (eds), *Future Sources of Global Conflict* (RIIA and Institute for International Policy Studies: London and Tokyo, 1995), ch. by Mayall.
Yergin, D., *Shattered Peace: The origins of the cold war and the national security state* (Penguin: Harmondsworth, 1977).

Nationalism

There is an enormous literature on this subject, and most general studies have good select bibliographies. However, recent works tend to dwell more on the character, origins and future prospects of nationalism than on its bearing on interstate conflict. Among recent and classic studies are the following:

Alter, P., *Nationalism*, 2nd edn (Edward Arnold: London, 1994).
Anderson, B., *Imagined Communities* (Verso: London, 1983).
Breuilly, J., *Nationalism and the State*, 2nd edn (Manchester University Press: Manchester, 1993).
Cobban, A., *Nationalism and National Self-Determination* (Oxford University Press: London, 1969).
Gellner, E., *Nations and Nationalism* (Blackwell: Oxford, and Cornell University Press: Ithaca, NY, 1983).
Kedourie, E., *Nationalism*, 3rd edn (Hutchinson: London, 1966).
Kedourie, E. (ed.), *Nationalism in Asia and Africa* (Weidenfeld & Nicolson: London, 1970).
Kohn, H., *The Age of Nationalism* (first pub. 1962; repr. Greenwood: Westport, CT, 1976).
Mayall, J., *Nationalism and International Society* (Cambridge University Press: Cambridge and New York, 1990).
Minogue, K. R., *Nationalism* (Batsford: London, 1967).
Seton-Watson, H., 'Unsatisfied nationalism', *Journal of Contemporary History*, vol. 6, 1971.
Seton-Watson, H., *Nations and States: An enquiry into the origins of nations and the politics of nationalism* (Methuen: London, 1977).

Smith, A. D., *Nationalism in the Twentieth Century* (Martin Robertson: London, 1979).
Smith, A. D., *Theories of Nationalism*, 2nd edn (Duckworth: London, 1983).
Tiryakian, E. A. and R. Rogowski (eds), *New Nationalisms of the Developed West* (Allen & Unwin: Boston, 1985).

Racial conflict

Barber, J. and J. Barratt, *South Africa's Foreign Policy: The search for status and security, 1945–1988* (Cambridge University Press: Cambridge and New York, 1990).
Berridge, G. R., *South Africa, the Colonial Powers and 'African Defence': The rise and fall of the white entente, 1948–60* (Macmillan: London, 1992).
DeConde, A., *Ethnicity, Race and American Foreign Policy* (Northeastern University Press: Boston, 1992).
Glazer, N. and D. P. Moynihan (eds), *Ethnicity: Theory and experience* (Harvard University Press: Cambridge, MA, 1975).
Mazrui, A., *Africa's International Relations: The diplomacy of dependency and change* (Heinemann: London, and Westview Press: Boulder, CO, 1977).
Mazrui, A. and M. Tidy, *Nationalism and New States in Africa* (Heinemann: Ibadan and London, 1984).
Moynihan, D. P., *Pandaemonium: Ethnicity in international politics* (Oxford University Press: Oxford and New York, 1993).
Nolutshungu, S. C., *South Africa in Africa: A study of ideology and foreign policy* (Manchester University Press: Manchester, 1975).
Schlesinger, A. M., Jr, *The Disuniting of America: Reflections on a multicultural society* (Norton: New York, 1992).
Segal, R., *The Race War: The world-wide conflict of races* (Penguin: Harmondsworth, and Viking Press: New York, 1967).
Shepherd, G. W., Jr (ed.), *Racial Influences on American Foreign Policy* (Basic Books: New York and London, 1970).
Tinker, H., *Race, Conflict and the International Order: From empire to United Nations* (Macmillan: London, and St Martin's Press: New York, 1977).
Vincent, R. J., 'Race in international relations', *International Affairs*, vol. 58, no. 4, 1982.
Wasserstein, B., *Britain and the Jews of Europe, 1939–1945* (Oxford University Press: Oxford and New York, 1979).

Structural conflict

Betts, R. K. (ed.), *Conflict after the Cold War: Arguments on causes of war and peace* (Macmillan: New York, 1994).
Buzan, B., *People, States and Fear: The national security problem in international relations*, 2nd edn (Harvester Wheatsheaf: Hemel Hempstead, 1991).
Cashman, G., *What Causes War? An introduction to theories of international conflict* (Lexington Books: New York, 1993).
Dickinson, G. L., *The International Anarchy, 1904–1914* (Allen & Unwin: London, 1926).
Diehl, P. F., 'Arms races and escalation: a closer look', *Journal of Peace Research*, vol. 20, no. 3, 1983.
Doran, C. F. and W. Parsons, 'War and the cycle of relative power', *The American Political Science Review*, vol. 74, 1980.

Gilpin, R. G., *War and Change in World Politics* (Cambridge University Press: Cambridge and New York, 1981).

Gray, R. C., 'Learning from history: case studies of the weapons acquisition process', *World Politics*, vol. 31, no. 3, 1979.

Herz, J. H., *Political Realism and Political Idealism* (Chicago University Press: Chicago, 1951).

Holsti, K. J., *Peace and War: Armed conflicts and the international order, 1648–1989* (Cambridge University Press: Cambridge and New York, 1991).

Jervis, R., 'Cooperation under the security dilemma', *World Politics*, vol. 30, no. 2, 1978.

Kratochwil, F., 'Errors have their advantage', *International Organization*, vol. 38, no. 2, 1984 [on Waltz's structuralism, pp. 312–19 only].

Levy, J. S., 'Organizational routines and the causes of war', *International Studies Quarterly*, vol. 30, no. 2, 1986.

Rotberg, R. I. and T. K. Rabb (eds), *The Origins and Prevention of Major Wars* (Cambridge University Press: Cambridge, 1989).

Suganami, H., 'Bringing order to the causes of war debate', *Millenium*, vol. 19, no. 1, 1990.

Waltz, K. N., *Man, the State and War: A theoretical analysis* (Columbia University Press: New York and London, 1959), chs VI–VIII.

Waltz, K.N., *Theory of International Politics* (Addison-Wesley: Reading, MA, 1979).

PART B
The instruments of conflict

5

Secret intelligence

Secret intelligence is not generally the most important of the 'instruments of conflict'. Nevertheless, there remain two good reasons why discussion of this topic should commence here. In the first place, states normally analyse the information gathered by their intelligence agencies *before* deciding how to pursue their foreign policies. In the second, political warfare or 'covert action' conducted by secret intelligence agencies provided much of the distinctive flavour of the cold war.

Until quite recently, secret intelligence received scant attention from scholars. This changed principally because of recognition that modern conditions make good intelligence on enemies more vital than ever and because, in spite of this and in spite of extraordinary technical advances in intelligence gathering, spectacular 'intelligence failures' continue to occur. Major public inquiries following such alleged failures – the Agranat Commission in Israel following the Yom Kippur War in 1973 and the Franks Commission in Britain after the Argentinian attack on the Falkland Islands in 1982, for instance – are symptomatic of the anxiety which these cases have generated. (These inquiries are also a rich source of evidence.) However, secret intelligence is also receiving more attention now because of revelations concerning the extent to which Allied intelligence shortened the Second World War, because CIA activities became an important domestic political issue in the United States during the 1970s, and because the collapse of the Soviet Union has resulted in unprecedented insights into the operations of the KGB. Not surprisingly, secret intelligence is no longer the 'missing dimension' of diplomatic history or international relations.[1]

This chapter will consider four main questions. First, what are the main functions of secret intelligence? Second, how have methods of intelligence collection changed since the Second World War? Third, why do 'intelligence failures' occur, and what can be done to avoid them? And fourth, what are the advantages and disadvantages of 'covert action'?

The functions of secret intelligence

Broadly conceived, secret intelligence has four main functions. The traditional, and still the most important, one is 'to obtain by covert means, and then to analyse, information which policy-makers cannot acquire by more conventional methods'.[2] While secret services seek information on a whole range of subjects, their most important task is usually to obtain information on the future plans and military capabilities of their actual and potential opponents. All information of this kind is conventionally known as 'strategic intelligence', as distinct from the 'tactical intelligence' sought by military commanders in preparation for and during battle.

Accurate assessments of external threats have always been important but are more so than ever today in view of the power, accuracy and speed of delivery of modern weapons; second chances are no longer so readily available. Moreover, overestimates of external threats, as in the case of the Soviet belief that Ronald Reagan's America – the 'main adversary' – was planning a nuclear first strike against it in the early 1980s, can be as dangerous as underestimates, since they can lead to wasteful overpreparedness and be interpreted abroad as aggressive – and provoke an equally aggressive response. The main task of American intelligence in the cold war was, of course, estimating the Soviet strategic threat.

Though at first this may seem surprising, states need to employ secret intelligence against their friends as well as their enemies, especially if they are important military allies. For the fact of the matter is that however close they are, friends never share all of their secrets. For example, the MacMahon Act, passed by Congress at the end of the Second World War, resulted in the exclusion even of Britain, America's wartime atomic research collaborator, from future access to United States nuclear secrets. Subsequently, China was denied access to the Soviet nuclear programme. States want to know the answers to two chief questions about their allies. First, their protestations notwithstanding, what contribution can they really make to the alliance? Secondly, are they reliable? If allies are intense economic rivals, as are the French and the Americans – notably in aerospace, defence, audio-visual electronics, and telecommunications – there is a further reason for espionage. In early 1995, against the background of a recent history of American allegations of French clandestine activity in the United States, France demanded the expulsion of five American citizens alleged to be engaged in industrial espionage.[3] Economic intelligence gathering has generally become more important since the end of the cold war, not least because secret services have been anxious to justify the large budgets to which they became accustomed during the long period of Soviet–American rivalry.

Because of the greater intimacy, it is generally easier to conduct secret intelligence gathering against friends than enemies, though the diplomatic consequences of discovery are more serious. Israeli intelligence is naturally targeted chiefly at the surrounding Arab states and the PLO but also at Israel's chief ally, the United States. This was confirmed with the arrest in November 1985 of Jonathan Pollard, an American Jew working in US naval intelligence for Israeli intelligence. It was underlined in 1990 by the evidence revealed in the memoirs of former Mossad agent Victor Ostrovsky (see 'Further reading'). US–Israel relations were made more difficult by these revelations and the American Jewish community, so vital to the support of Israel, was acutely embarrassed.

The inevitable corollary of secret intelligence gathering is the need for elaborate protection against it. This means not only the protection of general government secrets but the protection of the secret service itself against hostile penetration. (The possibilities which it provides for deception make a penetrated secret service more dangerous than having no secret service at all.) Thus 'counter-intelligence' is the second function of secret intelligence. This is sometimes conducted by separate organisations, for example Shin Beth in Israel and the Security Service in Britain. Counter-intelligence as well as foreign intelligence was controlled by the KGB in the Soviet Union,[4] while America's Central Intelligence Agency (CIA) also engages in both kinds of operation. (For the US 'intelligence community', see Box 5.1; for the British, Box 5.2.)

The third function customarily assigned to intelligence agencies is deception. Feeding other governments with 'disinformation' has obvious utility in wars or situations which threaten war, 'when its main purpose is to draw enemy defences away from a planned point of attack, or to give the impression that there will be no attack at all, or simply to confuse the opponent about one's plans and purposes'.[5] However, deception may also serve foreign as well as military policy, for example by misrepresenting to a rival's allies the rival's true feelings about them. Deceptions are usually uncovered before too long and are naturally corrosive of trust. They are thus best reserved for enemies, where there is no trust to be lost.

Box 5.1   The American intelligence community

According to information released into the National Security Archive in Washington DC, the 'community' is made up of twenty-five separate 'intelligence organisations'. Among these the main ones are as follows:

- National Security Council.
- Office of the Director of Central Intelligence.
- Central Intelligence Agency.
- National Security Agency.
- Defense Intelligence Agency.
- Army Intelligence and Security Command.
- Navy Operational Intelligence Center.
- Air Force Foreign Technology Division.
- Unified and Specified Command Intelligence Directorates.
- Bureau of Intelligence and Research (Department of State).
- National Reconnaissance Office.*

*Established in 1960 to manage satellite reconnaissance programmes for the whole intelligence community, the NRO became the most secret of its members. Its existence was not exposed until 1973, and it was not officially acknowledged until September 1992.

Box 5.2   The British intelligence community

The British intelligence community (if the history of rivalry within it will permit such a term) has three main components:

- *MI5*. Formally known as the 'Security Service', this organisation is Britain's counter-intelligence and counter-terrorism agency. However, the weight of its work shifts as the threats to national security themselves change. With the much reduced demand for operations against Soviet bloc intelligence agencies active in Britain brought by the end of the cold war, MI5 shifted far more resources into anti-terrorism, even wresting control of anti-IRA activities in Northern Ireland from the police. The cease-fire in the province in 1994 then had it once more looking for new work, chiefly in action against drug trafficking, money laundering, and organised crime. It is under Home Office control.
- *MI6*. Otherwise known as the Secret Intelligence Service (SIS), this is the foreign arm of British intelligence and operates under the control of the Foreign & Commonwealth Office. Its main regional interests are the Middle East and Eastern Europe.
- *GCHQ*. Based at Cheltenham, the Government Communications Headquarters specialises, like its US counterpart the NSA, in signals intelligence, including electronic intercepts and satellite monitoring. It is also under the control of the Foreign & Commonwealth Office.

The fourth function of secret intelligence is 'political warfare'. This is secret participation in the domestic politics or civil wars of other states, usually to defend a friendly government or overthrow a hostile one. In the latter case, it is commonly known as 'subversion'. Covert action was one of the principal weapons employed by the superpowers in the cold war. It has also been a source of considerable tension within the CIA, where there has been resistance to the idea of employing a secret service in such a role as well as to the activity itself.

Changing methods of collection

The traditional method of collecting intelligence is, of course, to employ spies. Men or women are sent into a target area with instructions to glean whatever they can by observation, eavesdropping or theft. However, in 1963 Allen Dulles, director of the CIA from 1953 until 1961, claimed that the attractions of this method had been greatly reduced by the complexity of modern targets as much as by the development of alternative, technological means. Agents capable of this kind of 'well-concealed reconnaissance', he maintained, were not likely to have the technical or scientific knowledge which would enable them to make sense of any discoveries which they made.[6] This may well have been generally true then and remains true of the intelligence services of most states today. However, revelations in the last years of the cold war about KGB operations to steal American high-technology secrets – especially those with military applications – demonstrated that a major agency at any rate could operate agents trained to a fairly high scientific and technical standard, and use them to some effect. Vladimir Vetrov, who worked for French intelligence within the scientific and technological division of the KGB's First Chief Directorate, revealed that in 1980 alone 'a total of 3,617 "acquisition tasks" had been under way, of which 1,085 had been successfully completed in the course of the year, producing over four thousand "samples" and more than twenty-five thousand technical documents'.[7]

The problem of technical ignorance will not in any case confront the 'planted' agent, whose very competence in a profession or trade makes possible insinuation into a target and the acquisition of information in the normal course of work as a trusted employee. One of the most successful planted agents uncovered in recent times was Gunter Guillaume, the East German agent who rose to become personal assistant for party matters to the West German chancellor, Willi Brandt, in 1972. He was arrested in 1974. Life is much more difficult for this kind of spy today, however, at least in the West, as a result of the sophistication of modern security vetting techniques.

With the traditional spy and the planted agent facing such problems, it is not surprising that 'human intelligence' ('HUMINT' in spook-speak) now places great reliance on the corruption, conversion, seduction or intimidation of men and women who are *already* members of a target institution, such as a foreign ministry, weapons research establishment, or – as in the case of Vladimir Vetrov, mentioned above – secret service. Such persons will know what sort of information is significant, and will not be as vulnerable to inquiries into their pasts. Priceless agents of this kind are known as 'agents in place'. Other important examples who have come to light in recent years include Colonel Ryczard Kuklinski, a CIA agent on the Polish General Staff at the beginning of the 1980s; Aldrich Ames, a middle-ranking CIA official recruited by the KGB in 1985 who was not exposed until 1994 and in the meantime enjoyed a spell as head of the Soviet section of agency counterintelligence; and Oleg Gordievsky, KGB resident in London in the 1980s, who had in fact worked for British intelligence since 1974.[8]

'HUMINT' has not been rendered obsolete by the appearance of 'spy satellites' and other forms of technical intelligence gathering. There are some kinds of information which are simply unobtainable by such means: for example, decisions taken so recently that they have as yet produced no externally detectable manifestations. A case in point was the decision of the Indian government in December 1971 to attack West Pakistan, which was immediately reported to the CIA by an agent in place within Mrs Gandhi's Cabinet.[9]

Thus, most states continue to disguise secret agents as members of their embassies, trade missions and other official and semi-official institutions with branches overseas (such as national airlines), and instruct them not only to pick up such information as they can by their own devices but also to secure and run agents in place. In 1982 the CIA created a new 'HUMINT' gathering committee. 'HUMINT' operations are easiest to run in countries where there is no strong tradition of secret police activity and there are marked ethnic or cultural affinities between the agents and their unwitting hosts. It was there-fore no great surprise to find, after unification in 1990, that West German intelligence was riddled to the top with agents in the pay of the East German Stasi. Guillaume had been merely the tip of the iceberg.

Despite the continuing importance of 'HUMINT', technological advances have made it possible at least for the major states to rely on safer, quicker and more accurate and reliable means than the secret agent where information on a vast range of vital targets is concerned. These targets include foreign com-munications (signals intelligence, or 'SIGINT'); nuclear weapons testing, pro-duction and deployment; troop manoeuvres; surface vessel and submarine movements; grain harvests; and the locations where hostages are known or suspected to be held. In the 1970s technological progress in intelligence gathering was spurred especially by the importance to successful arms control negotiations of the ability to 'verify' agreements, that is, to make sure that the other side was keeping its part of the bargain.

There is now a very rich variety of remote means for gathering intelligence, of which the spy satellite, relied on by the superpowers more and more after 1960, is only the best known. Moreover, this is no longer a technology over which the United States and Russia have a monopoly. Israel and France lead other powers entering this field. The capabilities of these remote means are also extraordinary, as was demonstrated once more by the information which they supplied to the coalition forces during the Gulf war in early 1991. Nev-ertheless, modern surveillance technologies are not without their problems and limitations. This became vividly clear when the hard information gathered by the West on the Warsaw Pact following German reunification (and the dissolution of the East German army) revealed that certain key assumptions about the Pact based chiefly on earlier electronic surveillance were inaccurate. It was discovered, for example, that the rate of advance of Warsaw Pact forces had been wildly overestimated.

Some modes of technical intelligence gathering have to face natural obstacles such as cloud-cover and darkness, while others are confronted by elaborate defences such as jamming, camouflage, decoys and the hardening of landline communications. Moreover, in some circumstances technical means may well be dangerously provocative, as was certainly the case with America's U-2 spy planes. Because of the present reliance of these technologies on far-flung networks of ground stations, they may also prove to be politically em-barrassing in relations with certain allies and other friendly states, and highly vulnerable in the event of radical changes in their regimes or in their governments' policies. The United States lost a number of ground-based 'SIGINT' facilities, most seriously those near the Soviet frontier in northern Iran, following the overthrow of the Shah of Iran in early 1979. The reliance of some surveillance technologies on politically problematical networks of overseas ground stations is reputed to be diminishing but it seems unlikely that it will be reduced dramatically in the foreseeable future.

Are intelligence failures inevitable?

Although it is clearly difficult even for the intelligence services of the great powers to obtain certain kinds of information, nevertheless an impressive consensus among scholars now maintains that the real problem of intelligence lies not in its collection but in its interpretation. The information is usually to hand; the problem lies in divining its significance. This is so difficult that 'intelligence failures' are widely believed to be inevitable. This conclusion was underlined when the world was surprised by Saddam Hussein's invasion of Kuwait in August 1990, despite detailed photographic evidence of military formations massing on the frontier. Most agencies, including Egypt's legendary Mukhabarat, though not the CIA and the DIA,[10] appear to have believed that he was merely attempting to intimidate the Kuwaitis.

Why is misinterpretation of raw intelligence such a common occurrence? Some reasons are common to misinterpretations both of intentions and of capabilities. First, an intelligence service's analysts may have been deliberately deceived by the opposition, for deception, as we know, is one of the subsidiary functions of secret intelligence. This is known to have happened prior to the Egyptian attack on Israel in 1973, when the Arabs sought to confirm the known Israeli belief that they were not ready for war by a whole variety of subtle diplomatic and disinformation strategies. Second, too much trust may be placed on assumptions about a rival's behaviour based on (accurate) knowledge of his past practice. This happened when the CIA refused to believe that the Soviet Union was installing nuclear missiles in Cuba in 1962 because Moscow had previously been opposed to 'adventurism' of this kind. The construction of predictive behavioural theories is unavoidable because the absence of conclusive evidence may leave no alternative to deduction. However, excessive reliance on such theories, perhaps encouraged by bureaucratic inertia, is obviously dangerous since the opposition may act 'out of character' for any number of reasons, including the fact that he probably knows what one *expects* him to do!

A third explanation of the misinterpretation of evidence collected by secret intelligence is really a variation on the second: the distortion of the image of the opponent by prejudice, whether racial or ideological. Following its sweeping victory over the Arabs in 1967 (coming as this did after earlier successes in

1948 and 1956), Israel had developed a contempt for Arab military prowess. This clearly contributed to a complacency which was shrewdly exploited by the Arabs in 1973. Conversely, the crude ideological prisms through which both sides in the cold war regarded each other probably contributed to an exaggeration of the mutual threat.

Finally, and perhaps most fatally of all, there is wishful thinking, the illogical but disturbingly easy jump from the *wish* that something might be true to the *conclusion* that it really is true. While the US Pentagon claimed to be 'winning' the Vietnam war, estimates of Communist strength produced by US military intelligence tended to be far lower than the (more accurate) estimates of the CIA. Wishful thinking is particularly dangerous because, like prejudice, it operates unconsciously, and when the evidence is ambiguous, as it often is, it provides a means of resolving the doubt. Wishful thinking, together with deception, were probably the main ingredients in the intelligence failure which occurred when Iraq invaded Kuwait.

If deception, excessive reliance on adversary images, prejudice and wishful thinking are the most common explanations of intelligence failures concerning both the intentions and capabilities of opponents, there are other explanations which are specific to each. An insurmountable problem confronts the secret service seeking to penetrate a rival's *intentions* when the latter has not yet decided on any course of action at all. How can intelligence know the other's plan if the other has none? Governments dominated by authoritarian individuals often seem to act on whim. In this connection it is interesting to note that British intelligence was exonerated from the charge of failing to give warning of the Argentine invasion of the Falkland Islands on 2 April 1982 on the very reasonable grounds that the Argentinian Junta 'probably' did not take the decision to launch the invasion until 31 March and 'possibly' not until 1 April, that is, the day before.[11] Even great powers sometimes seem to have no settled purpose, in the case of the United States chiefly because of a constitutional separation of powers. The rivalry for influence over foreign policy between the State Department, the National Security Council and Congress in certain periods since the Second World War (especially during the 1970s) must have caused acute problems to those sections of the KGB charged with determining US intentions.

As for *capabilities*, these present secret intelligence with two special problems. First, as Knorr reminds us, military success depends not only on quantitative factors which can be counted beforehand but also on qualitative ones which never fully emerge until fighting is well under way. These include 'troop-training and morale, military leadership, strategy and tactics, military intelligence and communications, the performance of arms under wartime conditions, the behaviour of allies, the ability of belligerent governments and publics to absorb casualties, and so forth'.[12] (Napoleon held that the relative importance of morale to *matériel* was three to one.) Second, as Knorr adds, 'all the elements that determine the military capability of a potential opponent in wartime are significant only relative to the capabilities of one's own side'[13] – Libya is powerful relative to Chad but weak relative to the United States, for instance. Hence estimating the capabilities of one's own side, with all the dangers of patriotic self-delusion which this presents, is also indispensable to any estimation of the capabilities of one's opponents. Quite rightly, Knorr concludes that 'the only true test of capabilities' is war itself.[14] (Knorr's analysis, of course, implicitly challenges the common view that it is easier to determine capabilities than intentions, since the latter – assuming they exist – are at least *in principle* knowable.)

The intrinsic difficulties facing correct intelligence analysis, principally by politicians, are enormous and some of them are clearly insuperable. This is why Betts is sceptical of the organisational reforms called for after each successive 'intelligence failure'. Making warning systems more sensitive should reduce the risk of surprise but will inevitably increase the number of false alarms, which in turn will undermine faith in all alarms. Creating rival intelligence agencies will increase the likelihood that false assumptions about an opponent will be challenged but may either make it impossible for the politicians to choose between rival estimates on any basis other than their own prejudices or simply induce paralysis. (In any case, the US intelligence community already contains twenty-five different organisations; see Box 5.1.) Separating intelligence analysis from policy-making may lead to greater objectivity but will reduce the political influence of the intelligence service and thus its ability to ensure that its view prevails within government, and so on. Not surprisingly, Betts concludes that intelligence analysis can only be marginally improved by organisational reform and that, therefore, intelligence failures are inevitable. He is undoubtedly right. By way of reassurance, however, he adds that 'seen *in perspective*, the record could be worse'.[15]

'Covert action'

When states use their intelligence agencies to support foreign friends or attack foreign enemies we speak of 'covert action' or 'political warfare'. Allies are secretly supplied with funds, advice, technical assistance, training and weapons. Enemies may become the targets of black propaganda, sabotage, economic disruption and even assassination. Such activity is by no means a monopoly of the CIA and the former KGB, as the sinking by French intelligence in the mid-1980s of the Greenpeace vessel *Rainbow Warrior* in a New Zealand harbour amply demonstrates. (The ship was proposing to inconvenience French nuclear testing in the South Pacific.)

Covert action has sometimes paid substantial dividends. American enthusiasm for the technique was fired by the effectiveness of the CIA's role in helping to prevent the victory of the Communists in the Italian general election in 1948, and of the Huks (Communist guerrillas) in the Philippines in the early 1950s. In 1955 the CIA played a similar role in the elections which consolidated the power of Ngo Dinh Diem in South Vietnam. 'The Company' also contributed to the downfall of nationalist leaders in Iran in 1953 (Dr Mossadeq) and in Guatemala in the following year (Jacobo Arbenz), and of the Marxist leader of Chile, Dr Salvador Allende, in 1973. Entering with gusto into the free-for-all in the Congo in the first half of the 1960s, by 1965 the CIA had also seen its chosen instrument, General Joseph Mobutu, emerge as president. In the 1980s Ronald Reagan, with his born-again ideological zeal to help 'freedom fighters' around the world, returned to 'special activities' with a vengeance and achieved at least one spectacular success: the withdrawal of Soviet forces from Afghanistan in the late 1980s, which was enormously influenced by the secret help given by the CIA to the Afghan *mujahideen*. According to Christopher Andrew, this was 'one of the most successful covert operations since the Second World War'.[16] The successes of Soviet intelligence in what 'Moscow Centre' called 'active measures' were achieved mainly in countries adjacent or near to its borders.

If the CIA has had substantial successes in the field of covert action, especially in the 1950s, it has also had serious failures. These have usually been the result of ignorance of local conditions or political vacillation, or both. Considerable failures were suffered in the Ukraine, Eastern Europe and Albania in the late 1940s and early 1950s, in Indonesia in 1958 (when it tried to sponsor a rebellion against President Sukarno), and, most spectacularly, in Cuba in 1961 – normally referred to as the 'Bay of Pigs' after the site chosen for the landing of the small CIA-trained exile army which was supposed, in some unspecified way, to be instrumental in the downfall of Fidel Castro. Subsequently, CIA activity in Laos and Vietnam ultimately came to nothing; it failed in a more discreet attempt to bring down Castro ('Operation Mongoose'); and it failed to prevent the Marxist MPLA from emerging triumphant in the succession struggle which followed the departure of the Portuguese from Angola in 1974–5. The Reagan administrations' success with covert action in Afghanistan was also seriously off-set by the failure of the miserable Iran-Contra affair, though this happened partly because the operation was run by amateurs from the National Security Council rather than professionals from the CIA.

'Covert action' is clearly the late-twentieth-century equivalent of gunboat diplomacy, and has been adopted as a result of the moral disapprobation which came to be attached after the Second World War both to 'imperialism' and to the use of force in international relations. Provided it works and *remains* covert, there can be no possible practical objection to it. It should also be borne in mind that it helps the major powers to protect their foreign interests without flagrantly intervening in the domestic affairs of other states, and thus helps to preserve the chief principle on which the states-system rests: the sovereignty of the state. The main argument against 'covert action' is that, if it is to be conducted on a scale sufficiently substantial to provide a good chance of success and if it is used repeatedly, it will be impossible to conceal either its role or the source of its direction. In other words, it will not be 'covert' at all and will thus attract the opprobrium which it was designed to avoid and undermine the principle it was designed to preserve. Lamenting America's excessive enthusiasm for covert action in the 1950s, Roger Hilsman, who was appointed director of the State Department's Bureau of Intelligence and Research by John F. Kennedy, remarks in his memoirs that:

> where one action, considered in isolation, might seem worth the cost of slightly tarnishing our image abroad, the cumulative effect of several hundred blots was to blacken it entirely. By the end of the Eisenhower administration our reputation was such that we got credit for almost everything unpleasant that happened in many countries.[17]

Furthermore, if there is to be any chance at all of preserving secrecy, it is probably inevitable that the responsibility for covert action should be handed to those most expert in acting by stealth, the agents of secret intelligence. But this risks compromising both the assets and the reputation of the intelligence gatherers among those in foreign countries whose trust they require. It was in substantial part as a result of its covert operations that the CIA attracted such unfavourable media and Congressional attention in the 1970s, and suffered serious harm as a result. Not surprisingly, the size and status of the CIA's covert action branch were severely reduced after the mid-1970s, though this was partly a result of the ending of the huge involvement in Vietnam. However, there will still be circumstances in which covert action will remain attractive and may well be the only option available.

Notes

1. Andrew and Dilks, *The Missing Dimension*.
2. *Ibid.*, p. 5.
3. *Financial Times*, 24 Feb. 1995.
4. In the successor Russian federation a separate organisation – the Federal Counter-Intelligence Service – was created. What remained of the KGB was christened the External Intelligence Service.
5. Dulles, *The Craft of Intelligence*, p. 144.
6. *Ibid.*, pp. 63–4.
7. Andrew, *For the President's Eyes Only*, p. 465.
8. Following his defection in July 1985, Gordievsky co-authored a best-selling book on the KGB with Christopher Andrew (see 'Further reading').
9. Powers, *The Man Who Kept The Secrets*, p. 206.
10. By the end of July both American agencies believed that evidence of invasion was only circumstantial – which it was – and preferred to accept the reassurances of the Egyptian and Jordanian leaders that Saddam would not attack, Andrew, *For the President's Eyes Only*, p. 518.
11. *Falkland Islands Review* ('The Franks Report'), January 1983, Cmnd 8787, para. 263.

12. 'Strategic intelligence: problems and remedies', Martin, *Strategic Thought in the Nuclear Age*, p. 81.
13. *Ibid.*
14. *Ibid.*
15. Betts, 'Analysis, war and decision', emphasis in original. For the more sanguine view, see A. E. Goodman, 'Dateline Langley: fixing the intelligence mess', *Foreign Policy*, no. 57, 1984–5 and S. J. Flanagan, 'Managing the intelligence community', *International Security*, vol. 10, no. 1, 1985.
16. *For the President's Eyes Only*, p. 493.
17. *To Move A Nation: The politics of foreign policy in the administration of John F. Kennedy* (Doubleday: New York, 1967), p. 86.

Further reading

Adams, J., *The New Spies* (Hutchinson: London, 1994).

Adams, S., *War of Numbers: An intelligence memoir* (Steerforth: South Royalton, VT, 1994).

Aldrich, R. J. and M. F. Hopkins, *Intelligence, Defence and Diplomacy: British policy in the post-war world* (Cass: London, 1994).

Andrew, C., *Secret Service: The making of the British intelligence community* (Heinemann: London, 1985); published in the USA as *Her Majesty's Secret Service* (Penguin Books: New York, 1987).

Andrew, C., *For the President's Eyes Only: Secret intelligence and the American Presidency from Washington to Bush* (HarperCollins: London, 1995).

Andrew, C. and D. Dilks (eds), *The Missing Dimension: Governments and intelligence communities in the twentieth century* (University of Illinois Press: Urbana, and Macmillan: London, 1984).

Andrew, C. and O. Gordievsky, *KGB: The inside story of its foreign operations from Lenin to Gorbachev* (Hodder & Stoughton: London, 1990; HarperPerennial: New York, 1991).

Andrew, C. and O. Gordievsky, *Instructions from the Centre: Top secret files on KGB foreign operations 1975–1985* (Hodder & Stoughton: London, 1991).

Berridge, G. R., 'The ethnic "agent in place": English-speaking civil servants and Nationalist South Africa, 1948–57', *Intelligence and National Security*, vol. 4, no. 2, 1989.

Betts, R. K., 'Analysis, war and decision: why intelligence failures are inevitable', *World Politics*, vol. 31, no. 1, 1978.

Betts, R. K., *Surprise Attack: Lessons for defense planning* (The Brookings Institution: Washington, DC, 1982).

Boren, D. L., 'The intelligence community: how crucial?' *Foreign Affairs*, Summer 1992, pp. 52–62.

Bower, T., *A Perfect English Spy* (Heinemann: London, 1995).

A Consumer's Guide to Intelligence (CIA: Washington, DC, 1994).

David, S. R., 'Soviet involvement in Third World coups', *International Security*, vol. 11, no. 1, 1986.

De Concini, Senator D., 'The role of US intelligence in promoting economic interests', *Journal of International Affairs*, vol. 48, no. 1, Summer 1994.

Dulles, A., *The Craft of Intelligence* (Harper & Row: New York, and Weidenfeld & Nicolson: London, 1963).

Ebon, M., *KGB: Death and rebirth* (Praeger: New York, 1994).

Eftimiades, N., *China's Intelligence Services: Structure, operations and methodology* (Cass: London, 1994).

Faligot, R. and P. Krop, *La Piscine: The French secret service since 1944* (Blackwell: Oxford, 1989).

Ford, H. P., *Estimative Intelligence: The purpose and problems of national intelligence estimating* (Defense Intelligence College: Washington, DC, 1989).

Freedman, L., *US Intelligence and the Soviet Strategic Threat*, 2nd edn (Macmillan: London, and Princeton University Press: Princeton, NJ, 1986).

Gaddis, J. L., *The Long Peace: Inquiries into the history of the cold war* (Oxford University Press: Oxford and New York, 1987), ch. 7.

Garthoff, R. L., *Assessing the Adversary* (The Brookings Institution: Washington, DC, 1991).

Goodman, A. E. and B. D. Berkowitz, 'Intelligence without the cold war', *Intelligence and National Security*, vol. 9, no. 1, 1994.

Grose, P., *Gentleman Spy: The life of Allen Dulles* (Deutsch: London, 1995).

Handel, M., 'Intelligence and the problem of strategic surprise', *Journal of Strategic Studies*, vol. 7, September 1984, pp. 229–81.

Hilsman, R., 'Does the CIA still have a role?', *Foreign Affairs*, vol. 74, no. 5, Sept./Oct. 1995.

Jeffreys-Jones, F., *The CIA and American Democracy* (Yale University Press: New Haven, 1992).

Jervis, R., 'Intelligence and foreign policy', *International Security*, vol. 11, no. 3, 1986/7, pp. 141–61.

Kerr, S., 'The debate on US post-cold war intelligence: one more new botched beginning?', *Defense Analysis*, vol. 10, no. 3, 1994, pp. 323–50.

Lustgarten, L. and I. Leigh, *In From The Cold: National security and democracy* (Oxford University Press: Oxford, 1994).

Mangold, T., *Cold Warrior: James Jesus Angleton, the CIA's master spy hunter* (Simon & Schuster: New York, 1991).

Marchetti, V. and J. D. Marks, *The CIA and the Cult of Intelligence*, revised edn (Dell: New York, 1989).

Martin, L. (ed.), *Strategic Thought in the Nuclear Age* (Johns Hopkins Press: Baltimore, and Heinemann: London, 1979), ch. by Knorr.

Maugham, W. Somerset, *Ashenden, or The British Agent* (Heinemann: London, 1928).

Neilson, K. and B. J. C. McKercher (eds), *Go Spy the Land: Military intelligence in history* (Praeger: Westport, CT, 1992).

Powers, T., *The Man Who Kept The Secrets: Richard Helms and the CIA* (Knopf: New York, 1979; Weidenfeld & Nicolson: London, 1980).

Prados, J., *The Soviet Estimate: US intelligence analysis and Russian military strength* (Princeton University Press: Princeton, NJ, 1986).

Prados, J., *Presidents' Secret Wars: CIA and Pentagon covert operations since World War II* (Morrow: New York, 1986).

Ranelagh, J., *CIA: A history* (BBC Books: London, 1992).

Reisman, W. M. and J. E. Baker, *Regulating Covert Action: Practices, contexts, and policies of covert coercion abroad in international and American law* (Yale University Press: New Haven, 1992).

Richelson, J. T. and D. Ball, *The Ties That Bind*, rev. edn (Unwin Hyman: Boston and London, 1990).

Robertson, K. G. (ed.), *British and American Approaches to Intelligence* (St Martin's Press: New York, 1987).

Roosevelt, K., *Countercoup: The struggle for control of Iran* (McGraw-Hill: New York, 1979).

Shlaim, A., 'Failures in national intelligence estimates: the case of the Yom Kippur war', *World Politics*, vol. 28, no. 3, 1976.

Shulsky, A., *Silent Warfare: Understanding the world of intelligence*, 2nd edn (Brasseys: London, 1994).

Stockwell, J., *In Search of Enemies: A CIA story* (Deutsch: London, 1978).

Sudoplatov, P., *Special Tasks: Memoirs of an unwanted witness – a Soviet spymaster* (Little, Brown: London, 1994).

Treverton, G. F., *Covert Action: The limits of intervention in the postwar world* (Basic Books: New York, 1987).

Woodward, B., *Veil: The secret wars of the CIA, 1981–1987* (Simon & Schuster: New York, 1987).

6

Force

Despite prophecies of its eclipse following both world wars of this century, force remains probably the most important instrument for the prosecution of conflict available to all states other than micro-states. The art of employing force in the service of foreign policy, for which much modern thought remains indebted to the Prussian military theorist, Karl von Clausewitz, is known as 'strategy'. While only the open exploitation of force will be the subject of this chapter, it should not be overlooked that, when states confine their actions to the diplomatic sphere, the possibility that force might be employed will sometimes be present as a 'silent calculation'.[1]

Contemporary strategy raises two main questions of a non-ethical kind. First, what *kinds* of strategy are employed by states? This is principally a question of concept.[2] Second, what are the advantages and disadvantages of the different strategies? This is a question of historical and practical judgement.

The most important distinction in strategy is the one made by Schelling between 'brute force' and 'coercion'. Force may be used to seize or hold an objective without regard to the wishes of an opponent; this is 'brute force'. But it may also be used simply in order to *hurt*, or threaten to hurt, an opponent *in order to compel a change of mind*; this is 'coercion'. As Schelling says: 'Pain and shock, loss and grief, privation and horror are always in some degree, some times in terrible degree, among the results of warfare; but in traditional military science they are incidental, they are not the object.' Where coercion is concerned, however, they are. The difference between brute force and coercion, therefore, is the difference between 'taking what you want and making someone give it to you, between fending off assault and making someone afraid to assault you'.[3]

There are three important strategies of brute force: the 'Napoleonic' strategy; the strategy of 'indirect approach'; and the strategy of 'protracted warfare'. As for coercion, this includes 'coercive bargaining' and 'deterrence'. The following analysis of these strategies, which will involve discussing them one at a time, should not be taken to suggest that in practice they are normally employed one at a time. This is far from being the case.

Brute force

The Napoleonic strategy

This strategy, sometimes also known as 'traditional strategy', is directed to the swift and complete destruction of the enemy's main military force in order to persuade the enemy that further resistance is useless. It was the most effective method of the Napoleonic era and is usually associated with Clausewitz. It is most suitably employed by a strong state confronting a weaker one.

Traditional strategy ran into great difficulties in the first half of the twentieth century, difficulties of which the world was reminded by the Iran–Iraq war which lasted from 1980 until 1987. These difficulties were a result partly of changes in military technology favouring the defensive against the offensive, and partly of the ability of the modern state to bring to the battlefield apparently infinite supplies of men and munitions. Perhaps above all, however, they were a result of the infinitely greater ease with which total mobilisation could be achieved following the rise of the ideology of nationalism (see Chapter 4). As the well-known French strategist, General André Beaufre, says: 'a decision is reached only after a prolonged period of mutual attrition out of all proportion to the issue at stake, at the conclusion of which both victor and vanquished emerge from the conflict completely exhausted'.[4] In short, in the twentieth century Napoleonic strategy descended into 'total war'. And, if the experience of the great wars was not enough, the development of the nuclear bomb and the long-range missile seemed to confirm the obvious irrationality of the Napoleonic strategy in modern conditions.

However, it is apparent that the reputation of traditional strategy suffered largely as a result of its failures in wars between wealthy, industrialised and relatively evenly matched powers; and because of the transparently suicidal implications of its employment at least in the earlier years of the cold war. It also lost credibility as a result of its spectacular failures when confronted by unconventional methods of warfare, as in Vietnam. But not all conflicts in the contemporary world are of these kinds and it is clear that traditional strategy continues to have important advantages to certain states in certain circumstances.

The first kind of modern conflict which invites employment of the Napoleonic strategy is that between a great power and a delinquent state within its sphere of influence, provided the delinquent is not so weak that it can be brought to heel by simple coercion. In 1956 the Soviet Union invaded Hungary in order to impose its authority, and repeated the exercise in Czechoslovakia in 1968 and in Afghanistan in 1979. With the same aim in view, the United States invaded the Dominican Republic in 1965, and in 1983 and 1989 physically removed governments of which it disapproved in Grenada and Panama respectively.

How effective has this strategy been for the great powers since the Second World War? The inescapable conclusion is that it has proved highly effective at an easily supportable cost. Not only was the immediate political objective achieved in each case but an important lesson of regional discipline was underlined. On top of this, the willingness to take military risks, which is believed to be so important to nuclear deterrence, was demonstrated, and valuable operational experience was acquired. Since – with the striking exception of Afghanistan – none of the invasions led to protracted fighting, the human and economic costs were not substantial. As a result, adverse domestic repercussions were generally minimal and sometimes governments even saw their popularity increase. Following Panama, the domestic approval ratings of US President George Bush rose to nearly 80 per cent.

The highest price that the superpowers paid for Napoleonic behaviour in their spheres of influence was damage to their international reputations in an era when much was being said about the rights of small states and the unacceptability of war. (The Soviet Union also had to worry about its effects on foreign Communist parties, especially in Western Europe.) However, this price can easily be exaggerated and usually is. Most states cannot afford to adopt a stand towards great powers that is too principled, and in practice neither great power lost an important friend or saw a vital initiative stall as a result of military action within its own sphere of influence. The speed with which the operations were carried out helped in this respect, for it is much easier for the lesser states to accept a *fait accompli* than to have to come to terms with a long-drawn-out, festering campaign. The American invasion of Grenada caused no more than temporary discomfiture to Anglo-American relations, despite Grenada's membership of the British Commonwealth and Britain's public condemnation of the action.

In early 1991, there also occurred a special case of this kind of conflict: UN-endorsed great power intervention against a smaller state in a sphere of vital interest rather than a sphere of influence. In an action beginning with air power and culminating in a '100-hour' ground battle, a US-led coalition devastated Iraqi forces in Kuwait (see Figure 6.1). This is discussed further in Chapter 12.

Traditional strategy is also effective in conflicts between more evenly matched states, provided they are not wealthy enough to sustain a prolonged war and are unable to use nuclear weapons even if they possess them. As Michael Howard says apropos such states:

> The forces which they have *en présence* with their first-line reserves are often all
> the strength they possess. For that reason their strategy can revert to a Napoleonic
> model. It is quite possible for them to destroy their enemy's entire available
> armed forces in a single battle or series of battles and leave him literally
> defenceless. At this level, war in the hands of skilful commanders and well-trained
> and equipped troops can still be a very effective instrument of policy.[5]

Particularly well-known examples of the Napoleonic strategy used in this sort of conflict are provided by the wars between India and Pakistan in 1947–8, 1965 and 1971, and above all by the six wars between Israel and its Arab neighbours which have taken place since the foundation of the state of Israel in 1948 (see Box 6.1). However, these are by no means the only cases. Other instances are provided by the Turkish occupation of northern Cyprus in 1974, the South African invasion of Angola in 1975, the Vietnamese occupation of

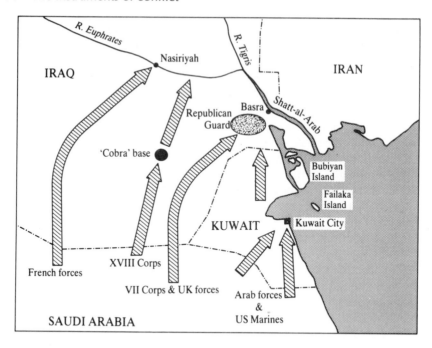

Figure 6.1 The 100-hour battle for Kuwait, February 1991 (Source: Reproduced from *Keesing's Record of World Events*, Longman: London, February 1991)

Kampuchea at the end of 1978, the retaliatory Chinese attack on Vietnam in early 1979, and the recapture from Argentina of South Georgia and the Falkland Islands by Britain in 1982.

Not all of these actions were successful, of course, and many of those which were considered to be successful failed to remove the sources of the conflicts which had occasioned them – and in some cases intensified the rivalries. In addition, it is important to remember that the failures sometimes occurred because the states involved were militarily and economically supported by one or other of the great powers. As a result, they approached *in effect* the level of military resilience which had rendered the Napoleonic strategy irrational in the two world wars of this century. This is particularly true of the Middle East, where, despite Israel's devastating defeat of the Arab armies in June 1967, the armies' main components were quickly rehabilitated with the help of the Soviet Union and it was only three weeks after that the first shots were fired in what came to be known as the 'War of Attrition'. Equally, it was rapid American resupply of its Defence Force which enabled Israel to recover from the initially successful Arab assault during Yom Kippur in October 1973.

But these are only qualifications. Napoleon himself was not always successful. Besides, as Osgood and Tucker point out, 'The fact that war does not always serve the interests of a particular state may only indicate its utility for

---

Box 6.1 The Arab–Israeli wars

- *The War of Independence, 1948.* Five Arab armies are repulsed by Israel following declaration of the new state in May.
- *The Suez war, October–November, 1956.* Israel launches a ground attack into Egypt in collusion with Britain and France; guerrilla bases are cleared and the Straits of Tiran opened to Israeli shipping.
- *The Six Day war, June 1967.* Israel launches a pre-emptive strike against Syria, Jordan and Egypt, seizing the Golan Heights, the West Bank of the River Jordan (including East Jerusalem) and the Sinai Desert up to the Suez Canal.
- *The War of Attrition, July 1967–August 1970.* Principally an artillery battle between Israel and Egypt across the Suez Canal, punctuated by air duels, commando raids and deep penetration bombing by Israel, this culminates in early 1970 in a major clash between Israeli jets and anti-aircraft defences massively reinforced by the Soviet Union.
- *The Yom Kippur war, October 1973.* Egypt and Syria launch surprise attacks on Israel on 6 October, the religious holiday of 'Yom Kippur' – the Jewish Day of Atonement. Bridgeheads initially seized by the Egyptians on the east side of the Suez Canal, together with early gains made by the Syrians in Golan, are clawed back by Israel after heavy losses and a counter-crossing of the Canal which encircles the Egyptian Third Army in Sinai.
- *The Lebanon war, June 1982–February 1985.* Israeli forces drive into south Lebanon in order to expel the PLO and reduce Syrian influence over the country. The PLO evacuates Beirut in September, but then Israeli forces become bogged down in fighting with Shiite Lebanese guerrillas. Complete withdrawal from Lebanon does not begin until February 1985.

---

another'[6] – for example, Vietnam in blunting the Chinese attack in 1979. Furthermore, great power backing on both sides of a conflict has not prevented traditional strategy from paying handsome dividends. In terms of prestige and defensive capacity, Israel's territorial gains in the 1967 war (see Figure 4.1) were of immense value. There is also little doubt that the advances made by the Egyptian army, which so shook the Israelis in the first days of the Yom Kippur war, did much to restore Egyptian standing and thus to strengthen Cairo's hand both in the Arab world and in subsequent negotiations with Israel and the United States.

Finally, it is necessary to add that there is a situation in which some strategists would like to see traditional strategy employed, namely in any major engagement between major nuclear powers themselves. This is the notion, which surfaced in the latter years of the cold war but still has relevance because of the proliferation of nuclear weapons, that the great powers should actually have a strategy for *nuclear victory* and not one merely for nuclear deterrence (discussed below). Partly because it is believed that this was always Soviet strategy anyway, partly because the increasing sophistication of weapons and communications technology suggested the possibility of more accurate targeting and greater control in nuclear war, and partly because of mounting disenchantment with the doctrine of 'assured destruction', this doctrine began to be influential in America in the late 1970s – though its origins could be traced through the 'Schlesinger doctrine' of the early 1970s back to the 'MacNamara doctrine' of the early 1960s.

As framed by Herman Kahn's disciple, Colin Gray, and with America's cold war posture towards the Soviet Union in mind, the theory of nuclear victory held that for any number of reasons nuclear deterrence (central or extended) *might* fail, and that in such an event the president would have no alternative but to demand 'a realistic war plan'.[7] Such a plan, he claimed, should not threaten Soviet civilian and economic life but the state machine itself – in view of its unpopularity and its concentration in Moscow, the Achilles' heel of the Soviet Union. The corollaries of such a nuclear war aim were, of course, that the United States should possess weapons sufficiently powerful and 'smart' to carry it out, and also develop much more effective methods for *defending its citizens* (as well as its missiles) against Soviet nuclear attack. In short, argued Gray, the United States should seek 'strategic superiority' over, rather than 'essential equivalence' with, the Soviet Union. Finally, a realistic plan for nuclear victory would not only make this more likely if deterrence should fail but also enhance the credibility of deterrence itself, thereby reducing the likelihood that nuclear 'war-fighting' would ever occur.

Not surprisingly, a number of problems with this approach were pointed out. First, translating nuclear war into the categories of traditional strategy (and thus 'operationalising' it) might encourage premature crossing of the nuclear threshold. Second, destruction of the state apparatus rules out the possibility of negotiating an end to any war. Third, since there is no practical experience of nuclear war, it cannot be assumed that, with homelands under direct attack, its direction would remain under firm, intelligent and humane control; it is at least as plausible that, as panic sets in and communications become dislocated, 'strategy' would disintegrate. Fourth, even if a nuclear offensive were to go well, the probable limitations of the defensive mode would mean that 'victory' would be very sour indeed. Finally, the defensive preparations entailed by such a strategy would seriously complicate arms control negotiations (discussed in Chapter 10).

Despite the weight of these objections, the logical force of the thinking of the 'new strategists' impressed the first Reagan administration. As a result, a programme to modernise US strategic forces was launched which culminated in President Reagan's dramatic announcement on 23 March 1983 of what came to be known officially as the Strategic Defense Initiative (SDI). At once styled derisively by its opponents as 'Star Wars', this was a programme of research into predominantly *space-based* defence designed to destroy enemy missiles before they re-enter the earth's atmosphere (see Box 6.2). However, SDI ran into widespread political and scientific hostility in both the United States and Europe and was denied much of the funding which the administration sought from Congress. Moreover, the initial research revealed that comprehensive population defence in nuclear war presented technical difficulties which had not been foreseen by early proponents of SDI, and would also be enormously expensive. Partly for these reasons, and partly because the thinking which spawned it seemed less appropriate with the ending of the cold war, enthusiasm for the SDI waned in the late 1980s.

Nevertheless, SDI research demonstrated the limited feasibility of some elements of strategic defence, and received a considerable boost from the high-technology successes of American arms in the war against Iraq. As a result, even though development of space-based strategic defence has now been virtually abandoned (see Box 6.2) in favour of upgrading existing ground-based anti-missile defence technology against threats from 'rogue states' such as Iraq, Libya and North Korea, it is unlikely that we have heard the last of it, particularly since it may well be nuclear powers substantially weaker than the former Soviet Union which the United States may want to coerce in the future. Against such powers 'strategic superiority', by definition, will be much easier to achieve.

The indirect approach

The second way in which 'brute force' can be applied as an instrument of conflict is by what the famous British strategist, Basil Liddell Hart, called the 'strategy of indirect approach'. The essence of this is to avoid immediate battle and instead to aim at the 'dislocation' of the enemy's forces by *movement* and *surprise*. At best this will make battle unnecessary, the political objective being achieved by 'pure strategy', while at worst it will so weaken the enemy that when battle is finally joined victory will be more economically purchased. The indirect approach is clearly suited to the weaker power in any conflict and found particular favour with Britain as a result of its weakness in land power relative to the 'continental' powers. During the deadlock on the Western Front in the First World War, this approach was adopted by the British in the Dardanelles campaign, designed to deprive Germany of its Turkish ally, draw the weight of the Balkans on to the side of the entente and, among other things, restore communications with Russia. The whole exercise was a disastrous failure, though in operational rather than conceptual terms. In the Second World War the strategy of indirect approach was employed with more success in the Middle East and southern Italy, though (significantly) it had been the subject of dispute with the Americans, whose greater

Box 6.2 Strategic defence

'Strategic defence' means the attempt to intercept and destroy incoming long-range ballistic missiles, ICBMs. This is extremely difficult since these missiles travel at enormous speeds, especially in their final stages, when they can achieve closing speeds of 12,000 miles per hour or 3 miles per second.

The main idea behind SDI was that the best chance of stopping such missiles was to employ 'layered defences', that is, a comprehensive suite of weapons capable of attacking ICBMs in all of their stages of flight: boost phase, post-boost phase (during which re-entry vehicles may be deployed), mid-course, and terminal phase. By providing more opportunities for interception, the overall destruction rate of incoming missiles would be maximised. Space-based defence systems, such as laser-armed satellites, would play a key role since in theory they could attack hostile missiles early in flight when their slower speed and brightly burning rocket engines would make them easier targets and when the highly toxic debris produced by a successful hit would fall back where it properly belonged rather than onto the territory of the defending state.

SDI thinking concentrated on two main types of technology as follows:

1. *Kinetic energy weapons.* These are missiles designed to destroy their targets by simply crashing into them; they may be space- or ground-based.
2. *Directed energy weapons (DEW).* Bearing an uncanny resemblance to the death rays of science fiction, these include chemical lasers, free-electron lasers, x-ray lasers and particle beams. The chemical and free-electron lasers were regarded as the most promising elements of DEW technology and were generally conceived as ground-based lasers which would be reflected to their targets off relay mirrors strung in space.

Development of space-based strategic defence systems flagged in the 1990s because of the end of the cold war and the huge costs and technical problems which they confronted. A functioning laser system, for example, is still thought to be beyond the reach of the United States, at least for the time being. Two other problems, however, have dented enthusiasm for space-based systems designed to hit ICBMs just after launch: first, this phase is very brief; secondly, there can be no certainty of knowing that the launch is actually hostile – it could be aimed at someone else, or carry a satellite rather than a warhead.

resources disposed them to look with more favour on the Napoleonic approach. The strategy was also well illustrated in this conflict by the use of strategic bombing and naval blockade, where the results have been more controversial. Finding themselves outgunned by Egyptian artillery along the Suez Canal, the strategy of indirect approach (using commando raids and deep penetration bombing) was also employed by the Israelis during the War of Attrition (see Box 6.1).

It is important to understand that Liddell Hart did not see the indirect approach as an alternative to the Napoleonic approach, each being more suited to different circumstances. On the contrary, he regarded the indirect approach as the *only* strategy and therefore as being *identical with strategy as such*. This is because he believed that, while the indirect approach is clearly indispensable for the weaker force, even the greatest army will achieve its victory more economically when this is employed. However, Liddell Hart was obsessed with the indirect approach and exaggerated its advantages (he went so far as to claim that it was 'a law of life in all spheres: a truth of philosophy').[8] The real truth is, as we have seen, that there are circumstances where Napoleonic strategy is to be preferred.

A particular limitation of the indirect approach is that it requires *time* to be effective. Of course, in a conflict between nuclear powers which starts at the conventional level, this may well be an advantage since it will provide an opportunity for diplomacy to intervene before irrevocable escalation to the nuclear level occurs. However, in other circumstances a speedy victory may be necessary in order to stifle the build-up of international or domestic opposition, or so that the enemy is unable to add to its strength, from either its own resources or the acquisition of new allies. The *fait accompli* has much to recommend it.

Protracted war

The final strategy of 'brute force' is protracted or revolutionary war, which is a variant of the strategy of indirect approach. Protracted war differs from the Liddell Hart conception in at least three ways. First, it tends to place more emphasis on the use of irregular forces, or 'guerrillas', though it is certainly not averse to the employment of regular forces for both positional and mobile warfare; it is thus not identical with 'guerrilla warfare' as such. Second, it attaches high importance to winning over the civil population of the territory on which the struggle is being conducted. Third, it involves attempting to defeat the enemy by demoralisation and physical exhaustion rather than by the kind of strategic checkmate which might result from surprise and brilliant manoeuvre. As a doctrine, protracted war came to prominence in the twentieth century and its outstanding exponent was Mao Zedong (Mao Tse-Tung), whose ideas were developed during the prolonged struggle of the Chinese Communists against the Kuomintang and the Japanese in the 1930s.

Protracted war is the strategy of a weak force operating among its own people and seeking the removal from power of indigenous opponents and/or foreign occupiers. It is, in other words, the characteristic strategy of a *movement* rather than a state, and was thus the typical strategy of the 'national liberation movements' which fought the European colonial regimes after the Second World War. It is strong emotional commitment and friendly terrain which make it likely that the strategy will eventually be successful, even if sometimes at extremely high cost in human life. The best-known examples of successful revolutionary war in the twentieth century are probably the Chinese Revolution and the wars fought in Algeria and Vietnam. The Arab Revolt against the Turks in the First World War was also successful, though the main effort came from the regular forces of the British commander, General Allenby; and in 1990 the 'Tamil Tigers' forced the Indian army out of Sri Lanka. There are also many other cases where adoption of protracted war proved highly effective, even if not in the end completely successful: for example, the war between Britain and the Boers in South Africa between 1899 and 1902 and the EOKA (National Organisation of Cypriot Struggle) campaign in Cyprus in the 1950s.

In view of the formidable reputation which the strategy of protracted war acquired in the 1960s and 1970s, especially after the Vietcong successes in South Vietnam, it is salutary to remember that it does not always prove effective. As Beaufre rightly insists,

> it can only succeed if the issue at stake is of far greater importance to one side than to the other (as in wars of colonial liberation) or [as in the case of the Arab Revolt and Vietnam] if it receives assistance from regular armed forces to which it acts as an auxiliary. . . .[9]

Neither of these conditions obtained for the Greek Communists during the civil war in the late 1940s; for the Cuban revolutionaries led into Bolivia in the mid-1960s by Che Guevara; for the *mujahideen* guerrillas in Afghanistan during the 1980s; or for the *peshmerga* guerrillas in northern Iraq, who rose (once more) against Saddam Hussein in early 1991. As a result, all of these operations failed, and there have been other striking failures, particularly in South America.

Nevertheless, revolutionary war is generally an effective strategy for internal war, and also plays an important role in *interstate* conflicts. This is because there are so many states where conditions are chaotic and central government authority over certain groups or regions weak or non-existent. The Reagan administration applied acute pressure to the leftist Sandinista government in Nicaragua by backing the 'Contras', while for a lengthy period Israel has sought to influence events in Lebanon by stiffening its various Christian militias. Perhaps most strikingly effective in recent years, however, was the policy of pre-Mandela South Africa of backing anti-government guerrillas operating in the black 'Front Line States', most notably in Angola (where it supported

UNITA until the peace agreements of December 1988) and in Mozambique (where it sustained the Mozambique National Resistance – MNR or 'Renamo'). By supporting the UNITA campaign in Angola, the South Africans denied a secure rear base to the Namibian guerrillas of the South West African Peoples' Organisation (SWAPO), ensured that the rust on the Benguela railway grew thicker, and kept the Marxist government of Luanda seriously off balance. By sustaining Renamo (as well as by applying other forms of pressure on Maputo), Pretoria forced the Marxist government of Mozambique to seek an accommodation with it.

Coercion

It will be recalled that coercion was defined as the use of force in order to hurt, or threaten, an opponent, the object of the exercise being to encourage second thoughts. When such a threat is made with the purpose of preventing aggression, we speak of 'deterrence'.

Deterrence

Deterrence is designed to forestall attack by convincing a potential aggressor that the costs of the contemplated action will substantially outweigh any possible gains. This strategy was hardly new but it achieved great prominence in the West in the 1950s because it was believed that there was no *defence* against the hydrogen bomb (vastly more destructive than the atomic bombs dropped on Japan in 1945) and the intercontinental ballistic missile (ICBM), which became the bomb's main delivery vehicle. With defence ruled out, *all* hopes came to be pinned on convincing any potential enemy that an attack would be suicidal.

In its early and simple form, deterrent strategy was terrorism writ large because it rested on the threat to reply to an attack – almost any attack – by wiping out not just the aggressor's industrial capacity but a great deal of the aggressor's *civilian population*. (In 1965 'assured destruction' was defined by the US Pentagon as 'the capacity to destroy one-fourth to one-third of the Soviet population and two-thirds of Soviet industry'.)[10] In the nuclear age people rather than military forces had become the targets. Indeed, it was common to speak of each great power 'holding hostage' the cities of the other as a guarantee of good behaviour. Not surprisingly, and quite properly, this situation was known as the 'balance of *terror*'.

Nothing could be simpler in conception than this strategy of deterrence. Wiping out the enemy's population is hardly a strategic task requiring the military skills of a Rommel, Montgomery, Patton or Giap. In fact, to call it a 'strategy' at all is an abuse of language. Nevertheless, accomplishment of the task or, more accurately, the ability to convince any potential enemy that the task can be accomplished, has been constantly eroded. The sources of difficulty have been technical developments, the economic burdens to which they have given rise, and the question mark which has always hovered over the rationality – not to mention the humanity – of threatening to annihilate the aggressor's population even after all that one cares about has been destroyed. Deterrence thus threw up problems of its own which had to be overcome if it was to remain 'credible'.

It is no good having the nuclear potential to burn up the enemy's population (to kill the hostages one is holding) if the enemy can eliminate that potential in a surprise 'first strike'. The first requirement of the credible deterrent, or of 'second strike' capability, is thus a strike force which can take *anything* which the enemy can throw at it and still have sufficient weapons left to be able to launch a devastating riposte. The best way to ensure the survival of the deterrent force is obviously to conceal its location. This is why great importance is attached to placing missiles in nuclear-powered submarines, which can prowl the ocean beds and lurk under the polar ice packs for long periods. Initially, though, it was necessary to rely on 'hardening' and dispersing the silos which housed land-based missiles, or trundling them across the desert or around country lanes in the event of warning of attack. Despite the high priority given by all the nuclear powers to submarine-launched ballistic missiles, land-based ones continued to be held in great numbers, especially by the Soviet Union, until the end of the cold war, and this sort of posture probably remains very necessary. It is also important to add that sheer numbers of warheads and missiles are an added guarantee of survivability since, obviously, the more one has, the more are likely to survive a first strike. (This is why the notion of 'overkill' in deterrence requires qualification.) The importance of concealment, dispersal and numbers is eloquently reflected in the traditional American policy of maintaining a 'triad' of nuclear forces: land-based missiles, submarine-launched missiles and bombers.

While it was never seriously suggested that the survivability of either the Soviet or American strike forces was in question at any point after the late 1950s, technical developments sometimes threatened it, or, put another way, promised the possibility of a successful 'counter-force first strike'. These developments included those which increased the destructive capacity of warheads, the speed with which missiles could deliver them, the ease with which they could evade interception, the accuracy with which they could be aimed and the ability with which their targets could be detected. It was in part a fear of the implications of these technical advances – summed up in the development of the multiple independently targetable re-entry vehicle (MIRV) – which provided the impetus to the Strategic Arms Limitation Talks (SALT) of the 1970s (see Chapter 10).

Survivability is, however, only the first requirement of effective deterrence. This in itself is of no use unless one's missiles and aircraft (such as the 'Stealth' bomber) are able to penetrate the enemy's defences. This is why supporters of 'mutual assured destruction' became alarmed at the end of the 1960s by the possibility that the superpowers would introduce anti-ballistic missiles (ABMs)[11] in order to protect their largest cities and industrial areas. (Ringing ICBM sites with ABMs was acceptable since this increased survivability.) Had this been done, and had it been supplemented by extensive provision of fall-out shelters, each side would have lost the fear for its own 'hostages' which was believed hitherto to have deterred it from launching a nuclear attack on the other. Having 'freed' their hostages, the strategic relationship between the great powers would have been restored to that which had prevailed in the pre-nuclear era; 'mutual assured destruction' would have gone out of the window and nuclear war would have become 'rational'. As a result, this possibility was another source of the impetus behind arms control talks, and severe limitations on the deployment of ABMs was one of the main provisions of SALT I, concluded in May 1972.[12] In 1983 these fears were resurrected by the announcement of the SDI programme, and had a similarly beneficial effect on arms control discussions between the United States and the Soviet Union.

The third requirement of effective deterrence is a reputation for military ruthlessness, since it is necessary to convince any potential aggressor of a willingness to retaliate, even if, following the destruction of one's own *society*, this will serve no strategic purpose and represent an act of grotesque cruelty against a people who may well be guilty of nothing more than political impotence or ordinary apathy in politics. As a result, states relying on nuclear deterrence must show no weakness or hesitation in using conventional force in daily support of their foreign policies. Schell's view is that the ruthlessness of American military action against North Vietnam in the last years of the Indo-China war was influenced more than anything by the need to preserve 'credibility', including nuclear credibility.[13]

However, a rider needs to be added to this last requirement of effective deterrence. This is that its stringency is clearly not as great in the case of deterrence of an attack on the homeland ('central deterrence') as it is in the case of deterrence of an attack on the territory of one's allies ('extended deterrence'). There are two reasons for this. First, with the destruction of all, or the great part, of one's own society there will remain no selfish incentive for restraint. Second, it is precisely in such circumstances that irrational decisions are likely to be made: *blind* anger and *blind* passion for revenge are likely to override any other feelings. Neither of these points could be made with regard to an attack confined to the territory of allies. It is thus only when a policy of extended deterrence is pursued in addition to homeland deterrence (America's traditional NATO posture towards Western Europe) that a reputation for risk-taking to the point of irrationality is important.

The final requirement for effective deterrence is not in one's own hands at all but in those of one's enemies. The enemy's government must employ similar criteria of rationality *and* be capable of making accurate cost-benefit calculations based upon them.

Of course, it does not follow that, just because these requirements of effective deterrence were met by both superpowers (as it seems they were), it was this which prevented the degeneration of the cold war into nuclear hostilities: it was not *necessarily* nuclear weapons which kept the peace. The United States probably never had any intention of attacking the Soviet Union, and the talk of 'liberating' Eastern Europe which was heard in America in the early 1950s may have been nothing more than election rhetoric. For its part, the Soviet Union may have had no desire to attack the United States or its allies in Western Europe. Nevertheless, though the contrary claim is frequently made, the success as well as the failure of deterrence is in principle knowable, since a decision to abstain from action is the product of reasoning in exactly the same way as a decision to engage in it; it is thus in principle equally penetrable by the historian. Moreover, the consensus among historians that nuclear deterrence explains the general restraint displayed by both great powers in the various crises of the cold war, including, most notably, the Cuban missile crisis in 1962, remains impressive.

Nevertheless, during the 1960s serious misgivings about the form of deterrence known as 'assured destruction' began to emerge. In particular, it was feared that a threat to obliterate the civilian population and industrial capacity of an enemy would not be a deterrent to a first strike *confined to military targets*, since carrying out such a threat would merely invite a follow-up from the enemy in kind. The credibility of extended deterrence also provoked scepticism, since it was difficult to believe that any state would risk national suicide for a third party. (This was the great worry of America's European allies after the United States itself became vulnerable to Soviet nuclear attack at the end of the 1950s.) In sum, many Western strategists became increasingly uncomfortable with the 'nuclear dilemma', dependence for security on threats the implementation of which could well lead to mutual annihilation.

Both of these doubts drove American deterrence policy in the same direction in the 1970s: to a belief in the need both for more regional conventional strength and for greater counter-force nuclear capability; in short, to a belief in the need for more military flexibility. On the role of regional conventional forces in the confrontation between the nuclear powers, Michael Howard wrote: 'Their object must be to make the use of nuclear weapons unnecessary while at the same time making the prospect of it convincing.'[14] On the role of greater counter-force capability, in the few kind words which he could find to say about American nuclear weapons policy at the end of the 1970s, Colin Gray wrote: 'A richer menu of attack options, small and large, would provide a president with less-than-cataclysmic nuclear initiatives should disaster threaten, or occur, in Europe or elsewhere.'[15] In short, the doubts about the credibility of 'assured destruction' led to much greater emphasis on the importance of *intrawar deterrence*, or coercive bargaining in a nuclear confrontation. (It is important to recognise that there remains a considerable difference between this and the theory of nuclear victory discussed earlier in this chapter. Both entail 'war-fighting' with nuclear weapons, it is true, but supporters of intrawar deterrence are prepared to pay a higher political price to end the war before an all-out exchange takes place.)

However, whether the drive towards greater nuclear flexibility *in relation to conflicts between great powers* really was the best route out of the 'nuclear dilemma' is by no means self-evident. It seems equally plausible that, as Lawrence Freedman and other opponents of the new strategists argue, the sheer incalculability of what might happen in such conflicts, *irrespective of the character and targeting capabilities of nuclear forces*, is sufficient to ensure deterrence.

Nuclear deterrence may well have encouraged restraint in the cold war but it cannot be assumed from this that it will have a similar effect if injected into other conflicts. Though both of the great powers had their 'revisionist' moments in the period between 1945 and 1990, their principal reflexes were to support the status quo. Furthermore, their technological and administrative sophistication made it possible for them to operate efficient control and safety measures for nuclear weapons, while their resources enabled them to make their strike forces invulnerable to surprise attack. To some of the states which now appear to be developing nuclear weapons in the midst of the most dangerous conflicts in the world – for example, in the Middle East and South Asia – not to mention the shaky successor states of the former Soviet Union, none, or few, of these things applies. In May 1990, for example, with tension boiling up again over the disputed territory of Kashmir, the American intelligence community seriously feared that an out-of-control Pakistani military command might launch a nuclear first-strike against New Delhi rather than risk another humiliation at the hands of the Indian army.[16] None of this is encouraging.

Coercive bargaining

Coercive bargaining is the other main form of coercion. It is sometimes known as 'compellance' or even 'coercive diplomacy' but the former is an ugly and unnecessary invention while the latter is a contradiction in terms. Coercive bargaining entails either the threat of pain or the causing of pain in an attempt to persuade an enemy to conform to one's will. In the offensive mode the enemy may be forced to surrender territory, in the defensive, to suspend an invasion in progress. In the defensive mode, coercive bargaining is one of the strategies which may be employed after deterrence has failed and is thus the same as what, in the nuclear context, is referred to as 'intrawar deterrence'. In conventional warfare it is now particularly associated with the pinpoint aerial destruction of key installations.

Coercive bargaining may or may not involve the use of the carrot as well as the stick but, in any event, it is always a more active and risky strategy of

Box 6.3   Operation 'Deliberate Force'

The use of massive NATO firepower on positions right across Serb-held Bosnia started on 30 August 1995, having been provoked by a mortar attack on Sarajevo marketplace three days earlier which killed at least

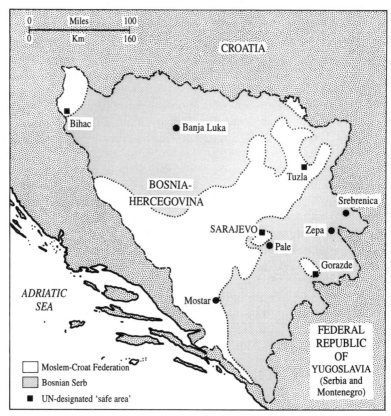

■ **Sarajevo** At least seven surrounding Serb-held districts hit by air strikes, says Bosnian Serb television. Nato aircraft and UN Rapid Reaction Force artillery pound gun emplacements, munitions factories and ammunition dumps. Nato reports heavy damage: huge clouds of smoke seen south of the city. EU officials fear five of their staff may have been killed.

● **Banja Luka** Communication facilities struck. 'Material damage is believed to be immense', says Serb radio.

● **Pale** No direct hits on town, but loud explosions heard throughout the night in the surrounding hills. At least seven dead, say Serb news reports. Nato renews attacks in late afternoon, with hits reported near main Serb headquarters.

■ **Tuzla** Nearby Serb positions attacked.

■ **Gorazde** Hilltop Serb communication facilities blasted and air defences hit.

● **Mostar** Serb positions bombed, with air defences especially targeted.

Source: Reproduced from the *Financial Times*, 31 August 1995

thirty-seven civilians. The main stated objectives of the operation, which was sanctioned by the UN and named 'Deliberate Force', were (a) to deter further Bosnian Serb attacks on UN-designated safe areas (involving notably the demand for the withdrawal of all heavy weapons from a 20 km exclusion zone around Sarajevo) and (b) the opening of Sarajevo's airport and land routes into the city. The unstated aims were to force the Bosnian Serbs to adopt a more accommodating attitude towards a US-driven peace plan for the former Yugoslavia (based on the *de facto* division of Bosnia within a formally united state), pre-empt military intervention on the side of the Moslem-led Bosnian government by member states of the Organisation of the Islamic Conference, and convince the Bosnian government and Croatian forces – which by this time had their tails up – that NATO had the answer.

The targets of UN Rapid Reaction Force artillery and NATO war planes flying from the US aircraft carrier *Theodore Roosevelt* in the Adriatic and bases in Italy, included munitions factories, ammunition dumps, heavy-gun emplacements, air-defence positions, and command-and-control facilities. The planes used laser-guided 'smart bombs' which usually score a direct hit. After three days, during which 500 air sorties were flown, 90 targets attacked from the air, and nearly 1,000 artillery shells fired, there was a pause to permit damage assessment and give the Bosnian Serbs time to comply with UN/NATO demands.

On 5 September, after the bombing pause had lasted for four days, NATO action against the Bosnian Serbs was resumed as punishment for their continuing failure to withdraw heavy weapons from around Sarajevo. Air attacks, approaching 200 a day, moved closer to Pale, the seat of the Bosnian Serb headquarters east of Sarajevo, and cruise missiles were thrown into the action. Not until 14 September, following progress in talks between the US special envoy Richard Holbrooke and the die-hard Bosnian Serb military commander, General Ratko Mladic, was there any let-up, when a 12-hour pause – which turned into an indefinite halt – was ordered. A deal, albeit an imperfect one, and agreed to on the Bosnian Serb side under pressures additional to NATO air power, had been reached on the relief of Sarajevo.

coercion than deterrence because it is actually designed to compel the enemy to *surrender a position or change some policy*. It thus threatens the enemy not only with material harm but also with serious loss of face. Nevertheless, the appeal of coercive bargaining is considerable. In contrast to all strategies of brute force – with the possible exception of the strategy of indirect approach – it 'offers the possibility of achieving one's objective economically, with little bloodshed, fewer political and psychological costs, and often with much less risk of escalation'.[17] However, coercive bargaining will only succeed if the victim can be persuaded that an escalation of 'punishment' will automatically follow refusal to comply with the will of the coercer, and if that prospect is worse than the consequences of compliance. Not surprisingly, it is a strategy which is only available to the stronger party to any conflict.

Hitler used coercive bargaining in order to absorb Czechoslovakia and Austria in the late 1930s, and President Truman's intimidation of the Japanese by atomic bombing was followed by the Japanese Emperor's surrender (though there is a view that the Japanese had already decided on this course). At least a 'modest success', according to a well-known study of the subject, was President Kennedy's use of coercive bargaining in the Laos crisis of 1960–1.[18] Israel has also had limited successes with this strategy in attempting to dissuade its neighbours from providing safe havens for its enemies (as did the 'old' South Africa), while Libya's enthusiasm for supporting anti-American terrorism in Europe and the Middle East cooled distinctly following attacks by US war planes on Libya in early 1986. Most recently, in August–September 1995, the relentless pounding of military targets in Serb-held Bosnia by NATO artillery, war planes, and even cruise missiles – one of the most spectacular examples of coercive diplomacy in the post-1945 period (see Box 6.3) – forced the Bosnian Serbs to remove their big guns from the immediate vicinity of Sarajevo and generally made them more disposed to the inevitability of a diplomatic settlement on terms which they had previously ruled unacceptable.

However, the very reasons which lead the stronger power to resort to coercive bargaining – fear of the human, material, diplomatic and domestic political costs of employing a strategy of brute force – may also vitiate the strategy. Aware of the constraints on the coercer, the victim may not believe in the threats of *further* escalation which are vital to the strategy. The terror bombing of North Vietnam by the United States did not bring Hanoi to its knees, and Khrushchev's threats to launch nuclear missiles against Britain during the Suez crisis in 1956 were shrugged off by the Eden government. In the absence of simultaneous pressure from President Milosevic of Serbia, together with recent military set-backs at the hands of Croatian and Bosnian government forces, it is also quite probable that the Bosnian Serbs would have proved far more resistant to NATO coercion in September 1995 – especially in light of the Russian hostility towards it.

Notes

1. Knorr, *On The Uses of Military Power*, p. 20.
2. I am not concerned here with the 'forms', or degrees of inclusiveness, of strategy which are depicted in the 'strategic pyramid' in Beaufre's *An Introduction to Strategy*. Beaufre's distinctions between 'total strategy', 'overall strategy' (of which there are four?) and 'operational strategy' seem to have served more to confuse than illuminate this area.
3. Schelling, *Arms and Influence*, p. 2.

4. *An Introduction to Strategy*, p. 28.
5. *The Causes of Wars*, pp. 92–3.
6. *Force, Order and Justice*, p. 161.
7. 'Nuclear strategy: the case for a theory of victory', p. 57.
8. *Strategy: The indirect approach*, p. 18.
9. *An Introduction to Strategy*, p. 27.
10. H. A. Kissinger, *The White House Years* (Little, Brown: Boston, and Weidenfeld & Nicolson and Michael Joseph: London, 1979), p. 215.
11. Now subsumed under the acronym 'BMD' (ballistic missile defence).
12. This interpretation is disputed by Henry Kissinger, whose personal role in 'back channel' negotiations with the Soviet leadership was of great importance in the SALT talks. According to Kissinger, neither side agreed to the ABM treaty out of doctrinal purity. The Russians, he says, agreed to it because they were afraid of being outstripped in an ABM race, while the Americans accepted it in order to persuade Moscow to limit *offensive* weapons, in which area the Russians were taking the lead. In the event, the United States abandoned the ABM programme altogether in 1975, following 'Congressional insistence and bureaucratic demoralisation', *The White House Years*, pp. 204–10.
13. J. Schell, *Time of Illusion* (Knopf: New York, 1976), pp. 9ff.
14. *The Causes of Wars*, p. 99.
15. 'Nuclear strategy: the case for a theory of victory', p. 63.
16. Intelligence reports to President George Bush at the time concluded that 'Pakistan had assembled at least six, perhaps ten, nuclear weapons, and might already have deployed them on its American-built F-16s'. India, of course, had a larger nuclear arsenal, C. Andrew, *For the President's Eyes Only: Secret intelligence and the American Presidency from Washington to Bush* (HarperCollins: London, 1995), pp. 516–17.
17. Craig and George, *Force and Statecraft*, pp. 189–90.
18. George, Hall and Simons, *The Limits of Coercive Diplomacy*, p. 77.

Further reading

In contrast to diplomacy and certain other subjects given prominence in this book, there is a vast and generally high-quality literature on force, or 'strategic studies'. It should therefore be understood that the following recommendations represent no more than a tiny fraction of the reading available.

General

Bayliss, J., K. Booth, J. Garnett and P. Williams, *Contemporary Strategy: Theories and policies*, 2 vols, 2nd edn (Croom Helm: London, 1987).
Beaufre, A., *An Introduction to Strategy* (Faber: London, and Praeger: New York, 1965).
Buzan, B., *An Introduction to Strategic Studies: Military technology and international relations* (Macmillan: London, 1987).
Clausewitz, Karl von, *On War*, ed. and trans. by M. Howard and P. Paret (Princeton University Press: Princeton, NJ, 1976; first publ. 1832).
Craig, G. A. and A. L. George, *Force and Statecraft: Diplomatic problems of our time*, 3rd edn (Oxford University Press: New York, 1995).
Freedman, L. (ed.), *War* (Oxford University Press: New York, 1994).

Howard, M., *The Causes of Wars* (Allen & Unwin: London, and Harvard University Press: Cambridge, MA, 1983).

Klare, M. T. and D. C. Thomas (eds), *World Security: Challenges for a new century*, 2nd edn (St Martin's Press: New York, 1994).

Knorr, K., *On the Uses of Military Power* (Princeton University Press: Princeton, NJ, 1966).

Osgood, R. E. and R. W. Tucker, *Force, Order and Justice* (Johns Hopkins Press: Baltimore, 1967).

Paret, P. (ed.), *Makers of Modern Strategy* (Princeton University Press: Princeton, NJ, 1986).

Schelling, T. C., *Arms and Influence* (Yale University Press: New Haven, 1966).

Shultz, R., R. Godson and T. Greenwood (eds), *Security Studies for the 1990s* (Brassey's: Washington, DC, 1993).

The indirect approach

Bond, B., *Liddell Hart: A study of his military thought* (Cassell: London, 1977).

Liddell Hart, B. H., *Strategy: The indirect approach* (Praeger: New York, 1954; first publ. London, 1941). NB: Among his many other books on strategic theory and military history, Liddell Hart published important histories of the two world wars: *History of the First World War* (Putnam: New York, 1971; Pan Books: London, 1972) and *History of the Second World War* (Putnam: New York, 1970; Pan Books: London, 1973). He also published two volumes of memoirs: *Memoirs*, 2 vols (Cassell: London, 1965; Putnam: New York, 1965–6).

Protracted war

Asprey, R. B., *War in the Shadows: The guerrilla in history*, 2 vols (Doubleday: Garden City, NY, 1975).

Laqueur, W., *Guerrilla: An historical and critical study* (Weidenfeld & Nicolson: London, 1977).

Laqueur, W., *The Guerrilla Reader: An historical anthology* (The New American Library: New York, 1977; Wildwood House: London, 1978).

Mao Tse-Tung, *Selected Military Writings* (Foreign Languages Press: Peking, 1966).

Urban, M., *War in Afghanistan* (Macmillan: London, 1987).

Vo Nguyen Giap, *The Military Art of People's War*, selected writings, ed. and intro. by R. Stetler (Monthly Review Press: New York, 1970).

Young, T., 'The MNR/RENAMO: external and internal dynamics', *African Affairs*, vol. 89, no. 357, 1990.

Coercive bargaining

Cable, J., *Diplomacy at Sea* (Macmillan: London, and Naval Institute Press: Annapolis, MD, 1985).

George, A. L., D. K. Hall, and W. E. Simons, *The Limits of Coercive Diplomacy* (Little, Brown: Boston, 1971).

Grove, E., *The Future of Sea Power* (Routledge & Kegan Paul: London, 1990).

Lauren, P. G. (ed.), *Diplomacy: New approaches in history, theory and policy* (Collier-Mac: London, and Free Trade Press: New York, 1979), ch. by Lauren ('Theories of bargaining with threats of force: deterrence and coercive diplomacy').

Nuclear weapons

Bobbit, P., L. Freedman and G. F. Treverton, *US Nuclear Strategy: A reader* (Macmillan: London, 1989) [includes a useful bibliographical essay].

Booth, K., *Strategy and Ethnocentrism* (Croom Helm: London, 1979).

Brown, H. (ed.), *The Strategic Defense Initiative: Shield or snare?* (Westview Press: Boulder, CO, 1987).

Brown, N., *New Strategy through Space* (Leicester University Press: Leicester, 1990).

Gray, C. S., 'Nuclear strategy: the case for a theory of victory', *International Security*, vol. 4, part 1, Summer 1979.

Gray, C. S., *Nuclear Strategy and National Style* (Hamilton Press: Lanham, and London, 1987).

Gray, C. S. and K. B. Payne, 'Victory is possible', *Foreign Policy*, no. 39, 1980.

Freedman, L., *The Evolution of Nuclear Strategy*, 2nd edn (Macmillan: London, and St Martin's Press: New York, 1989).

Halperin, M., *Nuclear Fallacy: Dispelling the myth of nuclear strategy* (Ballinger: Cambridge, MA, 1987).

Huntington, S. P. (ed.), *The Strategic Imperative: New policies for American security* (Ballinger: Cambridge, MA, 1982), esp. ch. by Betts ('Elusive equivalence').

Jervis, R., *The Illogic of American Nuclear Strategy* (Cornell University Press: Ithaca, NY, 1984).

Kaplan, F. A., *The Wizards of Armageddon* (Simon & Schuster: New York, 1983).

McGuire, M., 'Is there a future for nuclear weapons?', *International Affairs*, vol. 70, no. 2, April 1994.

Mandelbaum, M., *The Nuclear Revolution: International politics before and after Hiroshima* (Cambridge University Press: New York and London, 1981).

Mandelbaum, M., 'Lessons of the next nuclear war', *Foreign Affairs*, vol. 74, no. 2, Mar./Apr. 1995.

Nacht, M., *The Age of Vulnerability: Threats to the nuclear stalemate* (The Brookings Institution: Washington, DC, 1985).

Payne, K. B., *Strategic Defense: 'Star Wars' in perspective* (Hamilton Press: London, 1986).

Payne, K. B., 'Post-cold war deterrence and missile defence', *Orbis*, vol. 39, no. 2, Spring 1995.

Schroeer, D., 'Technological progress in the SDI programme', *Survival*, vol. 32, no. 1, 1990.

Segal, G., E. Moreton, L. Freedman and J. Bayliss, *Nuclear War and Nuclear Peace*, 2nd edn (Macmillan: London, 1988) [includes a useful bibliographical essay].

Sorokin, K. E., 'The nuclear strategy debate', *Orbis*, vol. 38, no. 1, Winter 1994.

Tucker, R. W., 'The nuclear debate', *Foreign Affairs*, vol. 63, no. 1, 1984.

Weinberger, C., *Fighting for Peace: Seven critical years at the Pentagon* (Michael Joseph: London, 1990).

7

Economic statecraft

Economic statecraft is the attempt to influence foreign states and other agents in world politics by 'relying primarily on resources which have a reasonable semblance of a market price in terms of money'.[1] These resources may be used as rewards (promised or delivered) or punishments (threatened or carried out); in short, they may be given, denied or taken away (see Box 7.1). When rewards are given openly and on a politically significant scale, we tend to speak of 'foreign aid'. When punishments are meted out in the same way, whether by states in pursuit of their own interests or by international organisations in defence of international norms, we now tend to speak of 'economic sanctions'. (There is a view that the term 'sanctions' should still be reserved solely for punishments administered in the interests of defending international standards, which certainly was its original connotation.)[2] This chapter will consider the requirements of successful economic statecraft ('the bases of economic power') and the utility of its most controversial components: foreign aid and economic sanctions.

The bases of economic power

No state can employ economic statecraft with any prospect of success unless it has a fair degree of economic power. This in turn depends upon four things: economic strength; the will to use it; skill in its application; and a reputation for its successful employment.[3]

'Economic strength' is the most important base of economic power and exists to the extent that a state, say state A, has either a monopoly over some economic good regarded as vital by another state, say state B, or has a monopsony (monopoly purchasing position) over some economic good which state B needs to sell in order to survive – *provided* state A is not similarly dependent on state B. Since most goods and services are in wide demand throughout the world economy, only very large states or groups of states like the EU are likely to have any real degree of monopsony, or market, power. If able to ban the export of a country's key product by mandatory resolution, the UN – as a universal body – naturally has the most monopsony power of all, as demonstrated by the effects of its resolutions prohibiting the export of Iraqi oil in the first half of the 1990s (see Box 7.2). However, even relatively small states may possess monopoly power if they are well endowed with natural resources in high demand, the known occurrence of which is limited. States which have only a low ratio of foreign economic transactions to gross national product,

---

Box 7.1   The forms of economic statecraft

Listed below are some of the most common ways in which states and international organisations employ economic statecraft.

Economic rewards   Economic sanctions

Financial

- Capital grants.
- Soft loans.
- Investment guarantees.
- Debt rescheduling.
- Encouraging private capital exports.

- Freezing bank assets.
- Suspending aid.
- Banning capital exports.
- Expropriation.
- Refusing debt rescheduling.

Commercial and technical

- Most-favoured nation (MFN) treatment.
- Reduced tariffs.
- Export or import subsidies.
- Export or import licences.
- Technical assistance training.
- Joint projects.
- Trade agreements.

- Export embargos (especially arms).
- Import boycotts.
- Withdrawing MFN status.
- Blacklisting firms trading with target.
- Dumping.
- Imposing quotas.
- Refusing licences.
- Pre-emptive purchasing.

---

for example the United States, are likely to be less vulnerable to monopsony power (exports being relatively insignificant to the economy as a whole) than 'trading states', for example Britain and South Africa. On the other hand, both kinds of state may be equally vulnerable to monopoly power exerted by a foreign rival.

To have 'economic strength' *vis-à-vis* a foreign target is not, however, sufficient. Economic statecraft also requires the absence of strong cultural resistance to political 'interference' or 'meddling' in foreign commerce and finance, together with adequate government control (direct or indirect) over them. If the will exists and the skill is available it is likely that the state in question will already have a diplomatically serviceable reputation for the political manipulation of economic strength. Of course, 'command economies' in the style of the former Soviet Union have traditionally been better endowed with these 'non-economic attributes' of economic power than market ones. As a general rule, therefore, market economies are more likely to obtain political influence via the dispensing of economic rewards than the threatening of sanctions (except where direct aid – 'taxpayers' money' – is concerned), providing they

---

Box 7.2   UN sanctions against Iraq

Four days after the invasion of Kuwait, on 6 August 1990 the UN
Security Council, under Resolution 661, imposed mandatory comprehensive sanctions on Iraq with the declared objectives of requiring Saddam Hussein to restore Kuwait's sovereignty and territorial integrity. To
enforce the sanctions, a naval blockade was authorised in Resolution
665 of 25 August, while Resolution 670 of 25 September confirmed that
sanctions applied to all means of transport, including aircraft.

   The rout of Saddam's forces in Kuwait in February 1991 not having
been followed by the collapse of his regime at home, a further mandatory sanctions resolution was passed on Iraq by the Security Council on
3 April 1991. Resolution 687, which represented the formal cease-fire
terms accepted by Iraq three days later, reaffirmed the measures introduced by the earlier resolutions though it exempted humanitarian items.
Among its declared objectives was the abandonment by Iraq of weapons
of mass destruction. The United States, the P5 member which has taken
the hardest line against Iraq, subsequently maintained that sanctions
cannot be lifted until Saddam's government has embraced all other
Security Council resolutions on Iraq, including Resolution 688, which
requires it to respect the human rights of its citizens.

   In part because of the costs of the long war with Iran in the 1980s and
the destruction inflicted during the Gulf War in 1991, but certainly in
substantial measure because of the sanctions imposed for five years
afterwards as well, real gross domestic product in Iraq is estimated by
the OECD to have shrunk by 35 per cent a year over that period. The
economy had been reduced to tatters, with per capita income only a
fraction of what it was in the boom years of the 1970s. Most telling was
the embargo on oil exports, on which Iraq had long been heavily dependent (dates are its only other significant export). Despite having the
world's second largest reserves of oil, even in 1995, with support for
sanctions ebbing in important quarters, it was still unable to move more
than 80,000–100,000 barrels a day, compared to a prewar daily export
capacity of 3–3.5 million.

---

extract the political price *before* the reward is granted. Since, however, the
only command economies left are weak and crumbling, the relative disadvantage of market economies in regard to the non-economic attributes of economic power is no longer politically significant.

   Where the preconditions for sanctions are concerned, it should also be
noted that even if a state has both a substantial degree of economic strength
vis-à-vis its target and the non-economic attributes of economic power, sanctions are unlikely to serve it well unless the target state regards the costs of
compliance as less than the costs of stubborn resistance. Thus, while serious

economic losses are not likely to be thought worth incurring in order to resist some small change in foreign policy, they may well be endured if the price demanded is a humiliating reversal of foreign policy and especially if it is an obvious and significant modification of domestic policy.

How useful is foreign aid?

Foreign aid may be employed in the service of foreign policy by holding out the prospect of either its donation, its continuation or its suspension. When used in the last way it is best thought of under the heading of 'economic sanctions' (see below). 'Foreign aid' is a rather elastic term but normally means the transfer of goods, services or investment capital from one state to another either without charge or (more frequently) at a rate somewhat below the market price. This may be done directly ('bilateral aid') or via the medium of some international organisation such as the World Bank ('multilateral aid'). Because they have sole control over it and because this makes it easier to extract a political price (or 'tie' it to purchase of their own exports), states normally prefer to give aid bilaterally (see Table 7.1). However, the major powers also have great influence over the intergovernmental aid agencies, so this rule needs qualification. Indeed, donor influence over recipients may be exerted more discreetly via the aid agencies.

According to the conventional definition,[4] 'aid' is not the only way in which a state can provide economic rewards to another state that it wishes to strengthen or cultivate. It is the most controversial, however, and embraces most of the techniques listed in the left-hand column of Box 7.1. It was regarded as a useful instrument in the struggle for influence in the Third World between the Soviet bloc and the NATO powers during the cold war, and also (especially in Africa) between the Soviet bloc and China after the Sino-Soviet split developed in the late 1950s. Its potency – political as well as economic – was generally believed to have been demonstrated by the contribution made by American assistance ('Marshall aid') to the recovery of Western Europe after the Second World War. During the cold war the radical left usually described Western foreign aid to the Third World as a 'tool of imperialism' and inflated its significance. Others saw it increasingly as a product of liberal guilt which was making little or no impact on the economic problems of the Third World and paid surprisingly few political dividends either. Since the early 1990s foreign aid has once more been at the top of the international agenda but this time as a possible means by which the G-7 countries (see Box 2.4) might sustain economic and political reform in the successor states of the former Soviet Union, especially in Russia itself (see Box 7.3).

How useful is foreign aid as an instrument of economic statecraft? Since the conditions for the successful employment of economic statecraft in general are exacting, it is not surprising that the record of foreign aid is mixed.

Box 7.3   Western aid to Russia

In early April 1992 a $24 billion financial package to Russia was announced by US President, George Bush, and Chancellor Kohl of Germany. This, however, understated the size of the assistance since it excluded deferral of principal payments of $7.2 billion that had already been granted in December 1991 by commercial banks and in January 1992 by official creditors. The package also provided for a GAB/IMF stabilisation fund of $6 billion in support of a pegged rouble rate. A significant element of the assistance was conditional on the implementation of economic reform, and failures in this regard led to delays in the disbursement of multilateral aid in 1992 and the non-activation of the stabilisation fund. (Disbursements from bilateral creditors and the EC, however, were larger than projected, and generally unconditional.) In April 1993 the G-7 countries announced a package of assistance for 1993 and beyond amounting to $43 billion (including technical assistance).

Source: B. V. Christensen, 'The Russian Federation in transition: external developments', Occasional Paper no. 111, February 1994 (IMF: Washington, DC).

Marshall aid certainly reinforced American policy goals (such as stabilising non-Communist governments and promoting European integration) in Western Europe after the Second World War; this was at a time when European governments could turn to no other quarter for help. On the other hand, the influence purchased by the superpowers via their aid programmes to the Third World during the cold war was less obvious and certainly more fragile. The chief reason for this, of course, was that neither superpower had a monopoly on the kinds of aid (including arms and training in their use) which were sought by the developing countries. The result was that any attempt to attach political strings to aid risked the recipient's desertion either to the Non-Aligned Movement (see Box 4.2) or – worse – to the other camp. This problem was compounded by the instability of many regimes in the Third World. Egypt provides a classic example, first relying on Western aid (especially in the construction of the Aswan high dam), then switching to the Soviet bloc in the mid-1960s, and finally returning in the mid-1970s to reliance on the West. Throughout this period Egypt retained considerable freedom of movement, both at home and abroad – *and* got the high dam built!

Foreign aid is not only difficult to utilise for political purposes because of the difficulty of achieving a monopoly over it. The will to employ it can be eroded by domestic hostility. This is likely to be considerable if the recipients of aid are believed to be ungrateful, or not using it for the purposes for which it was intended, and if aid programmes are thus *seen* – whether rightly or not – as 'ineffective'. ('Development' aid can actually lead to increased military spending if it frees resources which would have had to go into, say, agriculture in the absence of the aid. This is a well-known consequence of disbursements through the United States 'Economic Support Fund'.) Congressional opposition to the aid budget, which began to mount in the 1960s, has been a headache for successive American administrations; by 1989, against the background of huge budget and trade deficits, it had succeeded in reducing aid to only 0.15 per cent of US GNP (see Table 7.1). As Baldwin stresses, the less generous the aid is (other things being equal), the less effective it is likely to be; and the fact is that, contrary to popular belief, the size of American aid to the Third World has been at best moderate and at worst trivial when judged by various significant criteria. It has also been minuscule compared to Marshall aid to Europe.[5] Now US aid, which acquired an increasingly military flavour during the Reagan years, is concentrated on a relatively small number of countries of special political importance (see Table 7.2).

Table 7.1 Official development assistance by type and as a percentage of GNP, selected countries, 1989

	Bilateral (%)	Multilateral (%)	Aid as % of GNP
Canada	68.1	31.9	0.44
Denmark	55.7	44.3	0.94
Finland	61.6	38.4	0.63
France	82.3	17.7	0.78
Germany	64.2	35.8	0.41
Italy	60.6	39.4	0.42
Japan	75.6	24.4	0.32
Kuwait	87.3	12.7	0.54
Netherlands	72.2	27.8	0.94
Norway	60.1	39.6	1.04
Saudi Arabia	94.8	5.2	1.46
Sweden	70.9	29.1	0.97
United Kingdom	56.6	43.4	0.31
United States	88.9	11.1	0.15

Source
Adapted from OECD, *Development Cooperation, 1990 Report* (OECD: Paris, December 1990), Tables 47 and 52.

Table 7.2 The top six recipients of US official development assistance, selected years (percentage of total)

1970–1		1980–1		1992–3	
India	13.9	Egypt	12.6	Israel	13.0
Vietnam	10.5	Israel	11.5	Egypt	10.5
Indonesia	7.8	India	3.3	El Salvador	4.3
Pakistan	5.0	Turkey	2.8	Somalia	3.2
S. Korea	4.5	Bangladesh	2.2	Philippines	2.2
Brazil	3.6	Indonesia	2.1	Colombia	1.5

Source
OECD, *Development Cooperation, 1994 Report* (OECD: Paris, 1994), Table 45.

To be politically effective, aid programmes also have to be skilfully and sensitively administered. Neither superpower found this particularly easy during the long years of their cold war rivalry in the Third World. In Egypt, for example, Soviet advisers did not acquire a reputation for happy relations with the local population.

Nevertheless, it would be a mistake to conclude that because of the considerable problems facing the use of foreign aid as an instrument of economic statecraft its utility is generally low, and that the success of Marshall aid to Europe was a special case. To revert to the example of Egypt, it is clear that while the loss of Western influence here in the mid-1950s demonstrated the limitations of foreign aid, the subsequent increase in Soviet influence (which lasted for many years) testified to its potential. For if Moscow had been unable to step in with offers of arms and finance for the high dam it is highly unlikely that the Egyptian leader, Nasser, would have severed his links with the West and continued to be in a position to disrupt Western defence planning in the Middle East. When aid recipients change sides it is as mistaken to believe that this is evidence of the ineffectiveness of aid as to conclude that military defeat is evidence of the uselessness of force – it is for one party (on that particular occasion), but not the other.

Moreover, in assessing the effectiveness of aid it is vital to ask: For what purpose was it granted? If attention is confined to the employment of aid to change a recipient's behaviour, it should not be surprising – especially since levels of aid which are politically tolerable in the donor country are generally not high – if the results are poor. But aid is granted for a whole variety of purposes, and it is clear that in pursuit of some of these it is very effective. Aid (like propaganda) may reinforce existing patterns, which is why the former colonial powers concentrate their own dispersals on former colonies – Britain on poorer Commonwealth countries, France on francophone Africa, and the Netherlands on Indonesia. Alternatively, aid may help to consolidate changes in direction which have been initiated for other reasons, as when in 1977–8 the Carter administration made substantial economic promises to both Egypt and Israel which were conditional on their agreement to a peace settlement. Even if it has unintended consequences in the target country, aid may also be of great symbolic significance for the donor. Thus food aid donated to a famine-ravaged country such as Ethiopia may in effect do little more than keep a brutal military regime in power, but it will also underscore the benevolent intentions of the donor. Equally, military aid that merely allows resources which would have gone to the army to go instead into some other sector may still have the advantage of signalling an entente relationship (see Chapter 10).

The moral and economic collapse of Communism in the 1980s, together with the increasingly desperate economic plight of most Third World countries, placed the West in a much stronger position to extract a political price for aid. In southern Africa, for example, increasing aid-dependency on the West (among other things) contributed to the shift during this period towards multiparty democracy, free enterprise and a more accommodating attitude towards South Africa on the part of such erstwhile clients of the Soviet Union as Mozambique and Angola. (In 1988–9 'official development assistance' was equivalent to an astonishing 76.1 per cent of Mozambique's GNP.) It is also in this sort of situation that threats to cut off existing aid programmes are especially credible (see below). Nevertheless, different sources of aid within the West – the United States, the EU, Japan and the Nordic countries, as well as the aid agencies – still provide some latitude for recipient-country manoeuvre.

In sum, the utility of foreign aid depends on a whole host of factors. The only sensible question is thus not, 'How useful is foreign aid?' but, 'How useful are particular levels of particular kinds of aid for particular purposes in the context of particular distributions of economic power?'

Economic sanctions

The popularity of sanctions

Although economic sanctions are by no means a wholly twentieth-century phenomenon, there seems little doubt that since the First World War they have been used in support of an increasingly broad range of foreign policy objectives. Initially they were employed only as an auxiliary to military action or – as with the League of Nations – in attempts to halt military aggression. But since the Second World War they have also been employed to weaken the military potential of adversaries and 'destabilise' the governments of hostile smaller states. More recently sanctions have also been employed in order to encourage states to observe human rights, stop the spread of weapons of mass destruction, settle expropriation claims, restore democracy, and attack the growing problem of terrorism. Not surprisingly, the general incidence of their employment has grown and, despite mounting scepticism about their utility, 'the imposition of a whole range of economic sanctions and energetic diplomacy to persuade other countries to follow suit' is now, as Mayall points out, 'the standard reaction to a crisis'[6] – at least in the West. The first UN response to Iraq's invasion of Kuwait in August 1990 once more proved this point, and since then the Security Council has imposed mandatory economic sanctions on five more states: Serbia, Somalia, Libya, Liberia, and Haiti. Why did this reflex grow?

Probably the most important reason, ironically enough, was the triumph of liberal political theory – of which both the League and the UN were products – which occurred in the West during the course of the nineteenth century. This held (among other things) that war was irrational because it destroyed industry and interrupted commerce. Economic sanctions were thus preferable, not least because no state could long survive without the inestimable benefits of free trade. Since liberal theory blossomed at a time when economic 'interdependence' was believed to be growing rapidly and weapons were becoming more and more destructive, the appeal of economic sanctions is not difficult to understand. Then the alleged success of economic warfare in the two world wars was held to have provided substantial confirmation of its view, while the subsequent development of nuclear weapons seemed to prove beyond doubt the liberal claim that alternatives to war were more urgent than ever.

If it was liberal theory which spawned the idea of economic sanctions as an alternative to war, it was, in a further irony, an anathema to early liberalism which made possible its growth to maturity: the appearance of the interventionist state. In the East command economies were established, while in the Western market economies, particularly in Western Europe, the state sector grew considerably and indirect governmental control of the private sector became substantial. As a result, the political manipulation of foreign trade and international financial flows became much easier than hitherto. Furthermore, in the later 1970s and early 1980s objections to such manipulation were weakened by the economic nationalism provoked by recession.

Finally, economic sanctions are popular because, as with force, they have uses other than that of putting pressure on foreign states. Indeed, they may be employed even if they are believed to be ineffective in the latter regard.[7] They may, for example, be used to *symbolise* opposition to an unpopular regime, to deter others contemplating policies similar to those of the present adversary, and also to express 'adherence to a particular conception of international morality'.[8] Usually, too, economic sanctions are introduced in the hope that more than one of these purposes, and possibly others as well, will be achieved. A detailed study of the United States boycott of Castro's Cuba shows that American goals embraced all of the following: re-election for the Republicans in the presidential contest of 1960; showing other Latin American countries what they could expect if they chose the same path as Castro; symbolising the American belief in a *right* to exercise influence in Latin American affairs; cutting down on Castro's ability to *export* revolution as a result of Cuban poverty and preoccupation with domestic economic problems; and making it more difficult for the Cuban regime to portray itself as a successful model of Communism.[9]

How effective are economic sanctions?

Despite the multiplicity of purposes, particularly symbolic ones, that sanctions may serve, there remains great interest in their ability to influence the behaviour of target states, which is invariably the purpose for which they are ostensibly employed. How effective are they in this role?

On the face of it, the record of sanctions here has been poor, especially when employed in issues in which the stakes were high. League of Nations sanctions failed to prevent Mussolini's annexation of Abyssinia in 1935–6 and were abandoned with terminal implications for the League's authority. The NATO embargo on the supply of 'strategic goods' to the Communist countries, which was introduced in 1949, did not prevent the emergence of the Soviet Union as a nuclear superpower and was gradually scaled down. American economic measures against Cuba were no more effective in getting rid of Castro than were CIA covert operations. UN sanctions against Rhodesia, which lasted from 1966 until 1979 and which until August 1990 represented the only attempt by the world body to implement comprehensive, mandatory sanctions on a state, were certainly not the primary reason for the ending of white rule in that country; credit here must go principally to the revolutionary warfare of the 'Patriotic Front', which started at the end of 1972. The Arab League boycott of Israel failed to undermine Zionism; and, while the oil embargo imposed on Western states 'supporting Israel' following the 1973 war had some impact on the policies of Western Europe, it signally failed to move the United States, Israel's principal backer. The Organisation of African Unity (OAU) boycott of South Africa, launched in 1963, had no discernible impact on apartheid, while it was not so much official sanctions as the collapse of the confidence of private Western banks in South Africa in 1985 together with rising domestic violence which in the end forced Pretoria to start negotiating with the African National Congress (ANC). American sanctions against Panama in the late 1980s were no more effective in displacing General Noriega than they had been in the attempt to remove Castro. And UN sanctions against Iraq were rejected in favour of force by the 'Coalition' in January 1991, when it seemed unlikely that they would prise Saddam Hussein out of Kuwait. Despite remaining ever since (see Box 7.2), in late 1995 these sanctions had still failed to remove Saddam, guarantee his respect for political freedoms within Iraq, eliminate beyond reasonable doubt his ability to manufacture weapons of mass destruction, or calm outside suspicions of his aggressive intentions towards neighbouring states – the last three at any rate all being stipulated in various Security Council resolutions.

As already noted in the discussion of foreign aid (the suspension of which may itself be an important sanction), the chief problem confronting sanctioning states is the difficulty of obtaining anything like a monopoly position relative to their targets, whether in supply or market terms. For example, the UN oil embargo on Rhodesia (as well as other aspects of the UN campaign) was undermined by the oil conduit provided by friendly South Africa; the American boycott of Cuba was vitiated by Castro's ability to find an alternative market for his country's sugar in Russia; Arab sanctions against Egypt following Sadat's peace with Israel in 1979 were nullified by a massive rise in American aid and increased trade with Israel; and President Carter's attempt to punish the Soviet Union for its invasion of Afghanistan by the imposition of a grain embargo in 1980 was utterly defeated by the extent to which other producers, attracted by the high price offered – notably Argentina and Australia – were prepared to replace American grain in the Soviet market.

Sanctioning states face other problems as well. Being highly visible (like the use of force), sanctions tend to provoke a strong patriotic response in the target state, which stiffens the resistance of its regime. (However, sanctions also tend to raise the morale of any internal opponents of the regime; depending on the balance of forces, this may be more significant, as was the case in Rhodesia.) Some sanctions, especially commercial ones (see Box 7.1), also take time to mobilise and thus allow the victim opportunity to make defensive dispositions (see Boxes 7.4 and 7.5). Sanctions tend, furthermore, to produce administrative and juridical problems of great complexity and thus require extraordinary 'bureaucratic tenacity' to see them through – particularly, of course, in the market economies.[10] And where the sanction being threatened is the reduction or termination of aid, there is often such a strong bond of common interest between donor and recipient that the threat is simply not credible. (This has been all too apparent in the relationship between creditor and debtor countries since the onset of the debt crisis in the early 1980s: failure to grant debt rescheduling could have led to the collapse of the existing international financial regime.) Finally, unlike most kinds of conventional military force, economic sanctions tend to be undiscriminating in the damage which they inflict: in the complex and intricately intermeshed world economy, economic missiles, once more the commercial variety in particular, are almost by definition unguided. Not only do they have a nasty tendency to explode in the faces of those who launch them (a rise in unemployment figures following a trade embargo, for example) but they are likely to do as much harm to states adjacent to the target states as to the targets themselves. 'In the Rhodesian case,' says Renwick, who was a senior official responsible for Rhodesian affairs in the British Foreign Office and subsequently a highly successful ambassador to South Africa, 'it is at least arguable that they did *more* damage to the neighbouring countries than to the one to which they were applied.'[11]

Box 7.4   How states defend themselves against trade sanctions

When states are threatened with boycotts of their exports and restrictions on their ability to buy key commodities abroad (such as arms, oil, food, electronic and transport equipment), they characteristically resort to some or all of the following measures:

- Stockpiling.
- Diversification of markets and sources of supply.
- Import substitution.
- Exchange control.
- Rationing.
- Transport diversification.
- Clandestine trading – 'sanctions busting'.
- Counter-sanctions, i.e. commercial and/or financial retaliation.

Box 7.5 South Africa and trade sanctions

South Africa's policy of white racial domination ('apartheid') brought down upon its head commercial sanctions of one sort or another – and constant threats of more – for three decades preceding the irrevocable commitment to a multiracial constitution made in 1993. Arms embargoes, imposed mandatorily by the UN in 1977, were its biggest headache. Not surprisingly, therefore, South Africa provides the paradigm case of a state which had to take economic defence seriously, using all of the techniques listed in Box 7.4. It even created a 'Department of Unconventional Trade'.

Though South Africa's countermeasures proved very effective, it should be noted that it had special advantages which throughout the period meant that it never actually had to face *comprehensive* trade sanctions. These advantages included a long coastline with big, deep-water ports which would have made any naval blockade to enforce sanctions difficult and expensive; an increasingly broad-based and efficient economy, with manufacturing industry as well as food and mineral production, including coal; poor, weak neighbours heavily dependent upon it who would have suffered greatly in the event of comprehensive trade sanctions; trading partners with a visceral hostility to sanctions; key exports, notably gold, platinum and gem diamonds, whose minuscule physical proportions would have made them extraordinarily difficult to intercept; and a wealth of experience in 'sanctions busting' acquired during the years of its collaboration with the white supremacist regime in Rhodesia.

Nevertheless, there were two commodities which South Africa needed badly but which it could not produce adequately itself: oil and major weapons. It tackled the oil problem by stockpiling, rationing and – via the plants of the South African Coal, Oil and Gas Corporation (SASOL) – making oil from coal. But oil substitution was expensive and fuel was always a worry, not least because of the needs of the Defence Force. As for the arms embargo, the effects of this were certainly mitigated by the expanding production lines of ARMSCOR (the Armaments Corporation) and discreet foreign purchasing, probably by new-mined gold. However, Pretoria's inability to make or (after 1977) buy main weapons systems (especially advanced jet fighters) eventually told in the war against the Soviet-supplied Marxist government and its Cuban allies in Angola during 1988.

However, while it is true that it has been rare for economic sanctions to have been *decisive* in any major interstate conflict, it is illogical to conclude from this – though this was often done until quite recently – that they are rarely *effective*. Indeed, it is now well recognised that, though unlikely to be much use on their own in conflicts involving high stakes, sanctions may well be important when introduced in such conflicts as a *complement* to force, propaganda or diplomacy, especially if the target is small and weak. The quantitative study by Hufbauer *et al.* claims that one in two efforts to destabilise the governments of foreign rivals (usually 'small and shaky') succeeds and that economic sanctions make a modest contribution to this goal.[12]

There is now also ample evidence that economic sanctions are a still more effective weapon when employed in pursuit of modest policy goals, even when used alone. Thus Hufbauer *et al.* record that 'in not quite half of the modest policy change cases, the sender country made some progress in achieving its goals through the use of economic sanctions'.[13] This is helped by the fact that in such cases (for example, the US economic pressure on China which probably helped secure the release of the leading dissident Professor Fang Lizhi in June 1990) it is easier to employ sanctions with less fanfare than otherwise would be the case and thus to make it possible for the target to comply without significant loss of prestige. In conflicts over issues of relatively low priority, it is also more difficult for the victim to gain international support.

The successful use of sanctions in pursuit of relatively modest policy goals is, of course, a common feature of the relations between great powers (including 'regional' great powers) and their clients. This is because for *political* reasons clients find it difficult to make defensive economic adjustments with the help of other states. A case in point is provided by Soviet–Cuban relations in the late 1960s. At odds with Castro over the issue of encouraging armed revolution throughout Latin America, in late 1967 the Soviet Union slowed down deliveries of oil to Cuba and also insisted on more difficult terms in the trade agreements signed in the following March. These measures evidently hurt (gasoline rationing had to be introduced on 2 January 1968) and subsequently Castro not only moderated his position on armed revolution but adopted the unpopular position of support for the Soviet invasion of Czechoslovakia. In 1969 Soviet economic pressure was relaxed.[14] In southern Africa in 1976 the regional great power, South Africa, used unaccountable 'bottlenecks' on its railways to put the Rhodesians in a more accommodating mood towards the settlement which it was then anxious to promote.

It is not only in the relationship between great powers and their clients that sanctions are successfully employed. To help bring about the downfall of the Chilean Marxist, Salvador Allende, the United States applied economic pressure across a broad front in the aptly termed 'invisible blockade'. For its part, especially in the 1960s and 1970s, South Africa employed economic pressure not only to stiffen its faltering friends in the West but also to underpin its dominance of the entire southern African region. With the former it found its lucrative market (including the shipping market) and its ability to manipulate gold sales impressive weapons, while with the latter its transport network played an invaluable role (as with Rhodesia). Eloquent testimony to the potency of South African economic pressure on the black Front Line States was supplied in 1980 when the Front Line States were obliged to establish the

Southern African Development Coordination Conference (SADCC), principally in order to free themselves from the political consequences of economic dependence on the white south.

In sum, because of the exacting requirements of economic strength and the contingent difficulties of translating it into sanctions, this aspect of economic statecraft does not have any decisive punch in disputes between states involving high stakes. Nevertheless, economic sanctions are a useful auxiliary to other instruments of policy in such conflicts, especially when the victim is a small state with a weak regime. When used in a limited and discreet manner, even alone, they may also be effective in pursuit of modest policy goals, particularly in the relationships between great powers and their clients.

Notes

1. Baldwin, *Economic Statecraft*, pp. 13–14.
2. Doxey, *International Sanctions in Contemporary Perspective*, ch. 1, and Nossal, 'International sanctions as international punishment'.
3. This analysis is based on Knorr, *The Power of Nations*.
4. On difficulties with this definition, see Baldwin, *Economic Statecraft*, pp. 291–4.
5. *Ibid.*, pp. 298 and 320–2.
6. 'The sanctions problem in international economic relations', p. 631.
7. In his widely quoted 'Economic sanctions as a policy instrument', Barber distinguishes three objectives of economic sanctions: 'primary' ones, which are concerned with the behaviour of the target; 'secondary' ones, which are concerned with the domestic interests of the sanctioned; and 'tertiary' ones, which are concerned with 'broader international considerations, relating either to the structure and operation of the international system as a whole or to those parts of it which are regarded as important by the imposing states'. These distinctions are useful, but the labels applied to them are misleading. This is because they suggest a ranking of importance which needs to be historically established.
8. Mayall, 'The sanctions problem in international economic relations', p. 638.
9. Schreiber, 'Economic coercion as an instrument of foreign policy'.
10. Renwick, *Economic Sanctions*, pp. 78–9.
11. *Ibid.*, p. 91, emphasis added.
12. *Economic Sanctions Reconsidered*, p. 80.
13. *Ibid.*, p. 42.
14. Schreiber, 'Economic coercion as an instrument of foreign policy', pp. 403–4.

Further reading

General

Baldwin, D. A., *Economic Statecraft* (Princeton University Press: Princeton, NJ, 1985).
Huntington, S. P., 'Trade, technology, and leverage: economic diplomacy', *Foreign Policy*, no. 32, 1978.
Knorr, K., *The Power of Nations: The political economy of international relations* (Basic Books: New York, 1975).

Knorr, K. and F. N. Trager (eds), *Economic Issues and National Security* (Regents Press of Kansas: Lawrence, KA, 1977).

Foreign aid

Baldwin, *Economic Statecraft*, ch. 10.
Cassen, R. et al., *Does Aid Work?* (The Clarendon Press: Oxford, 1986).
McKinlay, R. D. and A. Mughan, *Aid and Arms to the Third World* (Pinter: London, 1984).
Minear, L., 'The forgotten human agenda', *Foreign Policy*, no. 73, 1988/9.
Hayter, T., *Aid as Imperialism* (Penguin: Harmondsworth, 1971).
OECD, *Development Cooperation, 1990 Report* (OECD: Paris, 1990). [This excellent statistical source, plus commentary, appears annually.]
OECD, *Geographical Distribution of Financial Flows to Developing Countries 1986–1989* (OECD: Paris, 1991).
Packenham, R. A., *Liberal America and the Third World: Political development ideas in foreign aid and social science* (Princeton University Press: Princeton, NJ, 1973).
Sewell, J. W. and C. E. Contee, 'Foreign aid and Gramm-Rudman', *Foreign Affairs*, vol. 65, Summer 1987.

Economic sanctions

Barber, J., 'Economic sanctions as a policy instrument', *International Affairs*, vol. 55, no. 3, 1979.
Doxey, M. P., *Economic Sanctions and International Enforcement*, 2nd edn (Macmillan: London, and Oxford University Press: New York, 1980).
Doxey, M. P., *International Sanctions in Contemporary Perspective* (Macmillan: London, 1987).
Hufbauer, G. C., J. J. Schott and K. A. Elliott, *Economic Sanctions Reconsidered: History and current policy*, 2nd edn (Institute for International Economics: Washington, DC, 1990).
Lindsay, J. M., 'Trade sanctions as policy instruments: a re-examination', *International Studies Quarterly*, vol. 30, June 1986.
Mansfield, E. D., 'International institutions and economic sanctions' [review article], *World Politics*, vol. 47, no. 4, July 1995.
Martin, L. L., *Coercive Cooperation: Explaining multilateral economic sanctions* (Princeton University Press: Princeton, 1992).
Mayall, J., 'The sanctions problem in international economic relations: reflections in the light of recent experience', *International Affairs*, vol. 60, no. 4, 1984.
Nincic, M. and P. Wallensteen (eds), *Dilemmas of Economic Coercion: Sanctions in world politics* (Praeger: New York, 1984).
Nossal, K. R., 'International sanctions as international punishment', *International Organization*, vol. 43, no. 1, 1989.
Olson, R. S., 'Economic coercion in world politics', *World Politics*, vol. 31, no. 4, 1979.
Renwick, R., *Economic Sanctions* (Harvard University Center for International Affairs: Cambridge, MA, 1981).
Rodman, K. A., 'Sanctions at bay? Hegemonic decline, multinational corporations, and US economic sanctions since the pipeline case', *International Organisation*, vol. 49, no. 1, Winter 1995.
Wu, Yuan-Li, *Economic Warfare* (Prentice Hall: Englewood Cliffs, NJ, 1952).

Case studies

Adler-Karlsson, G., *Western Economic Warfare, 1947–1967: A case study in foreign economic policy* (Almqvist and Wiksell: Stockholm, 1968).

Berridge, G. R., *Economic Power in Anglo-South African Diplomacy: Simonstown, Sharpeville and after* (Macmillan: London, 1981).

Berridge, G. R., *The Politics of the South Africa Run: European shipping and Pretoria* (Oxford University Press: Oxford, 1987).

Freedman, R. O., *Economic Warfare in the Communist Bloc: A study of Soviet economic pressure against Yugoslavia, Albania and Communist China* (Praeger: New York, 1970).

Hanlon, J., *Mozambique: Who calls the shots?* (Currey: London, 1991).

Hanson, P., *Western Economic Statecraft in East West Relations*, Chatham House Papers 40 (Routledge & Kegan Paul for the RIIA: London and New York, 1988).

Heikal, M., *Sphinx and Commissar: The rise and fall of Soviet influence in the Arab world* (Collins: London, 1978).

Lavy, V., 'The economic embargo of Egypt by Arab states: myth and reality', *The Middle East Journal*, vol. 38, no. 3, 1984.

Losman, D. L., *International Economic Sanctions: The cases of Cuba, Israel and Rhodesia* (University of New Mexico Press: Albuquerque, 1979).

Mastanduno, M., *Economic Containment: COCOM and the politics of East–West trade* (Cornell University Press: Ithaca, NY, 1992).

Ovenden, K. and T. Cole, *Apartheid and International Finance* (Penguin: Harmondsworth, 1989).

Paarlberg, R. L., 'Lessons of the grain embargo', *Foreign Affairs*, vol. 59, Autumn 1980.

Paust, J. J. and A. P. Blaustein, *The Arab Oil Weapon* (Oceana: Dobbs Ferry, NY, 1977).

Rouleau, E., 'America's unyielding policy towards Iraq', *Foreign Affairs*, vol. 74, no. 1, Jan./Feb. 1995.

Schreiber, A. P., 'Economic coercion as an instrument of foreign policy: US economic measures against Cuba and the Dominican Republic', *World Politics*, vol. 25, no. 3, 1973.

Strack, H. R., *Sanctions: The case of Rhodesia* (Syracuse University Press: Syracuse, NY, 1978).

Weintraub, S. (ed.), *Economic Coercion and US Foreign Policy: Implications of case studies from the Johnson Administration* (Westview Press: Boulder, CO, 1982).

8

Propaganda

To the extent that it is the manipulation of opinion by words alone, propaganda, by virtue of its characteristic contempt for facts and logic, is a perversion of the ancient art of rhetoric. But propaganda goes beyond this ancient art in two further senses: first, by exploiting pictures as well as words; and secondly, by conveying both through the channels of mass communication. In short, propaganda is the unscrupulous manipulation of public opinion by symbols carried through the mass media – political advertising.

In international politics the ends which propaganda serve are as varied as the aims of foreign policy itself. They typically include the encouragement of internal opposition to unfriendly regimes, which was the objective of American propaganda directed at the Soviet Union and its satellites during the cold war; and the splitting up of hostile alliances, which was the objective of Soviet propaganda directed at the European members of NATO during the same period and was the paramount objective of Iraq's propaganda directed at the uneasy coalition of Western and Arab states ranged against it during the confrontation in the Gulf in 1990–1. In wartime an essential objective of propaganda is undermining the morale of the other side's armed forces.

Like the other instruments of conflict, propaganda may be employed in more than one form, varying in both style of message and vehicle of delivery. Depending on its purpose, its target and the skill, ethics and resources (technical and financial) of the state employing it, propaganda may be subtle or crude and rely largely on the spoken word or on a mixture of the various modes of mass communication. For many years after the early 1950s, Egyptian propaganda was invariably shrill, emotional and unusually mendacious, and relied heavily on radio broadcasting – Cairo Radio's 'Voice of the Arabs'. This is because it was designed to foster nationalistic sentiment and periodically whip up war fever against Israel, and was directed at peoples with high rates of illiteracy. By contrast, the propaganda in Western Europe and the United States of apartheid South Africa was multifaceted, and in tone and content subtlety itself. This is because its main objective was to gain acceptance for South Africa as a legitimate member of the Western community of states, and was directed at highly literate and generally sceptical opinion leaders.

The use of propaganda in external affairs raises three main questions. First, why has it been so important in the twentieth century? Second, what does it need to be successful? And third, how effective in practice is it?

The rise of foreign propaganda

Though good propaganda is not usually cheap and rarely works overnight, its appeal, as either a companion or alternative to the other instruments of conflict (as well as to diplomacy), is obvious. It is cheaper and less dangerous than the use of force; it is cheaper than most forms of economic statecraft; and it is probably cheaper than many diplomatic actions which involve the exchange of concessions. 'To win without firing a shot', to convert or reason an opponent to one's point of view, is a possibility which must appeal to all except the masochist, the militarist and the misanthrope. But why in that case has propaganda only come to real prominence in the twentieth century?

As with economic statecraft, the appeal of propaganda has grown alongside the mounting fear of the destructiveness of modern weapons. It is no accident, therefore, that propaganda was the main instrument employed in the rivalry between the Soviet Union and the United States after 1945. Indeed, the very notion of 'cold war' is that of a relationship characterised not by genuine diplomacy, nor war, nor mutual neglect – but instead by a sustained and highly charged propaganda exchange. However, while the increased destructiveness of modern weapons may have encouraged the popularity of foreign propaganda as an *alternative* to force after 1945, this was not one of the reasons for its initial rise to prominence, which occurred during the First World War. In fact, at this juncture propaganda was widely regarded as nothing more than an auxiliary to warfare itself and thus actually inappropriate in time of peace.

In the West foreign propaganda began to grow in importance at the beginning of the twentieth century because political, social, military and technological developments conspired to produce both new incentives and new opportunities for its exploitation. Providing the incentives were the spread of democracy and the arrival of total war, that is to say, war requiring the mobilisation of entire societies. Democracy made public opinion politically important, and total war made it especially important in wartime. In the new circumstances, foreign governments could be influenced or even brought down by turning their publics against them.

As the motives for attempting to manipulate foreign public opinion became more and more compelling, so the means for accomplishing it improved, in both geographical range and potential effectiveness. The spread of literacy had been an important feature of the nineteenth century, and by the time of the First World War the development of large-scale publication of the printed word and photograph, together with the invention of the aeroplane and the balloon, had made it possible to drop leaflets by the thousand over enemy lines.[1] Moreover, the belief in the efficacy of allied propaganda during the First World War – in persuading the United States to join in as well as helping directly to defeat the Central Powers – made it impossible for the great powers to ignore the possibilities of propaganda in peacetime. Even the

British, disposed as they were to think of propaganda as a vulgar activity to which true great powers stooped only in the extremity of a major war, were forced to retain the skeleton of their wartime machine in the face of similar action by their rivals. Among these the Soviet Union stood out, for it had little military and economic strength in the first years after the Bolshevik Revolution and thus no alternative but to place great reliance on its propaganda machine – the Communist International (Comintern) – to protect the revolution by undermining the position of its enemies in their homes. That it should have attempted to do this in any case followed from the central Bolshevik belief in the revolutionary role of the working class in all capitalist states.

In the 1920s radio appeared on the scene (Radio Moscow was established in 1922) and in the 1930s the possibilities for international propaganda were further transformed by the widespread adoption of short-wave transmission. This had far greater range than anything which had preceded it. (1,500 miles is now considered the optimum range.) Taylor sums up the special qualities which made the new medium such an attractive weapon to the propagandist:

> It relied upon the spoken word and was thus more direct in approach and
> personal in tone than any other available medium. It was also immediate and
> extremely difficult to prevent. It was capable of reaching large numbers of people,
> regardless of their geography, literacy, political and ideological affiliation, or social
> status.

Because of its qualities, Taylor concludes, radio 'was of critical importance in any attempt to influence the audience of a closed society'.[2] When Britain launched the BBC's Arabic Service on 3 January 1938, following provocation by Italian broadcasts over the Mediterranean and Middle East, all of the great powers were exploiting foreign language broadcasts for propaganda purposes.

By this time, the use of foreign propaganda was also being encouraged by the successful use to which propaganda had been put *domestically* by the totalitarian dictatorships, apparently exploiting the unprecedented 'atomisation' which characterised modern 'mass societies'. Profoundly dislocated by industrialisation, urbanisation, war and recession, modern societies were widely believed to have witnessed the weakening or even collapse of institutions autonomous from the state, such as the extended family and the church. In such circumstances the individual stood naked and unprotected before the manipulators of opinion. Whereas in the nineteenth century it had been thought that 'the masses' would control the 'elites', by the middle of the twentieth century the pathetic condition of the masses was generating the opposite fear. It was not only the totalitarians who could exploit this condition abroad; what was sauce for the goose remained sauce for the gander.

During the Second World War propaganda was thus given serious attention by all of the participants, and afterwards became even more prominent, as already noted. The Comintern, which had been disbanded by Stalin during the war as a gesture of goodwill to the Western allies, reappeared as the

Communist Information Bureau (Cominform) in 1947. And in 1953, with the enthusiastic support of President Eisenhower (who believed that US propaganda had shortened the Second World War), American propaganda was put on a war footing with the creation of the United States Information Agency (USIA). By this time Radio Moscow and the 'Voice of America' (VOA) – latterly assisted by Radio Liberation (RL) and Radio Free Europe (RFE) – had already been on the air for some time (see Box 8.1). Today, all states of any weight devote resources to foreign radio broadcasting, among the better-known stations being the BBC's World Service, Deutsche Welle, and Israel Radio. Opposition movements invariably employ it as well (see Box 8.2).

Box 8.1 American radio stations in the cold war

Unlike most other countries, which have just one radio station, during the cold war the United States possessed several:

- *The 'Voice of America'* (VOA), a division of USIA which still survives, was the largest of these. It began broadcasting during the Second World War and by the end of the cold war was broadcasting in forty-three languages. It is the official mouthpiece of the United States. 'Radio Marti', a semi-autonomous branch of VOA, began broadcasting to Cuba in 1985.
- *Radio Free Europe/Radio Liberty, Inc.* (RFE/RL) was the other main broadcasting group. Based in Munich in West Germany, these stations were initially private ventures secretly supported by the CIA. However, following exposure of this connection, in 1971 the US Congress assumed responsibility for financing them both through the newly created Board for International Broadcasting. RFE (for Eastern Europe) first broadcast in 1950, while RL (for the Soviet Union) first went on the air in 1953. Until 1964 RL was known as 'Radio Liberation'. Unlike VOA, RFE and RL were specifically charged with operating as surrogate 'home services' for the countries to which they broadcast. In 1985 RL widened its orbit with the inauguration of 'Radio Free Afghanistan'.

In May 1987 the Soviet Union ceased all attempts to jam VOA broadcasts, and in November 1988 also stopped trying to jam RL. In 1993, with the cold war over, the United States began to wind down both RFE and RL but they were not taken off the air. Instead, in 1995 they were placed under a new 'Office of Surrogate Broadcasting' created within the US Information Agency. This was also given the task of administering both Radio and TV Marti and of developing the new station, 'Radio Free Asia', designed for broadcasting to the PRC, Cambodia, Laos, North Korea, Tibet and Vietnam.

Box 8.2   Rebel radios

It is not only states which invest in foreign radio broadcasting for political reasons. Opposition movements invariably use it as well.

For example, in its campaign against apartheid in South Africa, the African National Congress broadcast its own 'Radio Freedom' from five separate stations throughout the African continent: in Lusaka, Addis Ababa, Antananarivo, Luanda, and Dar es Salaam. For its part, UNITA, struggling to overthrow the Marxist MPLA regime in Angola from its base at Jamba in the south-eastern corner of the country, operated a station called 'Voice of the Resistance of the Black Cockerel'. According to the BBC monitoring service, this was based in South Africa.

Of course, propaganda in the cold war and in the other international conflicts which have occurred since 1945 has not been conducted solely by radio. Indeed, the other means employed seem to have grown daily more varied and exotic. Nevertheless, partly because of the introduction and huge growth in ownership of cheap transistor receivers (see Table 8.1), and partly because the jamming of signals remains difficult and costly, the enduring advantages of short-wave radio (which has itself benefited from new technology) have ensured that it has remained the pre-eminent medium for international propaganda. Indeed, the Reagan administration actually increased the proportion of the US propaganda budget devoted to radio broadcasting and broadened its range. Thus, in 1985 it launched both 'Radio Free Afghanistan' and 'Radio Marti', a Spanish-language surrogate home service directed at Cuba, while the 'Voice of America' resumed direct broadcasting to Western Europe after a break of twenty-six years – an index of mounting American alarm at the inroads then being made there by Soviet propaganda against US defence and foreign policies.

Despite radio's continued pre-eminence, television is also beginning to play a role in foreign propaganda. Hitherto, despite the great popular appeal of television and the spreading number of sets (see Table 8.1), 'transboundary television' has been severely limited by the short range of normal terrestrial broadcasts (typically about 100 miles) and by incompatibilities between different national systems. However, current trends in broadcasting suggest that things might be changing. These include improved terrestrial transmission techniques, direct broadcast satellites and the increasing availability of video cassette recorders and miniaturised receivers. On 27 March 1990 USIA launched 'TV Marti' (see Figure 8.1), with the object of finally toppling the creaking regime of Fidel Castro by bombarding Cubans with images of the Berlin Wall being torn down, the massive anti-Communist demonstrations in Czechoslovakia, and the revolution which unseated Nicolae Ceauşescu in Romania. Clearly, technology remains on the side of the propagandist.

Table 8.1 Radio broadcasting receivers per 1,000 inhabitants (selected years 1965–92) and television receivers per 1,000 inhabitants (1992)

	Radio broadcasting receivers				TVs
	1965	1975	1985	1992	1992
World total	170	254	344	376	160
Africa	32	69	152	170	38
Americas	617	851	978	991	408
Asia	28	61	145	184	73
Europe[1]	328	506	653	736	381
Oceania	171	816	964	990	375
Developed countries	486	778	966	1,050	498
Developing countries	32	59	143	177	61
Africa (excluding Arab states)	26	52	133	145	23
Asia (excluding Arab states)	27	60	143	182	72
Arab states	56	129	221	252	105
Northern America	1,173	1,747	1,984	2,013	800
Latin America and the Caribbean	137	183	314	360	166

Note: 1. Including the former Soviet Union.

Source: Adapted from UNESCO, *Statistical Yearbook 1989* and *Statistical Yearbook 1994*, Tables 6.8 and 6.9.

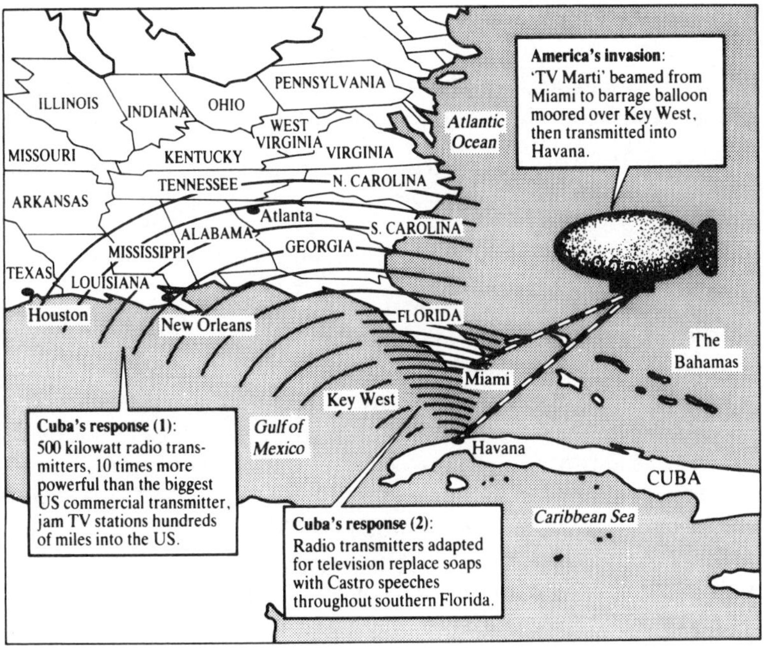

Figure 8.1 American television propaganda and Cuba (Source: Reproduced from the *Independent on Sunday*, 11 November 1990)

The ingredients of success

Understanding of the requirements of successful propaganda is now more sophisticated than it was when foreign propaganda was first introduced. This is largely a result of a vast amount of research into the effects of domestic propaganda on consumer preference (advertising), voting behaviour, violence, sexual practices, and so on. Accordingly, the old 'bullet theory' of propaganda, which held that the non-believer could be converted by 'paper bullets' and 'truth bombs', has been discredited. In its place has been substituted the view that propaganda is more likely to be effective when it is directed towards *reinforcing existing attitudes* rather than changing entrenched ones. (Though it is important to note that propaganda is still believed to be capable of *creating* attitudes on *new* issues.) Among other reasons for this, sociologists of mass communications have rightly pointed to the fact that the individual is not as vulnerable to manipulation as was earlier thought because the 'atomisation' of modern societies is, for the most part, a myth. The individual still acquires protection from 'primary groups' (such as work and neighbourhood groups), and in the West, at any rate, institutions autonomous from the state – including media institutions – continue to flourish.

To be successful, then, propaganda should first of all not be too ambitious. It should be carefully targeted at groups or populations where a degree of sympathy towards its message is known to exist, playing on existing prejudices, existing hopes and existing fears. Of course, this is preaching to the converted but it is certainly not a waste of time because, as Davison says:

> By reinforcing the convictions of those who are already favourably disposed, by providing them with evidence that their beliefs are correct, and by giving them information about what they might do to achieve their goals, the propagandist can often *stimulate action* on the part of people who are in basic agreement with him.[3]

For example, during the Palestinian *intafada*, Radio Al-Quds gave operational instructions to the peoples of the West Bank and Gaza: when to strike, and how and where to demonstrate. Action by sympathisers thus provoked by propaganda might in its turn alter domestic conditions in the target country and, depending on the character and success of the action, thereby help to change the attitudes of initially less sympathetic elements in the population. Hence, propaganda directed in the first instance at friendly sectors might indirectly work its influence over a broader field.

Naturally, there is little point in directing propaganda at sympathetic elements in a foreign country if they have no present or potential political influence, including the capacity to embarrass their governments. The Soviet target population of the 'Voice of America' consisted of 'the Soviet intelligentsia, young managers, scientists, and cultural and political leaders',[4] while Radio Liberty targeted the small dissident community. South African propaganda, particularly in the form of that subtle 'man-to-man movement', the South Africa Foundation, targeted mainly conservative politicians, businessmen and bankers.

Modest and judicious targeting is, of course, only a necessary condition of successful propaganda. It is also helpful if its message assumes the form of, or is coupled with, a *service* which is useful to the organisations or individuals which are in its sights. This fulfils the double function of attracting the attention of the target and inducing sympathy via gratitude – or at the least a vague feeling of being beholden. One of the most important ways in which this is done in radio propaganda is by broadcasting a large amount of straightforward entertainment, especially of the kind which is popular but frowned upon in the target state. Thus the American radio stations broadcasting to the Soviet bloc during the cold war all played a great deal of popular music and jazz, while Radio Liberty also put on the air readings from underground literature.

In addition, the style of a propaganda campaign must naturally be attuned to the idiom, customs and degree of sophistication of its target; and, above all, it must be plausible. To this end it is desirable if its organs are able to maintain an arms-length relationship with the state, an advantage more likely to obtain in liberal democracies than in any other kind of regime and one generally believed to have contributed greatly to the unrivalled prestige of the BBC's World Service and that great wing of Britain's 'cultural diplomacy', the British Council, despite the fact that both obtain their funds from the Foreign and Commonwealth Office.[5] American critics of US radio propaganda, with its history of CIA manipulation and continuing vulnerability to political pressure (in the case of VOA mainly through government influence over key appointments), regularly lament its consequent lack of 'credibility' and point to the BBC's charter as a model to emulate.

It is also because propaganda must be plausible that foreign policy and the use of the other instruments of conflict, together with domestic policy, should be coordinated with the use of propaganda as much as possible. 'Deeds speak louder than words', which is why the South Africa Foundation would always wring its hands and protest to the South African government each time some particularly flagrant act of racial discrimination occurred in the Republic and thereby gave the lie to the Foundation's claims.

The effectiveness of propaganda

Though exaggerated views of the effectiveness of foreign propaganda have been held, particularly in the first half of this century, it has never – unlike economic sanctions – been widely regarded as an alternative to force as an instrument of interstate conflict. Indeed, as already noted, it was seen at the beginning as nothing more than an auxiliary to war. Since the First World War it has certainly become established as a peacetime instrument as well, but none of the powers – not even the former Soviet Union – seems to have regarded it as an instrument with decisive possibilities, and this opinion is shared by scholars who have made its study their speciality. Nevertheless, the major powers spend considerable sums on it, and they are not alone in this. Furthermore, the palpable fear of hostile propaganda shown by some states is well documented. The British feared Cairo Radio in the 1950s; the Americans feared North Vietnamese propaganda during the Vietnam war; the Soviet Union seemed to fear American propaganda during the cold war (though the protests and defensive measures from which this fear is usually deduced may have been an exaggerated response, since pre-Gorbachev Moscow had an obvious interest in transferring the blame for bloc unrest from domestic conditions to 'outside interference'); the Chinese government feared the propaganda of the 'Goddess of Democracy' radio station to such an extent that in April 1990 it threatened to blow the ship carrying it out of the water; and the conservative regimes in the Middle East and secular regimes in North Africa have come to fear the propaganda emanating from Tehran since the overthrow of the Shah. It is interesting to note, too, that it was fear of subversive propaganda that even prompted the small states present at the Vienna Conference on Diplomatic Intercourse and Immunities in 1961 to insist, controversially, that foreign embassies might only install radio transmitters with the consent of the receiving state, the only qualification on the customary right of free communication between a mission and home.[6]

But to deduce that propaganda has some effect because a lot of money is spent on it and because some campaigns are feared is not sufficient. What is needed is historical analysis of the effectiveness of particular propaganda campaigns, that is to say, the campaigns of particular states on particular issues at particular times. And the problem here is that, while it is easy enough to judge when these have failed, it is much less easy to determine when they have succeeded or partially succeeded. If, consistent with the thrust of a particular campaign, attitudes are reinforced and action stimulated, is this a consequence of the propaganda campaign or a consequence of something else? In the case of states with organised ideological followers abroad, the difficulty is compounded by the problem of distinguishing between the influence of the oracle and the persuasiveness of its foreign disciples. Has Islamic fundamentalism flourished in the Lebanon chiefly as a result of the propaganda of Iran or of the local Hizbollah Party? Of course, the judgement is easier if no instrument other than propaganda was employed but it is extremely unlikely that this would have been the case.

Largely because of methodological difficulties, little research has been done on the impact of foreign propaganda, either by scholars or by the governments which put up the money for it. 'Incredibly', writes one commentator on US propaganda, 'the cost-effectiveness of these multimillion-dollar programmes has never been documented. In appropriations requests and congressional hearings, administration officials have simply *asserted* that US propaganda is effective.'[7] Moreover, estimates of radio and TV audience size, a crude index of 'effectiveness', are often based on surveys conducted by those agencies with a vested interest in exaggerating them – the radio stations or information agencies. (In August 1990 USIA was criticised by the investigative arm of the US Congress for survey methods which produced an estimated audience for TV Marti in Cuba of between 1 and 7 millions, while American diplomats judged that the audience was no more than 70,000.)[8] Nevertheless, certain opinions have been formed on the effectiveness of certain campaigns and it will be as well to consider at least an illustrative sample of them.

The assessment of Soviet propaganda's effectiveness by its principal student, F. C. Barghoorn, is cautious and, on the whole, he is inclined to play it down. In line with the general view, however, he suggests that it had some success in winning sympathy for the Soviet Union in the Third World in the 1950s and early 1960s. Here, stress on the industrial, military and space achievements produced by the 'Soviet model' of development found a responsive audience among peoples looking for quick solutions and still profoundly at odds with the 'colonialist' West. More recently, and in its more aggressive mode, Soviet propaganda was believed by the Americans to have contributed both to the fall of the Shah of Iran and to the anti-American direction subsequently taken by his successor, Ayatollah Khomeini. In this connection, the finger is pointed specifically at the radio station, 'National Voice of Iran'.

In the West itself, Soviet propaganda did not fall on entirely barren soil during the cold war, especially among the young. The manipulation of 'disarmament' and arms control proposals, and emphasis on the differences of interest between the United States and Western Europe, in particular, created some serious political problems for NATO. But fear of nuclear war and anti-Americanism – the twin sentiments on which Moscow played – were neither of them so strong as to give Soviet propaganda an edge over the anti-unilateralist and pro-NATO propaganda emanating from Washington and the other capitals of the Western alliance. Besides, few illusions about the disinterestedness or veracity of statements issuing from Moscow were held by the average citizen in the West, where contempt for Soviet propaganda was illustrated by the neglect of any measures to keep it out. The most effective countermeasure against Soviet propaganda was that taken by the Soviet bloc itself when, in August 1961, in order to prevent its residents fleeing to the West at the rate of roughly 1,000 a day, the Communist regime in East Germany, with Khrushchev's consent, erected the Berlin Wall.

What of the effectiveness of American propaganda? During the 1960s and 1970s the American propaganda machine was actually allowed to run down, both absolutely and relatively to that of the Soviet Union. This ' "unilateral" disarmament in the war of ideas'[9] was no doubt in part a result of detente, and in part a result of the mood of self-disgust which the Vietnam war brought over much of the American foreign policy establishment. But it was also a product of doubt about the effectiveness of American propaganda. In 1970, Bruce Oudes, a journalist and former USIA officer, wrote that it was 'hard to avoid suspicion that without the USIA the course of recent history would have been the same, except a bit less noisy'.[10] Ironically, RFE itself appears to have contributed to this scepticism by minimising its role in the Hungarian uprising in 1956 in order to deflect the charge that, by rashly suggesting that the arrival of American assistance was imminent, it had caused many unnecessary deaths among the counter-revolutionaries.

Under President Reagan, however, the tone of American propaganda became more aggressive and the machine was extensively refurbished, though it should be noted that, as its run-down had been caused by considerations other than those of effectiveness, so the same was true of its rejuvenation. Among these was the need to be seen to be *doing something* about the Russians (the same sort of argument which is advanced for economic sanctions) – an important advantage in light of the serious deterioration in Soviet–American relations at the end of the 1970s and the return to the United States of a mood of patriotic assertion. Nevertheless, more dollars for foreign propaganda were also justified on grounds of effectiveness. According to the Reagan administration, Radio Free Europe played an important role in encouraging the Prague Spring in 1968 and the emergence of the anti-Communist 'Solidarity' trade union movement in Poland in 1980. This was not just a Republican view. Writing in 1986, former National Security Adviser in the Carter administration, Zbigniew Brzezinski, claimed that RFE had 'almost single-handedly prevented Moscow from accomplishing a central objective: the isolation of Eastern Europe from the rest of Europe and the ideological indoctrination of its people'.[11] As the Communist regimes in Eastern Europe continued to weaken during the 1980s and finally collapsed at the end of the decade, there were more spectacular grounds for claiming the effectiveness of American propaganda – assisted, of course, by the BBC, Deutsche Welle, and others.

The confidence in the effectiveness of American propaganda in the 1980s may have been as excessive as the doubt about it in the 1970s. Nevertheless, it seems clear that the American radios (supplemented by other Western stations) played at least two important roles. First, they provided a channel of *internal* communication for dissidents within the Soviet bloc, by picking up messages from inside and then beaming them back. This helped dissidents in the Soviet Union itself, as well as in countries such as Poland, where Russophobia was intense and Radio Free Europe had its largest audience. One scholar even suggests that the inability of the Gomulka regime to localise the 1970 disturbances in Poland was the result of RFE broadcasts, and that this led to Gomulka's fall.[12] Secondly, the Western radios probably modified the climate of opinion within which decisions were made inside the Soviet bloc, shifting it in the direction of Western values and encouraging more general scepticism towards claims made by the bloc regimes. It is important to add, though, that this claim is impressionistic and is probably much truer of the states which were then still Soviet satellites, especially Poland, than of the Soviet Union itself. One of the first initiatives of the Clinton administration was to announce the phasing out of RFE and Radio Liberty, though this was not, of course, a vote of no confidence in their past effectiveness but an expression of the view that their job was now done.

Another well-known example of effective propaganda is provided by the broadcasts from the mid-1950s onwards of Cairo Radio's Arabic programme. The twin themes of the 'Voice of the Arabs' were the urgent need for Arab unity under the Egyptian leader, Colonel Nasser, and strident opposition to British imperialism and its 'lackeys' in the region. Nasserism swept through the Middle East in the second half of the 1950s, and there is broad agreement among students of the region that radio propaganda was one of its most potent weapons. In the light of its reputation, it is not surprising that Cairo Radio's transmitters in the suburbs of the city were the only non-military targets which Britain's prime minister, Anthony Eden, would allow the Royal Air Force to bomb at the time of the Suez invasion in 1956. (In the event, they were only off the air for three days.)

Defences against propaganda

Though Cairo Radio in the 1950s provided a very good example of propaganda used to great effect, this instrument is not always so potent, and not necessarily because of poor targeting or a low-quality product. Sometimes it simply fails to reach its target, usually as a result of *censorship*. The free flow of information across international frontiers is enshrined in international law – in the Universal Declaration of Human Rights, the radio regulations of the International Telecommunication Union and the Helsinki Accords – but this has not prevented many governments from taking exceptional measures to prevent foreign propaganda from reaching the eyes and ears of their citizens. Radio propaganda is the most difficult form of propaganda to obstruct, but this was achieved very effectively by the Japanese in the Second World War by the simple expedient of forbidding the ownership of short-wave receiving sets. In a similar move, in 1993 Communist China banned individuals and businesses from using or setting up satellite television dishes, which had even been appearing in remote villages, and in the following year Saudi Arabia announced equally draconian prohibitions against them. In the Hoxha era, Albania went to the lengths of seizing foreign newspapers from the trickle of tourists passing its frontiers. Moreover, though the liberal democracies themselves erect no significant barriers to foreign propaganda today, they have not always been so forbearing in earlier periods of peace. For example, in the 1920s Eisenstein's film *Battleship Potemkin* was denied commercial distribution in Britain and some other countries 'on the grounds that it might incite the working classes ... to imitate the example of their Russian counterparts'.[13]

However, it is obviously in authoritarian, and especially totalitarian, states, where absolute control over the content of the domestic media and control over the distribution of foreign media output are legitimate, that the best possibilities for the blocking of foreign propaganda are to be found. Nevertheless, even in 'closed' societies ownership of short-wave receivers usually has to be tolerated because use of short-wave is necessary for domestic broadcasting, as was always the case in the Soviet Union itself and in over 100 other countries. As a result, attempts to obstruct foreign radio propaganda have to be made in the following ways: by competing for the home audience by offering better programmes and more credible news bulletins (which may defeat the object); by watering down the content of the foreign broadcasts at source by diplomacy or some other means (in 1981 the RFE/RL office complex in Munich was bombed); or by 'jamming' – 'the transmitting of noise or program material on the same frequency as an unwanted incoming signal'.[14]

During the cold war, the Soviet Union tried all three of these means in order to neutralise the impact of Western radio propaganda but eventually came to rely, along with most of the other bloc countries, mainly on heavy jamming. There are two kinds of jamming: 'sky-wave' jamming, which intercepts the incoming signal after bouncing off the ionosphere and entails use of high-powered short-wave transmitters placed usually between 1,500 and 2,000 miles back from the target; and 'local' or 'ground-wave' jamming, which 'involves the use of scores of smaller, low power, short-range transmitters in tall buildings . . . in the area in which the signal is to be blotted out'.[15] All of this sounds impressive but in fact sky-wave jamming is never completely effective and does not work at all during the two to three hours of 'twilight immunity', while the range of local jammers is extremely limited. In practice, therefore, jamming is only really effective in the centres of large cities. (Television jamming is not much more successful.) In short, efficient totalitarians can do quite a lot to block foreign propaganda but even they can by no means succeed entirely. In one of the last shots of the 'cold war of words', the Soviet Union heavily jammed President Reagan's New Year's Day message to the Soviet people, broadcast on VOA on 1 January 1987. However, even in Moscow this was audible on some frequencies, and it was even more clearly heard in Leningrad.

Dangerous side-effects

Propaganda which exaggerates the strength of one's own side and minimises that of one's enemies may lead to self-delusion and provoke rash action. Of course, if the enemy is equally deluded by propaganda about one's invincibility the consequences will not be serious; indeed, they may be favourable, as was the case to some extent and for a limited period for Mussolini following the success of his propaganda about the new 'Roman Empire' being constructed in his Fascist state. However, if the enemy is *not* deluded – which is more common – the consequences of self-delusion may well be disastrous, as in the case of the Nazi propaganda which exonerated the German army from responsibility for defeat in the First World War, and the Egyptian propaganda which trumpeted the invincibility of the Arabs up to the moment of their humiliation by Israel in the Six Day War in 1967.

A second dangerous side-effect of propaganda, especially if it is radical in content and shrill in tone, is the blow to a state's prestige which will have to be endured if it is decided that a change in course is unavoidable. If the propaganda rests on the intellectual trivialities of ideology – with its characteristic litany of infallible deities and untouchable devils – the difficulty will be more acute still. In this way, propaganda might even trap a government into continuing on a course which changed circumstances have rendered unwise, even if its leaders have not fallen victim to self-delusion as well. Egyptian propaganda prior to the war in 1967 is also a good illustration of this danger, while the difficulties experienced by the United States and Communist China in seeking *rapprochement* in the early 1970s illustrate its more moderate form.

Finally, there is the danger that hysterical propaganda may fail to keep certain distinctions clear and may, as a result, end up antagonising one's friends, while merely amusing one's enemies. Once more, Egyptian propaganda in the 1960s is a case in point, failing as it often did to distinguish in its broadsides between 'Zionists' and 'Jews'. This weakened international support for the Arab cause, even on the political left.

Notes

1. The use of balloons for this purpose was not merely a quaintness of the First World War. Between 1951 and 1956 the Americans dropped 300 million leaflets over Eastern Europe from balloons launched in West Germany. See Mickelson, *America's Other Voice*, pp. 56–7.
2. Taylor, *The Projection of Britain*, pp. 189–90.
3. Davison, 'Political communication as an instrument of foreign policy', p. 33, emphasis added.
4. Adelman, 'Speaking of America: public diplomacy in our time'.
5. The World Service has always had editorial independence, but after the Foreign Office began funding it in 1938 the government gained the right to specify the languages broadcast and the relative importance given to them. However, after disputes in the 1980s, in 1994 the Foreign Office surrendered this influence, *Financial Times*, 2 Dec. 1994.
6. Article 27 (1), Vienna Convention on Diplomatic Relations, 18 April 1961.
7. Nicholls, 'Wasting the propaganda dollar', p. 132, emphasis added.
8. In 1993 the House actually voted to kill funding for TV Marti, though at the time of writing (October 1995) it still survives – as does Fidel Castro.
9. 'Can we win it?', *Public Opinion*, vol. 5, no. 1, 1982, p. 8 (contribution by Norman Podhoretz).

10. Quoted in J. F. Campbell, *The Foreign Affairs Fudge Factory* (Basic Books: New York and London, 1971), p. 169.
11. *Game Plan: A Geostrategic Framework for the Conduct of the U.S.–Soviet Contest* (The Atlantic Monthly Press: Boston, 1986), p. 233.
12. Lisann, *Broadcasting to the Soviet Union*, p. 156.
13. Short, *Film and Radio Propaganda in World War II*, p. 36.
14. Ronalds, 'Voices of America'.
15. Mickelson, *America's Other Voice*, p. 205.

Further reading

General

Browne, D., *International Radio Broadcasting: The limits of the limitless medium* (Praeger: New York, 1982).
Carr, E. H., *The Twenty Years' Crisis, 1919–1939*, 2nd edn (Macmillan: London, 1946), ch. 8, section (c).
Cohen, Y., *Media Diplomacy: The foreign office in the mass communication age* (Cass: London, 1986).
Davison, W. Phillips, 'Political communication as an instrument of foreign policy', *Public Opinion Quarterly*, vol. 27, 1963.
Davison, W. Phillips, *International Political Communication* (Praeger: New York, 1965).
Hale, J., *Radio Power* (Temple University Press: Philadelphia, 1975).
Manheim, J. B., *Strategic Public Diplomacy and American Foreign Policy* (Oxford University Press: New York and Oxford, 1994).
Martin, L. J. (ed.), 'Propaganda in international affairs', special edition of *The Annals of the American Academy of Political and Social Science*, vol. 398, November 1971.
Nason, J. O. H., 'International broadcasting as an instrument of foreign policy', *Millenium*, vol. 6, no. 2, 1977.
Qualter, T. H., *Propaganda and Psychological Warfare* (Random House: New York, 1962).
Short, K. R. M. (ed.), *Film and Radio Propaganda in World War II* (University of Tennessee Press: Knoxville, and Croom Helm: London, 1983).
Taylor, P. M., 'Back to the future? Integrating the press and media into the history of international relationships', *Historical Journal of Film, Radio and Television*, vol. 14, no. 3, 1994.

American propaganda

Adelman, K. L., 'Speaking of America: public diplomacy in our time', *Foreign Affairs*, vol. 59, Spring 1981.
Elliot, K. A., 'Too many voices of America', *Foreign Policy*, Winter 1989/1990.
Frederick, H. H., *Cuban–American Radio Wars: Ideology in international communications* (Ablex: Norwood, NJ, 1986).
Laqueur, W., 'Save public diplomacy: broadcasting America's message matters', *Foreign Affairs*, Sept./Oct. 1994.
Lisann, M., *Broadcasting to the Soviet Union: International politics and radio* (Praeger: New York, 1975).
Mickelson, S., *America's Other Voice: The story of Radio Free Europe and Radio Liberty* (Praeger: New York, 1983).

Nicholls, J. S., 'Wasting the propaganda dollar', *Foreign Policy*, no. 56, 1984.

Rawnsley, G., *Radio Diplomacy and Propaganda: The BBC and VOA in international politics, 1956–64* (Macmillan: London, 1996).

Ronalds, F. S., Jr, 'Voices of America', *Foreign Policy*, no. 42, 1979.

Short, K. R. M. (ed.), *Western Broadcasting over the Iron Curtain* (St Martin's Press: New York, 1986).

Sorensen, T., *The Word War: The story of American propaganda* (Harper & Row: New York, 1968).

Soviet propaganda

Barghoorn, F. C., *Soviet Foreign Propaganda* (Princeton University Press: Princeton, NJ, 1964).

Carr, E. H., *The Soviet Impact on the Western World* (Macmillan: London, 1946; repr. Howard Fertig: New York, 1973).

Leighton, M., *Soviet Propaganda as a Foreign Policy Tool* (Freedom House: New York, 1991).

Smith, D. D., 'Some effects of Radio Moscow's North American broadcasts', *Public Opinion Quarterly*, vol. 34, no. 4, Winter 1970–1.

British propaganda

Balfour, M., *Propaganda in War, 1919–1945: Organisations, policies and publics in Britain and Germany* (Routledge & Kegan Paul: London and Boston, 1979).

Black, J., *Organizing the Propaganda Instrument: The British experience* (Nijhoff: The Hague, 1975).

Rawnsley, G., *Radio Diplomacy and Propaganda: The BBC and VOA in international politics, 1956–64* (Macmillan: London, 1996).

Taylor, P. M., *The Projection of Britain: British overseas publicity and propaganda 1919–1939* (Cambridge University Press: Cambridge, 1981).

Arab propaganda

Loya, A., 'Radio propaganda of the United Arab Republic – an analysis', *Middle Eastern Affairs*, vol. 13, 1962.

Laqueur, W., *The Road to War: The origin and aftermath of the Arab–Israeli conflict 1967–8* (Penguin: Harmondsworth, 1969), pp. 30–3 and 105–7; published as *The Road to Jerusalem* (Macmillan: New York, 1968).

Taylor, P. M., *War and the Media: Propaganda and persuasion in the Gulf war* (Manchester University Press: Manchester and New York, 1992).

South African propaganda

De Villiers, L. E. S., *Secret Information* (Tafelberg-Uitgewers Beperk: Cape Town, 1980).

Gerber, L., *Friends and Influence: The diplomacy of private enterprise* (Purnell: Cape Town, 1973).

Hull, G., 'South Africa's propaganda war: a bibliographic essay', *African Studies Review*, vol. 22, no. 3, 1979.

Laurence, J. C., *Race, Propaganda and South Africa* (Gollancz: London, 1979).

Leonard, R., *South Africa at War: White power and the crisis in southern Africa* (Hill: Westport, CT, 1983), ch. 6.

McKay, V., 'South Africa's propaganda: methods and media', *Africa Report*, vol. 11, no. 2, 1966.

Meiring, P., *Inside Information* (Timmins: Cape Town, 1973).

Rees, M. and C. Day, *Muldergate: The story of the info scandal* (Macmillan: London and Johannesburg, 1980).

Rhoodie, E., *The Paper Curtain* (Voortrekkerpers: Johannesburg, 1969).

Rhoodie, E., *The Real Information Scandal* (Orbis: Pretoria, 1983).

PART C
The states-system

9

The 'constitution' of world politics

The formal ending of the cold war between East and West at the Paris summit in November 1990 does not alter the fact that conflict between states has been the dominant theme of the international politics of the twentieth century. However, as well as finding themselves in conflict over some issues, all states still share certain interests, not least over acceptable means for conducting their relations. Common interests of this kind find expression in agreed rules of international procedure which are in turn supported by (as well as being partially embodied in) practical international arrangements, or 'institutions', such as diplomacy. Together these procedural rules and these institutions compose a constitution of world politics which we refer to as the 'states-system'. With no recognised 'government' and no 'written' constitution like that enjoyed by the United States, the states-system may well be 'the loosest of all political associations'.[1] Nevertheless, while it is a frail constitution whose institutions for the most part lack organisational features, it still circumscribes in some degree the foreign activities of even the most revolutionary states.

Common interests

The more states share substantive as well as procedural interests (and values, of course) the stronger will be the states-system. However, it is not necessary for the system's members to have common interests in everything, nor for all states to be part of the minimal consensus. A states-system, like a state, can tolerate internal opponents provided its most powerful members – the great powers and other major states (see Chapter 1) – are in agreement on certain fundamentals. What are the *perceived* common interests (as opposed to the 'real' or 'objective' common interests)[2] of the major powers?

Until the late 1980s, the Soviet Union and the United States shared few interests. The attitude of the American Congress to foreign aid and the preference of Moscow for military over economic assistance did not suggest that the superpowers had a perceived common interest in the economic development of the Third World, though they were constantly urged to accept that they had. Since the Soviet Union still refused to participate in the institutions of monetary and commercial order created by the capitalist states after the war, the superpowers were also as far apart as ever on this. Nor could it be said, against the background of the Soviet invasion of Afghanistan and the American invasion of Grenada, that they shared an interest in the independence of all states, as opposed to the independence of their own. By the same token it could not be said that they shared an interest in peace at the sub-nuclear level, despite their frequent protests to the contrary. Nor did they share an interest in combating terrorism (the employment of random violence against civilians for political ends), with the result that Wilkinson was forced to note in 1986 that 'the record to date of international collaboration against terrorism is one of abysmal failure'.[3]

Nevertheless, even during the 'new cold war' in the early 1980s the superpowers possessed sufficient common interests to make the states-system work. For example, they demonstrated a common interest in the solution of many relatively non-political substantive problems. These included problems in the areas of international transport and communications (including space exploration), disease and pollution control (with particular attention, following the Chernobyl meltdown, to nuclear power stations), and so on. But, vastly more important, the superpowers shared a procedural interest, *the avoidance of nuclear war*. This was suggested by the slogan of 'peaceful coexistence' adopted by the Soviet Union in the mid-1950s, and the support which each power gave to the Vienna Convention on Diplomatic Relations in 1961; and it was confirmed by the postures struck by the superpowers following the intense fright of the Cuban missile crisis in 1962. These included the circumspection with which each treated the behaviour of the other in its acknowledged spheres of influence, the anxiety shown by both to restrain their clients in the world's most dangerous region (the Middle East), their joint hostility to the acquisition of nuclear weapons by third states, and their determination not to allow acute political differences either to overthrow existing arms control agreements or to interrupt for long their negotiations on new ones. The interest in not proceeding by the method of nuclear war was so strong and its implications so pervasive, that this alone was sufficient to make the great powers – ideological rivals though they were – work together. In short, a constitutional order in world politics was underpinned by the concrete foundation of nuclear fear.[4]

Though strong, this was nevertheless a slender basis for world order, and might have been destroyed – as some American strategists hoped – by unequal breakthroughs in the science and technology of nuclear defence. What has provided an infinitely more durable foundation for world order since the late 1980s is the transformation of the Soviet Union and Eastern Europe, and the 'new thinking' in foreign policy announced at that time by the Soviet leader, Mikhail Gorbachev. Acknowledging that 'class conflict' in world politics was a thing of the past, the new Soviet approach explicitly accepted that what united inhabitants of the 'common planetary home' was now more important than what divided them. Hence the emphasis on the urgent need for superpower cooperation in finding solutions to the 'regional conflicts' which had hitherto wrought such local destruction, strained their exchequers, complicated their diplomacy, and threatened to drag them into direct military confrontation. Hence, too, the much greater stress on collaborative approaches to old international problems like terrorism, old ones which had become much more serious (like environmental pollution, drugs and Third World impoverishment), and entirely new ones like the AIDS epidemic. 'Interdependence' had finally become a Soviet cliché as well.

In the course of jettisoning the ideological baggage of more than half a century, Mikhail Gorbachev also gave much greater emphasis in Soviet thinking to the United Nations, that temple of sovereign states held by Marxism-Leninism to be historically doomed. Russia, the successor state to the Soviet Union on the Security Council, has not markedly reversed this change of direction and now wants the UN to function as it was always supposed to function. After a period of intense hostility to the organisation, the United States now seems to share this view. In the economic sphere, too, the major powers seem to be acknowledging a greater common interest in providing a framework of order for the world's markets, as we saw in Chapter 2. The world has moved a long way in a few years.

Rules of procedure

The international rules of procedure, or 'rules of the game', are principally a distillation of the general principles codified in the peace settlements which followed the great wars of European civilisation (see Box 9.1). These rules are significant for their form as well as for their content, for the creation of order as such as well as for the content of that order. Order, a condition governed by rules irrespective of what the rules say and not to be confused with peace,[5] is important for two reasons: first, because in a complex world the routinisation of tasks which it implies enables governments to concentrate their limited resources on *new* problems; and second, because it makes the future more certain ('Just as long as we know!'). The second of these reasons is probably

---

Box 9.1   The peace settlements which shaped the 'constitution' of the states-system

- Westphalia, 1648 (the Thirty Years' War)
- Utrecht, 1713 (the War of the Spanish Succession)
- Vienna, 1815 (the Napoleonic Wars)
- Versailles, 1919 (the First World War)

The United Nations was created by *special* conferences held in the United States towards the end of the Second World War:

- Dumbarton Oaks, August–October 1944
- San Francisco, April–June 1945

the more important, for certainty is necessary for planning and planning makes possible the avoidance of unnecessary friction – so vital in the nuclear age.

As for the content of the international rules of procedure (other than those governing trade and finance, on which see Chapter 2), there are perhaps four important sets. First, there is the one which is expressly designed to prevent unnecessary collisions between all powers but especially between the great powers. Notable here are the rules delimiting the spheres of influence of the great powers, which used to be formal but in the contemporary climate are necessarily tacit. Second, there is the set designed to facilitate the peaceful resolution of those conflicts which occur, that is to say, the international laws of diplomacy. The third set of rules is that designed to give pause to any state with imperial ambitions, which includes the laws against the use of force as an instrument of national policy and (somewhat contradictorily) the precepts of the balance of power (to be discussed in detail in the following chapter). Finally, there is the set of rules designed to curb the barbarity and scope of war should conflicts descend to this: the international laws on neutrality, biological-chemical warfare, the treatment of prisoners of war, and so on.

Not all international rules of procedure (or rules of substance, for that matter) are dressed in the same style, as will be apparent from the last paragraph. Indeed, distinguishing them on the basis of the 'explicitness and formality with which they are communicated', Cohen identifies tacit rules, rules contained in the spirit of formal agreements, non-binding agreements, and international treaties and norms, thus making clear that international 'law' has no monopoly over the rules of the game.[6] It is, nevertheless, the law-like rules of the states-system which have attracted most attention and stirred up most controversy. As a result, they merit closer study.

International law is not handed down from an international legislature but is based mainly on the consent of states themselves, particularly that expressed through treaties (see Box 9.2). Furthermore, states cannot be compelled to take their international legal disputes to the International Court of Justice at The Hague, and there is no international police force to punish international law-breakers. It is for these reasons that there is widespread cynicism about the *effectiveness* of international law, the principal question concerning this subject in which students of international relations are interested. According to political theorists in the tradition of Thomas Hobbes and jurists in that of John Austin, international law is only 'observed' when it is in the interests of states to observe it, that is, when what it 'requires' is what the states would have done anyway: international law is at best 'merely morality'. It was in this vein that in 1916 G. Lowes Dickinson, employing an unforgettable metaphor, wrote that international law is 'as fragile as a cobweb stretched before the mouth of a cannon'.[7] Even Hart, himself no cynic, agrees that:

Box 9.2   Article 38(1) of the Statute of the International Court of Justice

This article lists the four 'sources' of international law as follows:

a. international conventions [including treaties], whether general or particular, establishing rules expressly recognized by the contesting states;
b. international custom, as evidence of a general practice accepted as law;
c. the general principles of law recognized by civilized nations;
d. . . . judicial decisions and the teachings of the most highly qualified publicists of the various nations, as subsidiary means for the determination of rules of law.

> The absence of these institutions [an international legislature, courts with compulsory jurisdiction, and centrally organised sanctions] means that the rules for states resemble that simple form of social structure, consisting only of primary rules of obligation, which, when we find it among societies of individuals, we are accustomed to contrast with a developed legal system.[8]

However, the cynical view of the effectiveness of international law does not withstand scrutiny. This is not surprising since it pays little attention to the facts of law observance, is based on a false analogy between conditions relevant to law observance within the state and those germane to the observance of international law, and begs the question as to why, if international law is so trivial, states spend so much time constructing and codifying it.

To begin with it is important to emphasise the conclusion of Louis Henkin, one of the few scholars to have given sustained attention to this question, that *'almost all nations observe almost all principles of international law and almost all of their obligations almost all of the time'*.[9] This fact only tends to be overlooked because there is vastly more international law than is commonly supposed[10] and precisely because its observance is so routine. Of course, a quantitative answer of this kind does not settle the argument, as Henkin is well aware, for it may still be true that states observe the great mass of international laws either because they do not consider them particularly important or because – having 'consented' to them – they coincide with what they would have done anyway. Certainly, too, some of the violations which still occur, such as the Iraqi invasion *and annexation* of Kuwait in 1990 and the 'ethnic cleansing' in the former Yugoslavia, are extremely serious. Nor is the argument settled by the demonstration that international law in fact resembles municipal law – in terms of the subjects' motives for non-violation, the extent of violation in both, and so on – more than is often believed; this is more a reminder of the weaknesses and complexities of municipal law than proof of the efficacy of its international counterpart.

What does begin to conclude the debate, however, is the central fact that states still routinely observe *important* international laws of procedure even when they have both the incentive and the ability to ignore them. Evidence of this was the decision of the British government to repatriate rather than to punish the Libyan diplomat responsible for the unprovoked and fatal shooting of PC Yvonne Fletcher in 1984, and the decision of the Libyan government itself to refrain from general attacks on British citizens and property in the aftermath of the American bombing of Libya in 1986 by aircraft based in Britain. Furthermore, where in the remaining cases states, in obeying international law, are indeed doing what they would *roughly* have done anyway, this is as often as not evidence of the law's efficacy. For, as Henkin points out, 'Law is generally not designed to keep individuals from doing what they are eager to do. Much of law, and the most successful part, is a codification of existing mores, of how people behave and feel they ought to behave.'[11] In short, the claim that international law is ineffective is based in part on ignorance of the facts and in part on a misconception of the purpose of law.

It is not difficult to understand why observance of international laws (and also the less formal procedural rules of the states-system) is so widespread even when states have the incentive and ability to violate them. States tend to observe international law as a result of habit, the characteristic reflexes of their highly bureaucratised agencies, and the activities of lobbies favouring it, especially in countries such as the United States where there are very strong domestic legal traditions. However, by far the most important reason is that *natural inhibitions* against law-breaking (especially violent law-breaking) exist in the relations between states which do not obtain in the relations between individuals.

In the first place, states, unlike individuals, rarely suffer from totally incapacitating infirmity or old age, and by virtue of the division of labour have no need to sleep at night. Hence, with the partial exception of the admittedly large number of micro-states, they are less likely to be caught off guard and are capable of retaliation against law-breakers, that is, of law enforcement by self-help. This may take the form of reprisals (though these may only involve the use of force if the law-breaking has taken the form of physical assault), countermeasures or demands for compensation. In the second place, most states have powerful friends whose reactions to an attack on the state(s) in question might not be predictable, whereas individual victims of assault or theft are less likely to have friends ready and able to stand by them. In the third place, states are small in number and subject to continuous and intense scrutiny, with the result that exposure of international law-breaking is much more likely than the revelation of domestic law-breaking. (Even the 'secret bombing' of Cambodia by the United States at the beginning of the 1970s did not stay secret for long.) Finally, because even the great powers are not so strong that they can dispense with negotiation, states tend to observe international law in order to avoid a reputation for unreliability which will lead other states to conclude that negotiating future agreements with them will be a waste of time. In short, the balance of power (see Chapter 10) is the foundation of international law.

It is important to add here that, if the natural inhibitions to law-breaking which exist in the states-system make a police force less necessary here than within the state, they also make one less desirable. For, given the way in which power is distributed, any attempt at enforcement would probably lead to war. This would be particularly dangerous, of course, if enforcement were attempted against one of the nuclear powers. It is for this reason that, through the veto on the United Nations Security Council, the great powers agreed that any of their number would be able to block collective action directed at itself. What is often regarded as the great weakness of the UN is therefore, in fact, a very considerable blessing.

Finally, it should be noted that while international law cannot survive in the absence of a balance of power there is often a serious tension between the two institutions. This is because preserving the balance of power sometimes requires actions from states of greater or lesser illegality. These include the subversion of threatening regimes, colluding in – or at least turning a blind eye towards – the lawlessness of one's allies and potential allies, and routine acts of espionage. The classic case of collusion usually cited is that which accompanied Mussolini's aggression against Abyssinia in the 1930s, which London and Paris felt had to be abetted in order to avoid driving the Italian dictator into the arms of Hitler. Equally, the Western powers (and others) effectively turned a blind eye to Saddam Hussein's invasion of Iran in 1980 because they were horrified by the prospect of the Islamic Revolution sweeping through the Middle East.

The demands of the balance of power, however, are not the only reasons which periodically prompt states to challenge, or connive in a challenge to, the sovereignty of other members of the states-system. Moreover, the principle of sovereignty, the most important corollary of which is the principle of non-intervention, is the key legal principle on which the system rests. For these reasons it is important to give further consideration to the problems posed by the occurrence of its obverse: intervention.

The problem of intervention

What is intervention? Why is it generally thought to be wrong? (Why, in other words, is 'non-intervention' a norm of international relations?) And in what circumstances, if any, is intervention nevertheless justified?

Intervention is action directed at a foreign state with the intention either of influencing some aspect of its domestic policy or of changing its regime. It is normally distinguished from outright annexation. The ultimate aim of an intervention may well be to influence the foreign policy of the state in question but the activity is still properly called intervention if it involves 'interfering' or 'meddling' in *domestic* affairs. An example of intervention with policy change in mind was provided by President Carter's 'human rights' campaign in the late 1970s, aimed at such countries as the Soviet Union, Iran and South Africa. An example of intervention directed at regime change was provided by the American overthrow and, indeed, 'arrest' of the Panamanian leader, General Noriega, in December 1989.

Not surprisingly, intervention is normally practised by great powers and regional great powers against weaker states. An intervening state may employ any or all of the instruments of conflict discussed in Part B of this book, and the appropriateness of the selection will affect judgements concerning the rightness of such intervention. (In 'just war' theory this is described as the doctrine of proportionality.) Intervention may also occur collectively, for example through the UN. This will also affect judgements concerning its rightness.

Despite the frequency with which intervention, in one form or another, occurs, the legal norm is non-intervention, or 'respect for sovereignty'. This is clearly expressed in Article 2 of the UN Charter (see Box 9.3) and the importance attached to it is best explained by describing what would happen in its absence. If it were regarded as normal that states *should* meddle in each other's domestic affairs the points of friction (already ample enough) would multiply hugely, all trust would dissolve, and civilised international relations would become impossible. Another argument in support of the norm of non-intervention is sometimes added. Particularly associated with the nineteenth-century English liberal, John Stuart Mill, and revived with the publication of Michael Walzer's controversial *Just and Unjust Wars* in 1977, this is the relativistic view that outside intervention denies to 'political communities' the right of self-determination and thus stifles that individual development without which virtue cannot flourish. There were echoes of this in President

---

Box 9.3   Excerpts from Article 2 of the UN Charter

The Organization and its Members . . . shall act in accordance with the following Principles.

1. The Organization is based on the principle of the sovereign equality of all its Members . . .
4. All Members shall refrain in their international relations from the threat or use of force against the territorial integrity or political independence of any state . . .
7. Nothing contained in the present Charter shall authorize the United Nations to intervene in matters which are essentially within the domestic jurisdiction of any state or shall require the Members to submit such matters to settlement under the present Charter. . . .

Bush's abstention from military intervention in Iraq in 1991 once the issue had become the character of the regime in Baghdad rather than the occupation of Kuwait.

Principally for the first of these reasons, it is rare to find governments claiming that they have a right to intervene in the domestic affairs of other states on purely ideological grounds: in order to 'convert the heathen' or wage a 'just war'. (Intervention to prevent 'counter-revolution' is a different matter, since this can be presented as being consistent with respect for sovereignty: 'We were asked to intervene by the recognised government.') In practice, of course, states sometimes find it impossible to resist the temptation (President Reagan in Central America, and Iran in Iraq, for example), but they rarely claim the right. Nevertheless, there is now wide agreement that there are other (that is, non-ideological) grounds on which the norm of non-intervention may be overridden, though their precise nature provokes huge controversy. Among these perhaps the most important are self-defence, massive abuse of human rights, and civil war.

All states have the legal right of self-defence, including the right to use force in self-defence. This means that there is a very strong case for saying that a state may intervene in the affairs of another state (by force if necessary), in order either to overthrow its government or to cripple its offensive military capability, *on two conditions*. The first is that it must have excellent grounds for believing that attack is imminent; the second is that it must have equally compelling evidence that such an attack would constitute a considerable threat. On both of these counts, Israel is generally believed, at least in the West, to have been justified in launching its pre-emptive attack on the Arab states in June 1967. The trouble is, of course, that most other cases are far less compelling: the American response to Castro's attempt to site Soviet nuclear missiles in Cuba in 1962; Iraq's invasion of Iran in 1980 (prompted in part by fears that Ayatollah Khomeini would stir up the Iraqi Shias against Baghdad); and the Israeli attack on the Iraqi nuclear reactor in 1981. Here it should be noted that great powers and regional great powers are tacitly allowed to intervene in neighbouring states on grounds of self-defence with manifestly less stringent conditions (provided they are not too heavy-handed). But this is in deference more to their power than to their rights. 'Spheres of influence' are a fact of life.

As for humanitarian intervention, this is morally (but not legally) justified to save one's own nationals in a foreign country, as when the Israelis launched their successful raid on Entebbe airport in 1976 in order to rescue Jewish (and mainly Israeli) passengers from a hijacked airliner. More controversially, it may be morally justified (though again not endorsed by international law) to save foreign nationals being subjected to massive abuse by their own governments. Luban argues that intervention is justified by the denial of 'socially basic human rights',[12] though Walzer limits the abuse to massacre, enslavement and the expulsion of very large numbers of people – so excluding, for example, widespread political murder and torture. Examples of military interventions designed, *among other things*, to end flagrant and exceptional human rights abuses of the kind contemplated by Walzer are provided by the Indian intervention in East Pakistan in 1971; the Vietnamese assault on the Kampuchean 'killing fields' of Pol Pot in 1978–9; the Tanzanian invasion of Idi Amin's Uganda in 1979; and the Western interventions in Iraq in 1991 (see Box 9.4). But clearly the conditions here also have to be stringent, especially where *military* intervention is being considered, since governments have mixed motives. The abuse must certainly be savage, probably involve hundreds of thousands of people, hold no prospect of abatement, and manifestly provide its victims with no hope at all of relying on 'self-help'. The intervention must also be likely to succeed at an acceptable cost both to the community in question and to the community of states. In short, the cure must not be worse than the disease. In any case, at least until the launch of Operation 'Deliberate Force' in 1995 (see Box 6.3) and despite claims to the contrary, it is not altogether clear that the early 1990s witnessed any significant weakening of the international legal norm prohibiting 'humanitarian war'. The Western interventions in Iraq on behalf of the Kurds and the Marsh Arabs were not authorised by the UN Security Council; the US military intervention in Somalia in December 1992 is irrelevant to the issue since no government existed to oppose it; and the introduction of US forces into Haiti

---

Box 9.4   'Safe havens' and 'no-fly zones' created in Iraq, 1991–2

In April 1991, following a massive exodus of Kurdish refugees from northern Iraq prompted by brutal government action against them, the United States, France and Britain intervened to create 'safe havens' for the Kurds inside Iraqi territory. In August the following year the same states imposed a 'no-fly zone' in the south of the country in order to offer more limited protection to the Shia 'Marsh Arabs' who were also suffering from the close attentions of the rump of Saddam Hussein's military machine. These actions were not, however, unambiguously authorised by the UN Security Council in its resolution on the crisis (Resolution 688) passed on 5 April 1991. While certainly determining that the consequences of government repression (refugees and cross-border incursions) 'threaten international peace and security in the region', demanding that Iraq cease this repression, and insisting that relief agencies be permitted access to its victims, Resolution 688 did not even hint at military intervention in support of these demands under the authority of the collective security provisions in Chapter VII of the Charter. It also reaffirmed 'the commitment of all Member States to respect the sovereignty, territorial integrity and political independence of Iraq and of all States in the area'.

in September 1994 to restore the government of President Aristide was in the event, and thanks in large part to the mediating skills of former President Jimmy Carter, sanctioned by the acting president in Port-au-Prince and thus unopposed.

Finally, intervention may be justified in a civil war if one party already has outside support. This is the neat argument that *counter*-intervention is justified provided its aim is merely to restore the local balance of forces which obtained prior to the *initial* intervention, thus permitting self-determination to operate. Acceptance of something like this view appears to have been implicit in the Soviet and American attitudes to 'regional conflicts' in the second half of the 1980s, in Angola and Afghanistan for example.

In sum, the norm of non-intervention is important to the stability of the *states-system* but may be overridden. Of course, general principles stating when this is permissible are easier to formulate than to apply. The special circumstances of each case must be carefully considered. It is also important to remember that when the norm is overridden, this does not need to take the form of *armed* intervention. Sanctions of other, less disruptive kinds are now very familiar. Even Mill allowed intervention by 'force of opinion', that is, foreign propaganda.

The institutions

The institutions of the states-system are of vital importance because they both embody and encourage adherence to the rules of the game. International 'institutions' in this sense are not to be confused with 'international organisations' such as the United Nations, although they all have organisational characteristics to greater or lesser degree. Rather, they are simply standardised modes of social behaviour which are typically pursued by distinctive groups. ('The army' is a familiar example of an institution in this sense which has highly developed organisational features, while 'the family' is a good example of one which does not.)

There are two outstanding institutions in the contemporary states-system and two subsidiary ones.[13] In the former category fall diplomacy and the balance of power (the latter understood principally as an alliance system of security) and in the latter, international peacekeeping and the UN welfare network. Discussion of these institutions will occupy the remainder of this book.

Notes

1. M. Keens-Soper, 'The practice of a states-system', in Donelan, *The Reason of States*, p. 29.

2. The concept of 'interests' is notoriously slippery. On this, see R. Scruton, *A Dictionary of Political Thought* (Pan Books: London, 1983), p. 229, and F. Kratochwil, 'On the notion of "interest" in international relations', *International Organization*, vol. 36, no. 1, 1982, though the latter is hard going.
3. P. Wilkinson, *Terrorism and the Liberal State*, 2nd edn (Macmillan: London, 1986), p. 284.
4. For an alternative view of the common interests of states, see Bull, *The Anarchical Society*, chs 1 and 2. Bull believes that states, like individuals, share an interest in the preservation of life, truth and property and, in addition, and in the following order, an interest in the preservation of the states-system itself, independence and peace. But his analysis has a very slender historical basis (his method seems to be to *deduce* the interests which states *must* share by virtue of their membership of a states-system), it is dogged by an ambiguity concerning the concept of 'common interests' (sometimes these are objective needs, as when he refers on p. 74 to the 'tendency' of states 'to lose sight of common interests', while sometimes they are subjective preferences, as when he says on p. 66 that, 'To say that x is in someone's interests is merely to say that it serves as a means to some end that he is pursuing'), and it fails to bring out the significance of the distinction in this context between the great powers and the rest.
5. It is a mistake to regard peace and order as synonymous since there appears to be nothing in principle to prevent states being at peace even in the absence of rules to govern their relations. If peace can be disorderly, order can be warlike. It all depends on the contents of the rules.
6. *International Politics*, pp. 50ff.
7. *The European Anarchy* (Allen & Unwin: London, 1916), p. 150.
8. Hart, *The Concept of Law*, p. 209.
9. *How Nations Behave*, p. 47, emphasis in original.
10. In 1979 Henkin recorded the number of agreements registered at the UN at 'more than ten thousand', adding that: 'There are thousands of agreements in effect which are not registered at the United Nations', *ibid.*, p. 47.
11. *Ibid.*, p. 93.
12. That is, rights whose satisfaction is necessary to the enjoyment of any other rights. They include rights to physical security and subsistence (food, water, clothing, shelter and healthy air), 'Just war and human rights', pp. 174–5.
13. In *The Anarchical Society*, Bull also treats war, the great powers, and international law as important institutions of the states-system, as well as altogether ignoring international peacekeeping and the UN welfare network. But while undifferentiated war may well be an 'institution' of *world politics*, in the sense used here, it is less easy to see it as an institution of the *states-system*. For war is by no means necessarily supportive of the states-system, and, where it is, it is as one of the mechanisms of the balance of power, as we shall see in the following chapter. War in general, therefore, is best thought of as an instrument of conflict, as in Part B of this book. As for the great powers, the difficulty in thinking of them as an 'institution' of the states-system is that there is only slender evidence of concertation in the contemporary period (though admittedly this has much increased of late), and to the extent that they nevertheless act in a manner supportive of the system that is to be seen in the roles which they play in the other institutions, in particular, the balance of power. It is noticeable that in discussing this Bull talks mainly about the great powers, and that in discussing the great powers he mentions first 'the actions they may take to preserve the general balance of power' (p. 208). By distinguishing between the great powers and the balance of power as separate institutions, Bull ends up making a distinction without a difference. The great powers of the contem-

porary states-system are thus best thought of as its dominant *members* rather than as an institution of it as well. Since there is no developed legal *system* in the states-system, it is also hard to conceive of international law as one of its key institutions, and thus better to regard it simply as the principal species of rule, as in this chapter.

Further reading

General

Berridge, G. R., *Return to the UN* (Macmillan: London, 1991), pt 2.

Brown, S., *International Relations in a Changing World: Toward a theory of the world polity* (Westview: Boulder, CO, 1992).

Bull, H., *The Anarchical Society: A study of order in world politics* (Macmillan: London, and Columbia University Press: New York, 1977).

Bull, H. and A. Watson (eds), *The Expansion of International Society* (Oxford University Press: Oxford and New York, 1984).

Clark, I., *The Hierarchy of States: Reform and resistance in the international order* (Cambridge University Press: Cambridge and New York, 1989).

Cohen, R., *International Politics: The rules of the game* (Longman: London and New York, 1981).

Commission for Global Governance, *Our Global Neighbourhood: The report of the Commission for Global Governance* (Oxford University Press: Oxford, 1995).

Donelan, M. (ed.), *The Reason of States: A study in international political theory* (Allen & Unwin: London, 1978), ch. by Keens-Soper.

Gilpin, R., *War and Change in World Politics* (Cambridge University Press: Cambridge and New York, 1981), ch. 1.

Goldstein, J. and R. O. Keohane, *Ideas and Foreign Policy: Beliefs, institutions, and political change* (Cornell University Press: Ithaca and London, 1993), ch. by Krasner ('Westphalia and all that').

Gorbachev, M., *Perestroika: New thinking for our country and the world* (Collins: London, 1987).

Haslam, J., 'The UN and the Soviet Union: new thinking?', *International Affairs,* vol. 65, no. 4, 1989.

Jackson, R. H. and A. James (eds), *States in a Changing World: A contemporary analysis* (Clarendon Press: Oxford, 1993).

James, A., *Sovereign Statehood: The basis of international society* (Allen & Unwin: London, 1986).

Mayall, J. (ed.), *The Community of States: A study in international political theory* (Allen & Unwin: London, 1982).

Mayall, J., *Nationalism and International Society* (Cambridge University Press: Cambridge and New York, 1990).

International law

Arend, A. C. and R. J. Beck, *International Law and the Use of Force: Beyond the UN Charter paradigm* (Routledge: New York, 1993).

Best, G., *Humanity in Warfare: The modern history of the international law of armed conflicts* (Methuen: London, 1983).

Bull, H., *The Anarchical Society,* ch. 6.

De Lupis, I. D., *The Law of War* (Cambridge University Press: Cambridge and New York, 1988).
Fawcett, J. E. S., *Law and Power in International Relations* (Faber: London, 1982).
Grenville, J. A. S. and B. Wasserstein, *The Major International Treaties since 1945: A history and guide with texts* (Methuen: London and New York, 1987), Introd.
Hart, H. L. A., *The Concept of Law* (The Clarendon Press: Oxford, 1961), ch. 10.
Henkin, L., *How Nations Behave: Law and foreign policy*, 2nd edn (Columbia University Press: New York, 1979).
Howard, M. (ed.), Restraints on War: Studies in the limitation of armed conflict (Oxford University Press: Oxford, 1979).
Howard, M., G. J. Andreopolous and M. R. Shulman (eds), *The Laws of War: Constraints on warfare in the Western world* (Yale University Press: New Haven, CT, 1995).
Merrills, J. G., *Anatomy of International Law* (Sweet & Maxwell: London, 1976).
Morgenthau, H. J., *Politics Among Nations: The struggle for power and peace*, 5th rev. edn (Knopf: New York, 1978), ch. 18.
Nardin, T. and D. R. Mapel (eds), *Traditions of International Ethics* (Cambridge University Press: Cambridge, 1992).

The problem of intervention

Beitz, C. R., 'Bounded morality: justice and the state in world politics', *International Organization*, vol. 33, no. 3, 1979.
Beitz, C. R., 'Nonintervention and communal integrity', *Philosophy and Public Affairs*, vol. 9, no. 4, 1980.
Bull, H. (ed.), *Intervention in World Politics* (The Clarendon Press: Oxford, 1984).
Donnelly, J., 'Human rights, humanitarian intervention and American foreign policy: law, morality and politics', *Journal of International Affairs*, vol. 37, no. 2, 1984.
Doppelt, G., 'Walzer's theory of morality in international relations', *Philosophy and Public Affairs*, vol. 8, no. 1, Autumn 1978.
Doppelt, G., 'Statism without foundations', *Philosophy and Public Affairs*, vol. 9, no. 4, 1980.
Falk, R. A., 'Intervention revisited: hard choices and tragic dilemmas', *The Nation*, vol. 257, no. 21, 20 Dec. 1993.
Gardner, R. N., 'International law and the use of force', Adelphi Paper No. 266, Winter 1991/92 (International Institute of Strategic Studies, London).
Klintworth, G., *Vietnam's Intervention in Cambodia in International Law* (AGPS Press: Canberra, 1989).
Lewy, G., 'The case for humanitarian intervention', *Orbis*, vol. 37, no. 4, Fall 1993.
Luban, D., 'Just war and human rights', *Philosophy and Public Affairs*, vol. 9, no. 2, 1980.
Luban, D., 'The romance of the nation state', *Philosophy and Public Affairs*, vol. 9, no. 4, 1980.
Matheson, N., *The 'Rules of the Game' of Superpower Military Intervention in the Third World 1975–1980* (University Press of America: Washington, DC, 1982).
Mayall, J., 'Non-intervention, self-determination and the "New World Order"', *International Affairs*, vol. 67, 1991.
Mill, J. S., 'A few words on non-intervention', in *Dissertations and Discussions, Political, Philosophical and Historical*, 2nd edn, vol. 3 (Longmans, Green: London, 1867; repr. J. M. Robson (ed.), *The Collected Works of John Stuart Mill*, Routledge & Kegan Paul: London and Toronto, 1963–).

Miller, K. E., 'John Stuart Mill's theory of international relations', *Journal of the History of Ideas*, vol. 22, no. 4, 1961.

Moore, J. N. (ed.), *Law and Civil War in the Modern World* (Johns Hopkins Press: Baltimore, 1974).

Roberts, A., 'Humanitarian war: military intervention and human rights', *International Affairs*, vol. 69, 1993.

Slater, J. and T. Nardin, 'Non-intervention and human rights', *Journal of Politics*, vol. 48, no. 1, 1986.

Tucker, R. W. and C. Krauthammer, *Intervention and the Reagan Doctrine* (Carnegie: New York, 1985).

Walzer, M., *Just and Unjust Wars* (Basic Books: New York, 1977; Penguin: Harmondsworth, 1980).

Walzer, M., 'The moral standing of states: a response to four critics', *Philosophy and Public Affairs*, vol. 9, no. 3, 1980.

Wasserstrom, R. A., 'Review of Walzer's Just and Unjust Wars', *Harvard Law Review*, vol. 92, December 1978.

Waters, M., 'The invasion of Grenada (1983) and the collapse of legal norms', *Journal of Peace Research*, vol. 23, no. 3, 1986.

Weiss, T. G., 'UN responses in the former Yugoslavia: moral and operational choices', *Ethics and International Affairs*, vol. 8, 1994.

Wheeler, N., 'Humanitarian intervention and the international community', *Interstate*, no. 45, 1994.

10

The balance of power

As in the state, so in the states-system, the control of violence is the most basic of all functions and the institution with ultimate decision in this area correspondingly the most important. We call this institution – though it is the source of much confusion – the 'balance of power'.

In the history of thought on the problem of what to do about interstate violence, however, the balance of power is only one of three principal schemes which have emerged, varying crudely according to the extent to which power within them is concentrated. At the one end, where power is most concentrated, is the idea of world government. This, however, has never appealed to states collectively as a result of the high value which they attach to their sovereignty, though more limited forms of 'integration' have been attractive following major conflicts, as with European integration after the Second World War. The record of the second scheme, collective security (see Chapter 12), which is mid-way along the continuum of the concentration of power, has been – at least until very recently – no more impressive. As a result, the third system, the balance of power, which stands at the end of the continuum where power is most dispersed, 'exists', as Inis Claude says, 'by default'.[1]

What, then, do we mean by the 'balance of power'? Have conditions since 1945, in particular bipolarity and nuclear weapons, been favourable or unfavourable to its efficient operation? What is the role of alliances and arms control in relationship to the balance of power? These are the main questions which the remainder of this chapter will address.

The 'objectives' of the balance of power

The 'balance of power' embodies the belief that any state's survival is best assured by reliance on its own military strength, allied where and when necessary to the military strength of others. In practice, therefore, the 'balance of power' means a system of big defence budgets plus military alliances and ententes.

The first point to grasp about the balance of power, however, is only implicit in the definition which has just been given. This is that its main objective is *not* to preserve international 'peace' but instead to preserve the security of states, particularly the big ones. (Another way of expressing this is to say that the main purpose of the balance of power is to preserve the states-system, or 'international stability'.) For states to preserve their independence war may, of course, be necessary. This is why it is illogical to claim, for example, that the nineteenth-century balance-of-power system 'broke down' with the outbreak of the First World War in 1914; what broke down here was diplomacy, merely one element, as we shall see, of the balance of power. (Though it is, of course, true that the horrific subsequent *development* of this war temporarily called into question the balance-of-power system.)

Having said all this, 'peace' is certainly a secondary objective of the balance of power, and has naturally pressed national security somewhat harder since the advent of nuclear weapons. Nevertheless, nuclear weapons have merely raised the finite political price which states are prepared to pay for peace within the balance of power; there is no evidence that they have raised it to infinity itself. The values and passions attached to independence, not peace, remain the primary objectives of the balance of power.

How the balance of power works

The balance of power is needed because of the possibility that states may seek to expand their frontiers or even challenge the whole basis on which international relations is conducted. Because early identification of such possibilities is a high priority of the system, vigilance is one of its most highly institutionalised features. This is seen in the resident embassy and its military attachés and also, as noted in Chapter 5, in the activities of secret intelligence.

If a 'revisionist' or 'revolutionary' power emerges to threaten the status quo powers, the latter will sometimes seek first to neutralise the former by diplomacy, even at the risk of being charged with 'appeasement' (seeking peace at any price). Governments rarely believe that a revolutionary power will allow its ambitions to be negotiated away but they usually want at least to go through the motions of diplomacy. First, negotiation buys time for the status quo powers to look to their defences. Second, it should remove any doubt as to whether or not the 'revolutionary' power is truly a revolutionary power, and thus make it easier to rally international resistance ('We tried talking to them but their demands were preposterous'). Third, it is even possible that brilliant diplomacy might dupe the leadership of the revolutionary power. In his classic work *A World Restored*, Henry Kissinger claims that Metternich thus outfoxed Tsar Alexander I of Russia.[2]

Despite brilliant diplomacy, the expansionist desires of the revolutionary power may remain unquenched. After diplomacy has fulfilled its other purposes, therefore, the next stage (assuming that there are more than two great powers in the system and ignoring for the moment the implications of nuclear weapons) is single-minded concentration on the construction, or refurbishment, of an opposing grand alliance. The point of this, it is important to emphasise, is not to create an 'equilibrium' of power between the two sides – a common misconception – but to give the grand alliance a *preponderance* of power and thus the capacity to dissuade the armies of the revolutionary power from venturing forth. Two points should be noted here in passing. First, following the sensible argument that security comes first, any state of strategic significance will characteristically be invited to join the grand alliance, irrespective of its domestic regime, provided only that it is hostile to the revolutionary power. (This point was well illustrated by the improvement in Sino-American relations well before the dilution of Communism in China, and by the West's reluctance to desert the anti-Communist though racist regime in South Africa.) Second, it is widely regarded as a useful feature of a balance-of-power system if there is one great power – the 'balancer' – which is so detached from the conflicts between the others that nothing will prevent it from throwing its weight on to the side of the status quo powers, whoever they are. This was the role played by Britain in the European balance. However, it is important to emphasise that in this special case of the balance of power, equilibrium, or 'balance', exists with the 'balancer' detached. When committed, the power of this state produces a preponderance in favour of the status quo (see Figure 10.1).

With a grand alliance of the status quo powers in place, the 'revolutionary' power will either be deterred from launching its aggression if it has any common sense (as is widely believed in the West to have been the case with the Soviet Union following the creation of NATO in 1949) or, if it does not, be crushed by war (as was eventually the case with Nazi Germany in the Second World War). However, if it comes to war, the fighting should ultimately be directed by the politicians and not by the generals, for the point of a balance-of-power war is not 'total victory' or 'unconditional surrender' – as the United States believed in the Second World War – but the replacement of the 'revolutionary' regime by a 'legitimate' one. This is important for four reasons. First, it preserves a 'weight' in the balance against a member of the

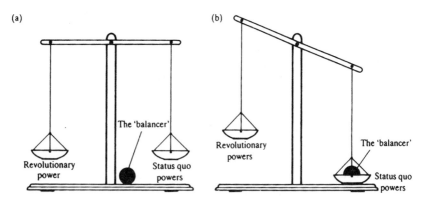

Figure 10.1 The role of the 'balancer': (a) 'equilibrium'; (b) preponderance in favour of the status quo

grand alliance perhaps made overambitious by the exhilaration of victory (France as a weight against Tsar Alexander after the overthrow of Napoleon, and West Germany as a weight against Alexander's successors following the overthrow of Hitler). Second, it avoids or, at any rate, reduces the sort of national humiliation which encourages the rebirth of revolutionary regimes ('the lesson of Versailles'). Third, it reduces the cost of the war to the grand alliance in terms of lives and resources. And fourth, if the grand alliance can succeed in making clear its essentially *political* strategy to the civil population, professional officer corps and military rank and file of the revolutionary state, it is more likely that domestic opposition will be encouraged.

In a multipolar balance of power, then, revolutionary power is met and checked by the temporary concentration of preponderant counter-power. This means alliance necessarily, and war possibly. In a system of sovereign states there is no other way of preserving the independence of its members: the balance of power derives from the logic of the system.

In what circumstances does the balance work best?

To say that the balance of power derives from the logic of a states-system is not to say, however, that it always works smoothly or even that its ultimate success in preserving the system is always assured. Like all things, it works better in some hands and in some conditions rather than in others. There is a common view that everything favoured the balance of power of the European states-system in the eighteenth and nineteenth centuries and that this accounts for its success during that period. It is also widely believed that many of these conditions ceased to exist in the twentieth century. What are the ideal conditions for the balance of power supposed to be, and is it true that these have disappeared?

The main conditions which are held to have favoured the operation of the balance of power in the European states-system are as follows. First, with power diffused among five great powers (Britain, France, Austria-Hungary, Russia and Prussia), there were sufficient players to make manoeuvre possible but not so many that it became too complicated. With a rough equality of power among these five, none was inclined to seek hegemony. In this 'multipolar' system there was an insular power, Britain, available to act as a 'balancer' should the need arise. Military power was uncomplicated and not subject to sudden changes in consequence of a volatile technology; it could thus be measured and its changes predicted with relative ease. The great powers were also by and large non-ideological in their outlook, which meant that the diplomatic mobility required by the system was not hindered by special affections between some states and special dislikes between others. Not altogether unconnected to the last point, none of the governments of the great powers needed yet to attune their foreign policies primarily to popular opinion. In addition, the engines of war were not yet so destructive as to threaten the obliteration of the whole world, and so war was still 'rational'. And finally, and most important of all, understanding and acceptance of the objectives and instrumentalities of the balance of power were encouraged by the shared culture of the five European great powers: all were gentleman players of the 'Great Game'.

All of this is persuasive. The claim is also plausible that many of these conditions ceased to exist in the twentieth century, and especially following the Second World War. Multipolarity was replaced by bipolarity (which by definition excludes the availability of a 'balancer'); military technology became vastly complex and subject to sudden spurts, while nuclear weapons revolutionised strategy; ideology secured a prominent place among influences on foreign policy, in the United States in part because of the need to take account of popular opinion; and the cultural homogeneity which underpinned the classical European balance disappeared. On the other hand, with the exceptions of South Vietnam and East Germany, no significant military powers (including Iraq) have disappeared from the world map since 1945 and at the great power level 'stability' has been manifestly preserved. No serious scholar or politician has ever suggested that this is the work of the United Nations, and it is abundantly clear that it is not the product of meekness. It is thus difficult to see what has been responsible if not the threat to revolutionary power of counter-power, that is to say, the efficient working of the balance of power. Why has the transformation of the circumstances which supported the European balance not made impossible the efficient working of the present global balance?

As for bipolarity, which in the mid-1990s still exists,[3] Waltz has advanced the controversial view that this is actually even more likely to produce a stable balance of power than multipolarity. The simplicity of a two-power balance and the greater ease of formulating agreed rules of procedure, he argues, reduce the fear, suspicion and miscalculation which flow from the uncertainties of a multipolar balance.[4] As far as it goes, this may be true but it overlooks the *drawbacks* of the rough equilibrium of power which obtains, by definition, in a bipolar balance. In this situation each side may be inclined to a pre-emptive attack in order to cash in on the advantage of surprise, as the depressing succession of Arab–Israeli wars amply demonstrates. Nevertheless (I hesitate to say 'fortunately'), nuclear weapons were invented and before long both the United States and the Soviet Union had achieved a second-strike capability (see Chapter 6). This made traditional notions of 'equilibrium' and – for that matter – 'preponderance' irrelevant since, whatever the mathematical relationship of force levels, neither party could have benefited from aggression. Neither surprise nor throw-weight provided guarantees of victory; the only consequence of all-out war would have been mutual destruction. In short, nuclear weapons have permitted the world to benefit from the advantages of bipolarity without having to suffer the disadvantages.

Furthermore, the rapid changes in the technology of nuclear weapons have not produced insurmountable problems for the system. This is partly because of great advances in technical intelligence gathering, and of developments in arms control (the latter will be discussed separately later in this chapter). As for the other changes – the greater impact of ideology and popular opinion on foreign policy, and the disappearance of the cultural uniformity of the European states-system – only two points need to be made. First, the fact is that neither ideology nor popular opinion had a decisive influence on Soviet foreign policy in the postwar period while, at least during the Nixon/Kissinger period from 1969 until 1976, ideology was at a discount in the United States as well.

Indeed, under the intellectual influence of Kissinger and the new sense of national limitations induced by failure in Vietnam, traditional balance-of-power pragmatism became a prominent feature of American policy. Second, and more important, the commitment of foreign policy elites to the rules of the 'Great Game' and their ability to play to the rules unhindered by swings in popular mood are in any case less important in a bipolar balance. This is because there is, by definition, no opportunity for diplomatic mobility at the great power level. In sum, bipolarity *plus* nuclear weapons, among other things, have favoured the balance of power, while bipolarity itself has rendered the other elements of the post-Second World War transformation less important. This transformation has thus not so much undermined the balance of power as altered its *style*.

Alliances

Bipolarity may have ruled out the opportunity for diplomatic mobility on the great power level but it has not, of course, ruled out the possibility of alliance formation and re-formation between the great powers and lesser states. Nor is this altogether without significance to the strategic relationship between the great powers themselves. Until 1991 the United States and the Soviet Union both led large alliances – NATO and the Warsaw Pact, respectively (see Boxes 10.1 and 10.2) – neither of which were merely disguised empires or security associations in which the leaders extended security but received none in return.[5] After the early 1970s there was also a considerable increase in diplomatic mobility between the great powers and the middle powers. For example, the Soviet Union moved nearer to ostensibly 'non-aligned' India, the United States gingerly concluded a *rapprochement* with Communist China in order to complete Kissinger's conception of 'triangular diplomacy' (see Box 10.3) and, following the formal dissolution of the Warsaw Pact in February 1991, erstwhile members started putting out very public feelers towards NATO. Alliances and similar associations have also played their traditional role in *regional*, multipolar balances, as in the Middle East, southern Africa,

---

Box 10.1   The North Atlantic Treaty Organisation (NATO)

The North Atlantic Treaty was signed in Washington on 4 April 1949. The key article of the treaty included the statement that 'an armed attack against one or more of [the parties] in Europe or North America shall be considered an attack against them all'.

Membership

1949	Belgium	Luxembourg	1952	Greece
	Canada	Netherlands		Turkey
	Denmark	Norway	1955	West Germany
	France	Portugal	1982	Spain
	Iceland	United Kingdom		
	Italy	United States		

In 1966 President De Gaulle withdrew France from the integrated military command and NATO headquarters were moved from Paris to Brussels.

The end of the cold war saw no enthusiasm in NATO for disbanding the alliance, mainly because of the unpredictability of political developments in the Soviet Union (subsequently Russia), but also because of the usefulness of the alliance organisation in coordinating collective responses to 'out-of-area' threats such as that posed by Saddam Hussein in the Gulf and conflict in the former Yugoslavia. With growing awareness that new friends could bring it extra strength and that the prospect of membership could be held out as a further incentive to the adoption of Western values in the countries of Central Europe and the former Soviet Union, NATO subsequently offered an entente-like relationship to them as a possible first step in this direction. This initially took shape with the creation of the *North Atlantic Co-operation Council* in December 1991, to which 22 states new to NATO circles (including Russia) were subsequently admitted. Three years later the NATO powers confirmed their willingness to admit new members provided they could demonstrate more than a transient attachment to liberal democracy and that they had made substantial progress in settling any disputes with their neighbours. In the meantime, the countries of the former Soviet bloc were invited to join a *Partnership for Peace (PFP)*, which promised more intimate military collaboration, including even joint exercises. Russia itself joined the PFP in June 1994 as its twentieth member. The four Visegrad countries (Poland, Hungary, the Czech Republic, and Slovakia) are usually mentioned as likely to be among the first admitted to full membership of NATO, though probably not before the year 2000. Russia's full membership has been ruled out and its hostility to NATO enlargement remains a serious problem for the alliance.

Box 10.2   The Warsaw Treaty Organisation (WTO)

The 'Warsaw Pact', as it was usually known, was concluded between the Soviet Union and its East European satellites in the Polish capital on 14 May 1955. 'In case of armed aggression in Europe', its signatories were assured of 'immediate assistance . . . with all means which appear necessary, including the use of armed force'. A United Military Command with headquarters in Moscow was established. Ostensibly created in retaliation for the granting of sovereignty to West Germany and its integration into NATO, formally the Pact represented little more than a multilateral synthesis of the series of bilateral treaties between Moscow and its satellites which had existed in most cases for nearly a decade; arrangements for Soviet control of their forces were also at least three years old by this time.

Membership

Albania	Hungary
Bulgaria	Poland
Czechoslovakia	Romania
East Germany	Soviet Union

Having sided with China in the latter's dispute with Moscow, in 1962 Albania was excluded from Warsaw Pact meetings and withdrew in 1968.

In the late 1980s the collapse of Communism in Eastern Europe spelled the end for the Warsaw Pact. In 1990 East Germany ceased to exist and in February 1991 the remaining six members formally dissolved the military wing of the Warsaw Pact at a meeting in Budapest.

---

and the Far East. No treatment of the contemporary balance of power – bipolar though it remains on the central strategic level – can therefore afford to ignore the modern alliance.

An alliance is a contractual commitment entered into by two or more states to engage in cooperative military action in specified circumstances (though the commitment may be only one-sided, as in the case of the Japanese–US Security Treaty, 1970). The hallmark of the alliance is not so much its formality as the precision or firmness of the commitments to co-belligerency which it contains. Alliances are usually defensive but may be offensive. If they are offensive they tend, for obvious reasons, to be secret. In contrast to alliances in the classical states-system of Europe, modern alliances tend to be larger, more concerned with *internal* threats, to have permanent planning and executive machinery and a high level of military integration. The emphasis on peacetime preparations is a function of the expectation that the earliest stage of modern war is likely to be decisive.

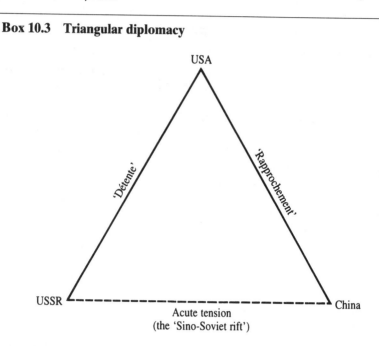

Box 10.3   Triangular diplomacy

At the beginning of the 1970s, when Henry Kissinger was National Security Adviser to President Nixon, the United States determined to create a 'triangular' relationship with the two major Communist powers, predicated on the assumption that an early end to the Sino-Soviet conflict was not in sight. This involved improving relations with Moscow (*détente*) and creating as near normal diplomatic relations with Peking as possible (*rapprochement*). The diplomatic rationale of this policy was to place the United States in a position to extract unrequited concessions from each by simply threatening to move closer to the other in the absence of payment. The balance-of-power rationale was to signal to the Soviet Union that the United States would 'not remain indifferent' to a Soviet attack on China.

It is important to note, however, that states may make weaker military commitments to other states than those embodied in the alliance. The most common alternative is the entente, a form of military liaison well illustrated by the relationship between the United States and Israel (much strengthened in the 1980s). Some of the former Soviet Union's 'treaties of friendship and cooperation' with Third World countries, such as Angola, also created ententes, while NATO's current 'Partnership for Peace' (see Box 10.1) also approaches a relationship of this kind. The essence of an entente is that military commitments are implicit rather than explicit, deriving either from a formal agreement for *consultation* in the event of a crisis, or from some kind of practical military collaboration, for example in arms sales, military assistance agreements, military research and development, manoeuvres or arrangements for the use of bases. Ententes, in other words, suggest strongly that the parties are sympathetic to each other to the point that they will stand shoulder to shoulder in war but contain no firm promises. The modern concept derives from the Anglo-French 'entente cordiale' of 1904. Unilateral declarations such as the Nixon Doctrine (which spelled out in broad terms what America's allies, especially those in South East Asia, could expect of it in the early 1970s), and even public statements about military strategy in general which have fairly clear implications for particular relationships, are other ways in which states can make military commitments to other states.

Despite the clear contemporary importance of alternatives to the alliance, this particular form of military relationship obsessed scholars in this area during the cold war. This is partly because of the high visibility and obvious importance of the most notable cold war alliances, and partly the result of a feeling that there were so many sources of strain upon them that superpower alliances, at any rate, were obsolete. In this connection, heavy emphasis was normally placed on the corrosive effects of nuclear weapons.

Two main arguments have for some time been advanced in support of the view that nuclear weapons undermine alliances. The first is that a power with the deterrent capability which nuclear weapons provide does not need the additional increment of strength which an alliance supplies. This, however, is unconvincing. A major nuclear power such as the former Soviet Union or the United States may not need allies for the small increment of *nuclear* strength which they can provide but the fact remains that during the cold war, at any rate, they needed them for a whole variety of other purposes. These included conventional military assistance, intelligence-gathering facilities and diplomatic cover (the United States was very anxious for 'allied' assistance in the Vietnam war for this reason). Alliances also provided legal justifications for superpower interventions designed to preserve the political status quo, and served to mark out those areas which each regarded as 'vital' to its interests. Conversely, small nuclear powers such as France or Britain may need the nuclear guarantees of a friendly superpower in order to deter a hostile one. In the last connection, it is noticeable that while in 1966 France left the North Atlantic Treaty *Organisation*, it did not cease to be a signatory of the *Treaty*.

The second and more important of the arguments supporting the view that nuclear weapons undermine alliances is that the thought of nuclear war is so appalling that no 'ally' *not itself attacked* can be trusted to keep any promise of military assistance, since it will know that this could well provoke its own destruction. This is a telling point and certainly helps to explain the unease about America's NATO guarantee which was manifest among its West European allies after the United States became vulnerable to nuclear attack from the Soviet Union (probably towards the end of the 1950s). However, this unease over 'extended deterrence' was not fatal to NATO. This is because, if nuclear weapons rendered the American guarantee less trustworthy than it probably would have been in an earlier epoch, they also rendered awesome even the remote possibility that it might be implemented. Altogether, then, nuclear weapons had less influence on alliances than has sometimes been imagined. The Warsaw Pact has collapsed but this had nothing directly to do with nuclear weapons. Rather, this was chiefly a result of the moral and economic eclipse of its dominant member, the Soviet Union.

Alliances versus ententes

It has already been noted that alliances are only one way in which states might make military commitments to other states, and that the entente is an alternative. An important question which is often overlooked is why this should be so. Kann, an exception in this regard, replies that ententes possess the advantages of alliances without the disadvantages.[6] On this argument, while ententes have the same operational significance as alliances, their lower visibility and general fuzziness enables them to be emphasised or played down as the sensitivities of different constituencies require; this includes hostile states, in regard to which ententes are less provocative. These characteristics also allow them to be dissolved when the circumstances which encouraged their growth change, without the 'credibility' of the participants being called into question; by contrast, the floodlit preciseness of alliances creates 'straitjackets' which lock states to commitments long after they have ceased to be useful out of fear that withdrawal will compromise their 'credibility'. In short, since ententes are less 'entangling' than alliances, they are less likely to impede that fluidity of alignment and realignment which is the essence of balance-of-power diplomacy.

Ententes, however, also have their drawbacks. For example, weak commitments are less likely to be honoured in a crisis, especially when governments are internally divided on the proper course to follow. Partly for this reason and partly because entente commitments are less likely than alliances to generate pressure for force build-ups and joint military planning, ententes are generally less efficient in the deterrence role. The vagueness and open-ended character of ententes (consultation agreements excepted) may also encourage policy drift and are more likely to lead to friction between the partners over questions of responsibility.

In what circumstances, then, if any, should alliances be replaced by ententes? The clear commitments of the alliance are obviously best when, in face of a 'clear and present danger', states wish to pool their strength for deterrence (which rests on *convincing* the enemy that retribution is certain), and when there are no serious political drawbacks to making their relationship highly visible. Such were the circumstances of NATO between its creation in 1949 and the collapse of the Soviet Union in 1991. On the other hand, the entente is preferable where the threat is less serious, or where the threat certainly is serious but the need for maximum deterrence is qualified by either the practical or political difficulties in the way of co-belligerency. Thus, the short-lived Soviet–Mozambique entente, which spanned the late 1970s and early 1980s, reflected both the unlikelihood that South Africa would launch a conventional military assault on the new Marxist regime in Maputo and the equal unlikelihood that, if it did, Moscow would be able to do anything about it. To take another example, the Anglo-South African entente, the most visible components of which were the Simonstown Agreements of 1955, reflected the nervousness of Afrikaner nationalist leaders at the prospect of a bilateral alliance with the old imperial enemy (an 'African NATO' was another matter) and the nervousness of the British at the thought of over-identification with apartheid.

Arms control

Arms control in a limited sense is not a recent invention. In 1868 the St Petersburg Declaration banned the use of exploding bullets and in 1922 the Washington Naval Conference restricted the battleship and aircraft carrier programmes of the great powers. In the 1960s and early 1970s arms control became much more ambitious, producing a host of agreements between East and West which peaked with SALT I and II (see Box 10.4). Following this, however, arms control found itself under mounting attack from all sides. Disarmers reviled it on the grounds that at best it had not worked and at worst it had actually fuelled the arms race, while cold warriors denounced it by alleging that it had allowed the Soviet Union to 'catch up' with and possibly even outstrip the United States in that vital competition. With the ending of the cold war the fortunes of arms control are once more riding high. What is 'arms control'? Can it be reasonably expected to reinforce the balance-of-power system, or is it – as its 'right-wing' critics in effect claim – *in principle* at odds with it?

It is perhaps best to begin by emphasising that 'arms control' is not the same as 'disarmament', though it is true that in common usage the two are now virtually synonymous. Disarmament, which is predicated on the false theory that weapons cause wars, has traditionally meant either the complete abolition or at least the drastic reduction of all, or certain categories of particularly dangerous, armaments. It was effectively killed off as a serious proposition by the vulnerability to the dictators which even the limited post-First World War disarmament left Europe in the 1930s. (The UN Charter has nothing like the emphasis on disarmament which is contained in the Covenant of the League of Nations.) By contrast, the theory of arms control accepts that national armaments are a clear corollary of a states-system. Nevertheless, on

---

Box 10.4   The golden age of arms control

Soviet–American arms control negotiations produced their first significant breakthroughs in the period from the late 1950s until the late 1970s. The following were probably the most important agreements:

- Antarctica Treaty, 1959.
- Partial Test Ban Treaty, 1963.
- Hot Line Agreement, 1963.
- Latin American Nuclear Free Zone Treaty, 1967.
- Treaty on the Exploration and Use of Outer Space, 1967.
- Nuclear Non-proliferation Treaty, 1968.
- Seabed Treaty, 1971.
- Agreements on Measures to Reduce the Risk of Outbreak of Nuclear War, 1971.
- Agreement on the Prevention of Naval Incidents, 1972.
- Agreement on Cooperation in Space, 1972.
- ABM Treaty, 1972.   ⎱ Strategic Arms
- Interim Agreement on the   ⎰ Limitation
  Limitation of Strategic Offensive Arms, 1972.   ⎰ Talks (SALT I)
- Agreement on the Prevention of Nuclear War, 1973.
- Final Act of the Conference on Security and Cooperation in Europe ['Helsinki Final Act'], 1975.
- Treaty on the Limitation of Strategic Offensive Arms, 1979 (produced by SALT II; not ratified by the US Senate).

---

the assumption that potential enemies have a common interest in avoiding war (a reasonable assumption where *nuclear* enemies are concerned), it also believes that the outbreak of war can be rendered less likely by agreement between potential enemies on measures to establish and subsequently reinforce mutual deterrence. This modest view has been at the heart of arms control in the nuclear age: its main aim has been to stabilise the existing strategic relationship between the Soviet Union (subsequently Russia) and the United States, a deterrent relationship widely believed to have been responsible for the preservation of global peace for the greater part of the post-1945 period. Subsidiary objectives of arms control have been to reduce the geographical scope and ferocity of war should it occur, for example by creating 'nuclear-free zones' and banning the use of chemical-biological weapons. To this extent 'arms control' agreements embrace elements of disarmament.

Even so, it cannot be emphasised too strongly that the main object of genuine arms control negotiations is manipulation of the structure of a strategic relationship (superpower or any other) in such a manner that the disinclination of both sides to launch a surprise attack is strengthened. It is for this reason that there is as much concern with the character and deployment of weapons as with their numbers. Contrary to popular belief, therefore, arms control may actually require an increase in certain kinds of armament by one or both parties – for example, an increase in the number of less vulnerable weapons at the expense of more vulnerable ones. It makes obvious sense, however, to stabilise mutual deterrence at the lowest possible level of armaments. As a result, arms reduction where possible is an important – if secondary – objective of arms control. In short, arms control is the art of preserving mutual deterrence at the lowest possible cost. This also embraces measures to improve crisis avoidance (especially through 'confidence-building' actions such as the permitting of observers to attend large military manoeuvres) and crisis management. The 'Hot Line Agreement' of 1963 was the earliest of measures in the latter area.

If potential enemies are committed to stabilising mutual deterrence by agreement, important problems nevertheless remain. Arms control will not prosper if the general level of tension is high, and will also be slowed down if developments in military technology are rapid and complex. In the latter connection, the trend towards multipurpose weapons, such as the cruise missile, initially presented difficulties since these cannot be simply classified as either 'strategic' or 'tactical', 'nuclear' or 'non-nuclear'. The most serious problem confronting arms control, however, has always been that of verification, that is, of ensuring that the other side honours its commitments by actually observing the steps which it has agreed to take. States have been traditionally reluctant to allow their rivals deep inside their military establishments ('on-site inspection'), as the recent history of the attempts by the International Atomic Energy Agency (IAEA) – supported most powerfully by the United States – to gain access to suspected nuclear weapons projects in Iraq and North Korea amply demonstrates. Moreover, even if intrusive inspection is permitted, a deeply suspicious state will be hard to convince that its enemy is not taking prohibited measures in secret. In 1981 Israeli aircraft bombed the nuclear reactor being built by the French in Iraq, even though this was subject to inspection by the IAEA designed to prevent it from being used to produce nuclear weapons. Advances in satellite reconnaissance have done much to alleviate the problem of verification but have by no means solved it altogether.

In the light of this brief outline, it will be obvious that arms control, by definition, is supportive of a balance of power based on the strategy of deterrence and is, indeed, a most important ingredient of it. However, it seems unlikely that it has the same role to play in a balance of power based on traditional strategy (see Chapter 6), whether involving nuclear weapons or not. For, while in such a balance all parties are likely to retain an interest in preventing accidental war and in keeping the scope and ferocity of any engagement within limits, it is less clear that they will have any other interest in military negotiations. After all, if war – including nuclear war – is believed to be rational, potential enemies will have an interest in striving for sufficient power to be able to 'win' it, that is, for military preponderance. This, unlike mutual deterrence, can hardly be expected to provide an appropriate subject for agreement between them.

Conclusions of this kind, together with a belief that the Soviet Union remained an aggressive, revolutionary power, appear to have been behind the coolness towards arms control shown by the Reagan administration, which, as noted in Chapter 6, had come to think increasingly of nuclear weapons in terms of traditional strategy. It was thus not surprising that the SALT II Treaty (1979) was never ratified by the US Senate (though in practice it was substantially honoured by both sides). New negotiations were soon entered into but little progress was made until the late 1980s, when the advent of Mikhail Gorbachev led to a dramatic improvement in Soviet–American relations and the inauguration of a second 'golden age' of arms control. Among other developments, this saw the signing in 1987 of a treaty eliminating Soviet and American intermediate-range nuclear forces from Europe. The 'INF Treaty', as it was known, went into force in June 1988. At the Paris summit in November 1990 which formally ended the cold war a treaty on Conventional Armed Forces in Europe (CFE) was signed which imposed equal ceilings on non-nuclear forces between the Atlantic and the Urals.[7] Most strikingly of all, the Strategic Arms Reduction Talks (START), which were designed to make substantial cuts in long-range nuclear missiles and had proceeded so fitfully in the early and mid-1980s, were successfully concluded in 1991. These provided for a one-third reduction in the strategic forces of both sides. Furthermore, in 1993 a START II agreement provided for cuts in deployed Russian and American strategic nuclear warheads to between 3,000 and 3,500 by the year 2003, and banned MIRVed land-based missiles altogether. Finally, in 1995 a major conference in New York decided to extend the Nuclear Non-Proliferation Treaty indefinitely. None of these agreements was perfect, and disarmers were not disarmed by them. But they were not a bad record for arms control.

Notes

1. *Power and International Relations*, p. 93.
2. pp. 266–9.
3. As William Walker has recently pointed out, 'Russia's territorial losses, economic reverses and the deterioration of its conventional forces have tended to increase the value attached to its [still considerable] nuclear forces', *International Affairs*, vol. 71, no. 4, p. 845 [book review].
4. *Theory of International Politics*, ch. 8.
5. Though alliances of the latter kind, under 'treaties of guarantee', do exist. For a useful taxonomy of alliances, see Holsti, *International Politics: A framework for analysis*, pp. 103–7.

6. 'Alliances versus ententes'.
7. By mid-1995 the provisions of this treaty, the completion of which was imminent, had resulted in the destruction of tens of thousands of weapons and the relocation of many more.

Further reading

General

Buzan, B., *People, States and Fear: An agenda for international security studies in the post-cold war era* (Harvester Wheatsheaf: Hemel Hempstead, 1991), ch. 4.
Claude, I. L., Jr, *Power and International Relations* (Random House: New York, 1962), chs 1–5.
Deutsch, K. W. and J. D. Singer, 'Multipolar power systems and international stability', *World Politics*, vol. 16, 1964.
Gaddis, J. L., *The Long Peace: Inquiries into the history of the cold war* (Oxford University Press: Oxford, 1987).
Gilpin, R., *War and Change in World Politics* (Cambridge University Press: Cambridge and New York, 1981), pp. 85–96.
Gulick, E. V., *Europe's Classical Balance of Power* (Norton: New York, 1967), chs 1–3.
Haas, M., 'International subsystems: stability and polarity', *American Political Science Review*, vol. 64, no. 1, 1970.
James, P. and M. Brecher, 'Stability and polarity: new paths for inquiry', *Journal of Peace Research*, vol. 25, no. 1, 1988.
Kissinger, H. A., *A World Restored: The politics of conservatism in a revolutionary era* (Gollancz: London, 1977; first pub. Boston, 1957).
Organski, A. F. K. and J. Kugler, *The War Ledger* (University of Chicago Press: Chicago, 1980).
Review of International Studies, 'The balance of power', vol. 15, no. 2 (special issue), 1989.
Rosecrance, R. N., *International Relations: Peace or war?* (McGraw-Hill: New York, 1973).
Waltz, K. N., *Theory of International Politics* (Addison-Wesley: Reading, MA, 1979).

Alliances

Allison, R., *The Soviet Union and the Strategy of Non-Alignment in the Third World* (Cambridge University Press: Cambridge and New York, 1988), ch. 4.
Bayliss, J., K. Booth, J. Garnett and P. Williams, *Contemporary Strategy*, vol. 1, 2nd edn (Croom Helm: London, 1987), ch. by Booth.
Beer, F. A. (ed.), *Alliances: Latent war communities in the contemporary world* (Holt, Rinehart & Winston: New York, 1970).
Berridge, G. R., 'Ententes and alliances', *Review of International Studies*, vol. 15, no. 3, 1989.
Carpenter, T. G., 'Special issue on the future of NATO', *Journal of Strategic Studies*, vol. 17, no. 4, December 1994.
Dunbabin, J. P. D., *The Cold War: The great powers and their alliances* (Longman: London and New York, 1994).
Gallois, P. M., 'US strategy and the defense of Europe', *Orbis*, vol. 7, no. 2, 1963.

Grosser, A., *The Western Alliance*, trans. Michael Shaw (Macmillan: London, 1980; first pub. Paris, 1978).

Holsti, K. J., *International Politics: A framework for analysis*, 5th edn (Prentice Hall: Englewood Cliffs, NJ, 1988), pp. 101–10.

Holsti, O. R., P. T. Hopmann and J. D. Sullivan, *Unity and Disintegration in International Alliances: Comparative studies* (Wiley: New York, 1973).

Imam, Z., 'Soviet treaties with third world countries', *Soviet Studies*, vol. 35, no. 1, 1983.

Kann, R. A., 'Alliances versus ententes', *World Politics*, vol. 28, July 1976.

Kissinger, H. A., *American Foreign Policy*, 3rd edn (Norton: New York, 1977), pp. 65–78.

Liska, G. F., *Nations in Alliance: The limits of interdependence* (Johns Hopkins Press: Baltimore, 1962).

Morgenthau, H. J., *Politics Among Nations: The struggle for power and peace*, 5th rev. edn (Knopf: New York, 1978), pp. 188–200.

Osgood, R. E., *Alliances and American Foreign Policy* (Johns Hopkins Press: Baltimore, 1968).

Rothstein, R. L., *Alliances and Small Powers* (Columbia University Press: New York, 1968).

Spiegel, S. L., 'US relations with Israel: the military benefits', *Orbis*, vol. 30, no. 3, 1986.

Suhrke, A., 'Gratuity or tyranny: the Korean alliances', *World Politics*, vol. 25, no. 4, 1973.

Talbot, S., 'Why NATO should grow', *The New York Review of Books*, 10 Aug. 1995.

Treverton, G. F., *Making the Alliance Work: The United States and Western Europe* (Macmillan: London, 1985).

Walt, S. M., *The Origins of Alliances* (Cornell University Press: Ithaca, NY, 1987).

Arms control

Bull, H., *The Control of the Arms Race* (Praeger: New York, 1965).

Carter, A., *Success and Failure in Arms Control Negotiations* (Oxford University Press: Oxford, 1989).

Goldblat, J., *Arms Control: A guide to negotiations and agreements* (International Peace Research Institute: Oslo, 1994).

Koulik, S. and R. Kokoski, *Conventional Arms Control: Perspectives on verification* (Oxford University Press for SIPRI: Oxford, 1995).

Newhouse, J., *Cold Dawn: The story of SALT* (Holt, Rinehart & Winston: New York, 1973).

Schelling, T. C., 'What went wrong with arms control?', *Foreign Affairs*, vol. 64, no. 2, 1985/86.

Schelling, T. C. and M. H. Halperin, *Strategy and Arms Control* (Twentieth Century: New York, 1961).

Simpson, J., 'The birth of a new era? The 1995 NPT Conference and the politics of nuclear disarmament', *Security Dialogue*, vol. 26, no. 3, 1995.

Spanier, J. W. and J. L. Nogee, *The Politics of Disarmament: A study in Soviet-American gamesmanship* (Praeger: New York, 1962).

Talbot, S., *Endgame: The inside story of SALT II* (Harper & Row: New York, 1979). [This includes the full text of the SALT II agreement.]

Talbot, S., *Deadly Gambits: The Reagan administration and the stalemate in nuclear arms control* (Knopf: New York, 1984; Pan Books: London, 1985).

Towle, P., *Arms Control and East–West Relations* (Croom Helm: London, and St Martin's Press: New York, 1983).
Willrich, M. and J. B. Rhinelander (eds), *SALT: The Moscow agreements and beyond* (Free Press: New York, and Collier Mac: London, 1974).

NB: There is a vast specialist literature on arms control and most general works on contemporary strategy contain a substantial treatment of the subject.

11

Diplomacy

Diplomacy is not foreign policy. Foreign policy is the attitude struck by one state towards another; diplomacy is one of a number of instruments employed in order to make that attitude persuasive. It would, however, be wrong to describe diplomacy as an 'instrument of conflict' and thus place it in the same category as secret intelligence, force, economic statecraft and propaganda. Like these, it is certainly an instrument of foreign policy; however, only diplomacy emphasises the idea that states have common, as well as conflicting, interests. Diplomacy, in other words, is an institution *of* the states-system in a way in which what I have called the 'instruments of conflict' are not.

The functions of diplomacy

Diplomacy has a good many functions but there is wide agreement that its chief one is negotiation. De Callières (see Box 11.1), to whom modern diplomatic theory owes so much, was emphatic on the point. Negotiation in international politics is a technique of regulated argument which normally occurs between delegations of officials representing states, international organisations or other agencies. It takes place with a view to achieving one or other of the following objectives: identification of common interests and agreement on joint or parallel action in their pursuit; recognition of conflicting interests and agreement on compromise; or, more often than not, some combination of both. A highly significant special case of negotiation seeking the second of these objectives, which often provokes cries of moral outrage, should also be mentioned. This is the surrendering of an interest in one dispute in return for the gratification of an interest in a more important one. This procedure is known alternatively as 'horse-trading', seeking a quid pro quo, looking for 'a package deal', negotiating 'on a broad front', or, following its popularisation by Henry Kissinger, 'linkage'. A spectacular success for linkage was achieved in late 1988 when the South Africans agreed to leave Namibia. They did this not because they finally acknowledged a legal obligation to vacate the territory but because the Cubans agreed, *in exchange*, to withdraw their own forces from Angola.

Negotiation is not an activity which can proceed fruitfully in any conditions. The time must be ripe, which means that the parties should have abandoned hope of achieving their objectives by other means, for example by war. Less obviously, the talks must also take place *in secret*. The first reason for this is that such talks unavoidably reveal weaknesses as well as strengths. It is bad enough having to reveal these to the other side; having to reveal them to the

---

Box 11.1   François de Callières, 1645–1717

De Callières made his mark as a man of letters and then achieved a long-nurtured ambition when in 1693 he entered the diplomatic service of Louis XIV (at that juncture seeking a peaceful end to the Nine Years' War). After a relatively short but successful diplomatic career, De Callières published his most important book *De la manière de négocier avec les souverains* (The Art of Negotiating with Sovereign Princes), which appeared in March 1716, exactly a year before his death.

A distillation of his experience and the diplomatic customs of his age, this work is remarkable for abandoning the prevailing habit of writers on diplomacy to dwell either on the law or on the attributes of the 'perfect ambassador'. Instead, De Callières' attention is firmly fixed on the conditions which doom states to a permanent diplomacy, the vital role which this plays in a states-system and the consequent need for diplomacy to become a profession. With his unprecedented *political* thrust, De Callières was really the father of diplomatic theory.

His book was highly regarded throughout Europe in the eighteenth century but slipped from sight in the nineteenth. His reputation was revived by two British diplomats at the end of the First World War: Ernest Satow, who quoted extensively from De Callières in *A Guide to Diplomatic Practice* (1917), which subsequently became the unchallenged manual of the profession; and A. F. Whyte, who was alarmed by the trend towards conference diplomacy and in 1919 published an English translation of De Callières' classic in an attempt to revive the 'old' diplomacy. In 1983 a new, critical edition of De Callières, on which the above account is based, was published by Maurice Keens-Soper and Karl Schweizer (see 'Further reading').

---

whole world might prove highly damaging. Second, negotiations involving conflicting interests have to be conducted in secret because success in such negotiations inevitably means that each side will have to settle for less than its ideal requirements. This means that certain parties – a domestic interest or a foreign friend – will have to be in some measure 'sold down the river'. If those parties are aware of this at the time they might well be able to sabotage the negotiations. As Kissinger says: 'The sequence in which concessions are made becomes crucial; it [the negotiation] can be aborted if each move has to be defended individually rather than as part of a mosaic before the reciprocal move is clear.'[1]

Negotiation is not an activity for which everyone is fitted. Most international negotiations – even between allies – are difficult enough without being made more so by abrasive and discourteous behaviour. Neither can negotiation be successful unless there is a minimum of trust between the parties: trust in the truth of what is being said and trust in the promises being made. Hence, honesty is among the other attributes of the successful diplomat. And so, too, is precision of language, not only because the misunderstanding to which vagueness and muddle can lead is likely to result in actions inconsistent with agreed objectives but because this can lead to the charge of bad faith and thus vitiate subsequent negotiations. Indeed, such is the importance attached to precision of language in diplomacy that Harold Nicolson, the most widely quoted twentieth-century writer on the diplomatic art in the English language, goes so far as to say that diplomacy is 'a written rather than a verbal art'.[2] (However, ambiguity or 'fudging' can sometimes play a constructive role in negotiations when the parties concerned are in agreement on the more important issue confronting them but cannot reconcile their differences on a lesser, though related, matter on which the world nevertheless expects them to pronounce. In such circumstances it is better to 'fudge' or 'paper over' these differences with deliberately vague language rather than to allow them to undermine the whole negotiation. An important case in point is the vagueness of the 1978 Camp David Accords on Palestinian national rights.)

Negotiation typically proceeds through three stages: pre-negotiation (putting out feelers to establish the need to negotiate, agreeing the agenda and procedure); the formula stage (agreeing the broad shape or general principles of a settlement); and the details stage (fleshing out the formula). It may be assisted by a carefully chosen venue, appropriate deadlines, judicious use of media management, mediation by third parties (see below), and appropriate packaging of any agreement reached. In some cases negotiation may also be assisted by the assurance of great power guarantees of any settlement which the powers can endorse. Such guarantees, albeit vague and very guarded, were a marked feature of settlements in regional conflicts in the 1980s, for example in Afghanistan and south-western Africa.

Diplomacy, however, is by no means concerned exclusively with negotiation. Among its other important functions are the conveying and clarifying of messages between governments, the gathering of information, the symbolic demonstration of the state's legitimacy and splendour, the protection of a state's citizens abroad (strictly speaking, 'consular' work), and the cultivation of friendly relations. The latter should not be scorned or regarded simply as an excuse for staggering from one cocktail party to the next. Feelings of respect and 'cordiality' between states can smooth the general course of business and may sway a nicely balanced argument the right way in an hour of dire need. But the less tangible functions of diplomacy are often overlooked, and many diplomats today find themselves in the absurd position of having to engage in export promotion in order to stave off political attacks.

The attack on diplomacy

Diplomacy was practised in the Near East in the second millennium BC but its marked institutionalisation only began with the creation of the resident ambassador in the city-states of Renaissance Italy. In the seventeenth century the dubious doctrine of the extraterritoriality of embassies was legally recognised, and, in the eighteenth, the 'diplomatic corps' and its dean or 'doyen' emerged. (The doyen is the longest-serving ambassador in a capital city, whose task is to negotiate with the host government on matters affecting all diplomats accredited to it.) The next landmark was the Congress of Vienna in 1815, at which, among other things, 'a system of determining precedence among diplomatic missions consistent with the doctrine of the equality of states'[3] was agreed. (Quarrels over precedence had previously brought some states to the verge of war.) And in 1961 Vienna was once more the scene of another important step for the institution of diplomacy when the Vienna Convention on Diplomatic Relations was signed. This instrument codified and modernised the international law of diplomacy and has since been ratified by the vast majority of states (153 at 31 December 1989). Two years later the Vienna Convention on Consular Relations was also signed.

Diplomacy came to be institutionalised in the states-system (via the permanent mission) for a number of compelling reasons. One was the extreme difficulty of foreign travel and communication until late in the nineteenth century, and another was the parallel growth of international law. But diplomacy became a vital institution above all because only rarely was any one state able simply to seize what it wanted. In the absence of overwhelming power, negotiation was inescapable. Diplomacy, in other words, took root in centuries of multipolarity. Nevertheless, in the twentieth century it has been under attack from two quarters: first, from those who reject the activity in principle; and second, from those who acknowledge its importance but object to its traditional style.

To begin with, the *principle* of diplomacy has come under attack from ideologists of all hues. It was attacked by the Bolsheviks after the Russian Revolution in 1917, by the Chinese Communists between 1949 and the early 1970s, and by the Islamic fundamentalist regime in Iran following the overthrow of the Shah in 1979. Diplomacy was also held in low regard in the United States until the late 1960s (when disasters in Vietnam produced unprecedented feelings of national weakness), though this was an antipathy fostered as much by geographical isolation and enormous power as by the pronounced moralistic and legal strains in American foreign policy. Ideologists, whose tests of truth are unique and whose arrogance is absolute, cannot reason and compromise with their opponents but rather kill, convert or – if their power is too great – ignore them. In the 1930s the principle of diplomacy also came under attack from the supporters of 'appeasement', who made 'peace' their priority in dealings with the dictators and thus brought diplomacy into disrepute via parody. Finally, diplomacy was temporarily abused by the new states in the late 1950s and the 1960s because they tended to regard it as a conspiracy of their late colonial masters.

As if this has not been enough, even among the friends of diplomacy there has been hostility to the *style* in which it has been traditionally conducted.

This sort of opposition really began when admirers of 'democratic' practice blamed the 'old diplomacy' and its 'secret treaties' for the First World War. All treaties in future, they demanded, should be replaced by 'open covenants [which are one thing] *openly arrived at* [which is quite another]'. Though conceived as an attack on diplomatic style, the campaign for 'open diplomacy', associated with the American president, Woodrow Wilson, was actually an attack on diplomacy itself. This is because any attempt to conduct negotiations in public can only lead to posturing for the benefit of outside audiences and will thus be more likely to make matters worse – as in the General Assembly of the United Nations.

Diplomacy has been attacked not only for unnecessary secrecy but also (at least in the West) for drawing its professionals too exclusively from the upper circles of society, and encouraging them to devote their attention to 'high politics' at the expense of economics. It is also alleged that the need for diplomats to be in residence in foreign capitals is much reduced since rapid advances in transport and communications now make it possible for politicians or home-based foreign ministry civil servants to make swift, direct contact with their foreign counterparts. Finally, it has been held, at least since the First World War, that the danger and geographical extent of modern problems and the great growth in the number of states have made 'bilateral' diplomacy simply too slow and 'multilateral' or 'conference' diplomacy thus unavoidable. How has diplomacy adapted itself in the face of these considerable pressures, both on the activity itself and on its traditional style?

Survival and adaptation

The unusually ideological character of the twentieth century has certainly contributed to long periods in which diplomacy has been at a discount: war and propaganda have often seemed to be the hallmarks of this epoch. However, the balance of power has preserved the states-system through thick and thin and thus maintained the situation in which diplomacy is unavoidable, namely, that in which not even the strongest power is able simply to seize what it wants. Within months of the October Revolution the Bolsheviks had realised that the social structure of the rest of Europe was not going to be razed to the ground and had started to conduct a diplomacy of their own with the surrounding capitalist states, thus swiftly reversing the famous announcement of the first People's Commissar of Foreign Affairs, Leon Trotsky, that he would just 'issue a few revolutionary proclamations to the people and then close up shop'.[4] During the 1960s the cold war between the United States and the Soviet Union gave way to serious negotiations, first on the ground rules of their conflict and then on more substantive issues. Imperial distractions and economic disintegration in the late 1980s confirmed the Soviet disposition to seek negotiated solutions with the Americans. (American diplomats had endured Moscow, and Soviet diplomats enjoyed Washington even in the worst days of the cold war.) Furthermore, at the height of its isolation from the West, in 1966 China retained diplomatic missions in forty-eight states, while during the 1970s, fearful of Soviet attack and less and less impressed by the merits of self-reliance, the Chinese came in from the cold altogether. By this time, too, most of the 'new states' had lost their suspicions of traditional diplomacy and were as heavily involved in it as their slender budgets would permit. Though it is true that embassies have been attacked by mobs, this has only occasionally (as in Tehran) been with the connivance of governments.

Diplomacy as such, then, has manifestly survived, though it is true that its *form* has changed considerably. The change in form has two aspects: changes in the personnel of diplomacy, and changes in its context.

Technical experts

Technical experts feature vastly more in modern diplomacy than they did in earlier days. They were not, of course, entirely unknown in traditional diplomacy – the embassy's military attaché has a long history, and statisticians were employed at the Congress of Vienna in 1815 – but the range and complexity of the issues on the agenda of contemporary diplomacy have increased their prominence enormously, whether they be economists, agronomists or experts in arms control or acid rain. Technical experts also enter diplomacy via the increasingly direct contact between the whole range of government departments of different states which has been taking place in recent years.

Political leaders: 'summitry'

Substantially in response to the potency of television, politicians are also playing a much greater role in diplomacy, though this is much more controversial than that performed by the experts. A distinction should be made here, however, between 'summits' of political leaders and meetings of politicians at lower levels. Thus, while the latter may make serious individual contributions to international negotiations, especially when an impasse has been reached, summitry usually plays a somewhat different role, though in part a *diplomatic* one none the less.

Heads of government, especially if they are also heads of state, are usually in no position to make any individual, direct contribution to international negotiations and it is as well if they do not try to do so. As David Watt says: 'with their massive egos, their ignorance of the essential details and their ingrained belief in the value of back-slapping ambiguity, [they] simply mess everything up'.[5] Besides, since heads of government personify regimes and always attract great publicity, it is difficult for them to contemplate bringing a summit to a scheduled end without something substantial to present to their followers. Hence they are always in danger either of making unwise concessions in order to achieve a 'success' (which, because of the greater loss of face, are more difficult to retrieve when made by a head of state rather than by a professional diplomat), or of breaking off negotiations prematurely if it seems that they will not be able to gain everything they had promised. As remarked by George Ball, whose blast against summitry should be read by every head of state as well as by every student of international relations, 'theatre and sound policy are rarely compatible'.[6] The unfortunate result of the personal encounter between Hitler and Chamberlain on the eve of the Second World War is a sobering illustration of the risks of summit meetings.

Fortunately, the pitfalls of summitry are now widely recognised and are, therefore, usually avoided – at least in the relations between major states. This is achieved by ensuring that excessive expectations are not aroused; that the greater part of the negotiations are concluded before the summit actually begins; and that any remaining details are wrapped up by the professionals prior to the scheduled signing ceremony. But if the heads of government thus have little to do other than sign any agreements and pose for the cameras, what, if anything, is the positive contribution of summitry to diplomacy?

Summits certainly allow government leaders to take the measure of each other in person, though whether this is a better means of obtaining this kind of knowledge than others – the reports of professional diplomats and intelligence agencies, for example – is probably an open question. They also force heads of government 'to focus on the international dimension of problems they usually see in domestic terms'.[7] They make linkage easier by pulling together bureaucratically separate strands of policy. And they can be very helpful in setting deadlines for important negotiations and breaking last-minute deadlocks; if negotiations have to be completed in their essentials *before* a summit begins, the summit itself is an excellent discipline. Certainly, great quantities of midnight oil were burned in order to bring the SALT (arms control) negotiations to virtual completion before the arrival in Moscow of President Nixon in May 1972, while the proximity of leaders on this occasion allowed for a relatively speedy settlement of remaining differences. A similar process preceded the signing of the INF Treaty during the Reagan–Gorbachev summit in Washington in December 1987.

In short, it is clear that especially when summits are held regularly, when they are in effect institutionalised, they are of the first importance in maintaining diplomatic momentum on an issue or range of issues. Following the advent of Mikhail Gorbachev, summitry became an institution in East–West relations (see Box 11.2) – and arms control, the settlement of regional conflicts and other matters benefited accordingly. But it should not be forgotten that for varying lengths of time summitry has also been an important institution of the Commonwealth, the 'Front Line States' in Africa, the Arab League, the European Union (the 'European Council'), the 'Group of Seven' Western

---

Box 11.2   The Reagan/Bush–Gorbachev summits, 1985–90

These summits, like previous US–Soviet summits, were dominated by discussions of the nuclear balance and arms control. The exception was the one-day summit held at Helsinki in September 1990, which was called to discuss the Gulf crisis.

Geneva	19–21 November 1985
Reykjavik (Iceland)	11–12 October 1986
Washington	7–10 December 1987
Moscow	29 May–2 June 1988
Malta	2–3 December 1989
Washington	31 May–3 June 1990
Helsinki	9 September 1990

---

economic powers, Central and South America (the 'Rio Group'), francophone Africa (the annual 'Franco-African Summit'), and other regional groupings.

Another important diplomatic function of summits, and especially of meet-the-people foreign tours and *ad hoc* meetings, is to clarify intentions by dramatic *symbolism*. (To the extent that foreign and domestic publics, as well as foreign governments, are part of the audience, this is obviously propaganda as well as diplomacy.) The purpose may be to underline an existing commitment, as when President Kennedy visited West Berlin in 1962 and addressed the words '*Ich bin ein Berliner*' to an increasingly hysterical crowd in the Rudolph Wilde Platz. It may be to emphasise the sincerity of a new policy priority, as when the Egyptian president, Anwar Sadat, made his 'historic' visit to Jerusalem in November 1977, or when President Bush met the leaders of the South American drug-producing countries at the 'Cocaine Summit' held in the Colombian seaside resort of Cartagena in February 1990. It may be to set the seal on a new friendship, as when Benazir Bhutto of Pakistan met Rajiv Gandhi of India in December 1988. Or the purpose of the summit may be to advertise broader feelings of regional solidarity: when Arab leaders meet they are usually cherishing the so far futile hope that their gathering will symbolise the unity of their peoples.

Conference diplomacy

The changes in the context in which modern diplomacy occurs have been even more dramatic than those in the personnel of diplomacy, and the biggest transformation here has been the switch to an emphasis on diplomacy in a conference setting, to multilateral rather than bilateral diplomacy. This is a response to the great increase in the number of states, and the huge growth in the length of and the urgency attached to dealing with the international agenda.

There are two main kinds of multilateral conference: *ad hoc* and permanent. The *ad hoc* conference, such as that held between the Americans, the Israelis and the Egyptians at Camp David in 1978, is one called up when the occasion demands and dissolved when agreement is reached or failure to agree is acknowledged. Such conferences, however, have other distinguishing features, which align them squarely with traditional diplomacy. Only interested parties are invited, the agenda is agreed beforehand, the chair is a dignitary of the host government, and – most importantly – unanimity is required for agreement. By contrast, permanent, or standing conferences (sometimes misleadingly known as 'international organisations'), such as the United Nations, the International Monetary Fund and the Organisation of African Unity (OAU), have diplomatic delegations permanently accredited to them and a permanent secretariat typically headed by a 'secretary-general'. In further contrast to *ad hoc* conferences, permanent conferences often have a deliberative group which is wider than that of the 'interested parties', and characteristically adopt a 'parliamentary' style of proceeding: they debate in public; they have a non-specific agenda; and they wield votes (only rarely, as in the World Bank, weighted to give more influence to the bigger members) in order to determine the outcome.

It will be clear from the foregoing that permanent conferences in practice often have little to do with diplomacy and even exacerbate tensions between states. The General Assembly of the United Nations – where each member state is encouraged to speak up even on issues which have only the remotest connection with its interests – is particularly notorious for conducting propaganda in the name of diplomacy, and among its more significant consequences in this regard was its contribution to the general deterioration in relations between the United States and the Third World in the 1970s. It was awareness that the United Nations was a diplomatic minefield which produced the early reluctance of Finland and Mexico to serve on the Security Council and which clearly contributes to the continuing refusal of the Swiss people to join the UN at all. However, proper attention to the anti-diplomatic side of permanent conferences such as the United Nations should not be allowed to obscure the fact that they usually have a pro-diplomatic aspect as well. The UN – despite the reputation which it acquired in the United States in the 1970s for being 'a dangerous place' – is no exception to this rule.

Diplomacy at the UN

Apart from mediation by the Secretariat (see below), the United Nations fulfils two main diplomatic roles. It legitimises diplomacy and it provides a convenient forum for general diplomatic activity. In all of these regards – if not in others – the UN is currently enjoying a remarkable revival. (Though it should not be overlooked that the UN has always been of the first importance to the diplomacy of states too poor to afford extensive networks of bilateral representation.) This revival has been prompted by developments both inside and outside the organisation. These include the institutionalisation of 'secret' diplomacy in the Security Council (which began with the process of informal consultation and informal private meetings of the Council at the end of the 1960s), the election of the very fine Peruvian diplomat Javier Pérez de Cuéllar as secretary-general in 1981 and his re-election in 1986, the positive response of the General Assembly in 1986 to Western pressure for reform and, above all, the thaw in US-Soviet and Sino-Soviet relations. But the UN also has a unique combination of attributes which places it in an unrivalled position to assist in the diplomatic settlement of acute international conflicts.

As a diplomatic forum the UN is especially significant for making possible discreet direct discussions, usually of an exploratory nature, between states (or between states and organisations such as the PLO) which have no formal relations and, as a result, either cannot afford to be *seen* talking to each other or can but because of the absence of formal relations do not find this easy. (The UN was an important point of contact between the United States and the MPLA government of Angola during the period preceding the successful conclusion of the Angola/Namibia accords in December 1988, and also between the United States and North Korea in the 1993–4 period.) Why is the UN so valuable in this regard? First, it has near universal membership. Second, heads of government and foreign ministers regularly attend the annual opening of each new session of the General Assembly in September. Third, the permanent missions are normally staffed by diplomats of high calibre, a fact which is by no means unconnected to the vitality and importance of the city of New York and the proximity of this city to Washington, capital of the most powerful state in the world.

There is a difference between the permanent UN missions and peripatetic statesmen of unfriendly states exploiting their legitimate proximity in New York (or some other UN venue) in order to make *discreet contact*, and the use of the UN's imprimatur in order to make it easier for hostile powers to enter *publicly admitted negotiations* and, following this, perhaps retreat from dangerous postures without losing face. This is the difference between the diplomatic forum of convenience and the diplomatic legitimising functions of the UN. The operation of the latter is seen most obviously in limited international conferences of the kind convened by the UN on the Middle East in Geneva in December 1973, with their avowedly 'ceremonial' roles, but is *also at work in the Security Council itself*. Indeed, the Security Council is a permanent example, and the most important of all examples, of the operation of this role. (The UN may serve, too, to legitimise mediation efforts conducted by others, as it did with the labours of the Western Contact Group on Namibia in the late 1970s and early 1980s.)

The United Nations is not the only body which can legitimise contact and thus provide an opportunity for bitter enemies to save face. States, a group of states in a region, and regional organisations can all do this. But the UN is normally the best placed. This point is most tellingly developed by Conor Cruise O'Brien in his brilliant, rambling essay, *The United Nations: Sacred drama*. The United Nations, points out O'Brien, enacts a highly publicised drama, principally in the General Assembly but also in the Security Council and other 'theatres'. It is 'sacred' drama, he adds, less conventionally, because it originates in fear and prayer, in this case fear of and prayer addressed to man. It is, in other words, at the United Nations, and only at the United Nations, *that common humanity expresses through varied and complex ritual its dedication to peace.* In addition to being a forum and a stage, therefore, the United Nations is also a shrine, and the secretary-general its 'high priest'.

At the United Nations, then, there is an authority before which all sovereign states may kneel without loss of dignity. For the big powers there is no other. Who else can *they* defer to? UN resolutions are especially important when they sanctify the retreat of a big power that wants to climb down from a position in which it cannot remain without serious risk of dangerous and possibly suicidal military conflict with a rival. The classic examples are Britain and France during the Suez crisis and the Soviet Union in the Cuban missile crisis. This lesson was further underlined by the role of the United Nations in Angola/Namibia in 1988. But by handing responsibility to the United Nations (however it chooses to deal with it) the big powers may also obtain an excuse for 'expedient but inglorious' *non-intervention*,[8] as the United States did during the Hungarian counter-revolution in 1956, Britain did in Cyprus in 1974, and the Soviet Union did in Lebanon in 1982. As Brian Urquhart says: 'The Secretary-General may not be able to *solve* the problem, but at least his efforts give the pretext for resisting domestic pressures for action that might well be fatal.'[9] In short, the UN can sanctify inaction as well as retreat.

The United Nations (together, it should be added, with certain other permanent conferences) is by no means the only vehicle which hostile states may employ in order to preserve, or re-establish, discreet diplomatic contact. Indeed, severing diplomatic relations has in recent times become so commonplace as a political gesture that old alternatives to the exchange of ambassadors have been used more extensively than ever and at least one new one has been invented. Underground diplomacy, its head occasionally appearing on the surface, now flourishes.

Interests sections

States have long entrusted their interests in a hostile state to the embassy of a state with which both are on friendly terms. Because of their policies of neutrality, Austria, Switzerland and Sweden have been especially popular choices. However, it is now common to find a state's interests in a hostile state being protected by a small group of its *own* diplomats operating from the embassy of a third state. 'Interests sections', as they are known, were first employed by the United Kingdom when seven African states broke off relations with London as a protest at the weakness of its response to the unilateral declaration of independence in 1965 by the white supremacist party controlling the self-governing British colony of Rhodesia. With the agreement of these states, British 'interests sections' were established in the embassies of third states in their capitals.

Though the effectiveness of interests sections is impaired by their smallness, the extreme hostility – in some cases – of their immediate environment, and other factors, at least they ensure that a presence *inside* the countries concerned is maintained. This makes it at least a little easier to conduct the general business of diplomacy.

During the Falklands war, a British interests section was established in the Swiss embassy in Buenos Aires, and following the rupture in US–Iran relations after the overthrow of the Shah an Iranian interests section was opened in the Algerian embassy in Washington. The Algerians also provided protection to an Iraqi interests section in Washington after the Gulf war in 1991; in London, the courtesy was provided by Jordan. However, as well as being employed as a means to salvage something from a dramatically deteriorating relationship, interests sections may be created as the first step towards normality in an improving one. Thus in 1986, against the background of a thaw in relations between Israel and Eastern Europe, the governments in Jerusalem and Warsaw, which had enjoyed no diplomatic relations for almost twenty years, agreed to exchange interests sections. Their first tasks were to process visa applications and foster cultural links, but it was clear that, if things went well, the new diplomatic connection would be upgraded.

The diplomatic corps in third states

Direct contact between hostile states may also be made within the diplomatic corps resident in a third state with which each has diplomatic relations. This was an important means employed by the United States and the People's Republic of China during the long years of their dangerous rivalry following the revolution in 1949, when Warsaw and Paris were the cities where their diplomatic proximity was most usefully exploited. The so-called ambassadorial talks were important for producing limited agreements on sensitive subjects (chiefly to do with nationals detained by both sides), providing a facility for 'diplomatic radar',[10] soothing the nerves of allies and neutralists, raising the propaganda price of a resort to force ('Why did they do that? We were still talking!'), and preparing the ground for the subsequent *rapprochement* in the early 1970s. More recently, in the 1988–94 period, the Beijing diplomatic corps was the discreet setting for similar negotiations (at political counsellor level) between the United States and North Korea, principally over the allegation that Pyongyang was secretly developing nuclear weapons.

The strategy of exploiting coincidental proximity in third states has the obvious disadvantage that the diplomats of the unfriendly states are likely to have been chosen for their knowledge of the third state rather than for their knowledge of each other's country. It is also likely that they will lack the authority to discuss the most sensitive issues, while certain debts may need to be incurred to the government of the third state in order that their discussions might prosper. Nevertheless, the record reveals that these obstacles are surmountable, not least because of the incentive provided by great secrecy which these meetings can provide.

Diplomatic rites of passage

Direct contact between hostile states may also be made by the high-powered teams of mourners which they despatch to attend important state funerals. 'Funeral diplomacy', which goes back at least to the Feast of the Dead celebrated by the Algonkians of the Upper Great Lakes of Canada in the seventeenth century and probably much further, and is normally a special case of summitry, became an especially pronounced feature of international politics in the 1980s as a result of the highly advanced age profile of the Soviet leadership. Brezhnev, Andropov and Chernenko all died in fairly quick succession between late 1982 and early 1985, and their funeral rites were attended by huge numbers of foreign dignitaries and professional diplomats. Almost all of these wanted discussions with the new Soviet leadership as well as with each other. Particularly worthy of note in the first category of talks (between the bereaved and the delegations of mourners) were the encouraging conversations held between Andropov and the Pakistani leader, General Zia ul-Haq, at Brezhnev's funeral in November 1982 (Islamabad was embroiled indirectly with Moscow over the bitter conflict then raging in Afghanistan). Interesting as an illustration of the second category (talks between the mourning delegations themselves) were the fruitful discussions held between the East German leader, Erich Honecker, and Chancellor Kohl of West Germany at the funerals of both Andropov and Chernenko. These were the first occasions on which the leaders of then-divided Germany met.

State funerals become 'working funerals' because of the proximity at them of so many world leaders. Even the enemies of the bereaved government can attend without serious fear of attack from supporters at home or friends abroad; paying respects to the dead is above reproach in all cultures of which I am aware, including that of the New York mob. State funerals are generally times of political truce. But the atmosphere of these occasions is also generally conducive to diplomacy. In Western cultures, at any rate, funerals are

customarily junctures for reflecting on the transitoriness of life and the petti-
ness of so many of its squabbles; and state funerals are usually a time for
urging a more energetic search for peaceful solutions to the world's problems.
Moreover, unlike most ordinary funerals, state funerals signify birth as well as
death – the birth of a new leadership – and with it the sense of new
opportunities.

Having said this, not all state funerals are equally appropriate screens for
diplomatic encounters. It would be surprising if local variations in ritual and
the strength of feeling associated with them did not have a bearing on this.
Furthermore, it seems reasonable to suggest that the funeral of an elderly
statesman who dies a natural and expected death, where the atmosphere is
likely to be calm and reflective, will normally provide a more appropriate
setting than the highly charged atmosphere suffusing the funeral of a young
leader cut down by an assassin. Certainly, there is less evidence of diplomacy
at the funeral of President John F. Kennedy, who was shot to death in Dallas
in November 1963, than at the Soviet funerals of the 1980s.

Independence-day celebrations also provide an ideal cover for diplomatic
contacts between unfriendly states. The champagne atmosphere of these occasions is obviously far different from the sombre, reflective mood of the state
funeral, but this means that at least the sense of new beginnings is even
stronger. Besides, good spirits generally inspire camaraderie. At the celebrations attending Namibia's independence on 21 March 1990, South Africa's
new leader, F. W. de Klerk, shook hands with the PLO's Yasser Arafat and
held confidential discussions with the Soviet foreign minister. (The latter
encounter was the highest-level meeting ever held between Moscow and Pretoria.) As one observer of these events commented, 'there was something in
the air which encouraged diplomatic promiscuity'.[11]

The special envoy

Direct contact between hostile states may also be made by the simple expedient of despatching a high-ranking government official (or even minister) on a
temporary visit. This may be public or secret, depending upon the odium
which it might be expected to attract or the alarm which it might be reckoned
to excite. Secret ones, of course, tend to be better known after the event.
Henry Kissinger's secret visit to China during the fragile early stages of the
rapprochement with the United States, and the extraordinary visit to Tehran
of President Reagan's own national security adviser, Robert MacFarlane, who
was trying to put together the notorious arms-for-hostages deal, are cases in
point. So, too, are the forays made by the South Africans into black Africa in
1974, and the excursion made by Israel's new foreign minister, Moshe Dayan,
to India in 1977, travelling on scheduled Alitalia flights and disguised by dark
glasses and a large straw hat. (In the same year he also travelled to Morocco,

disguised this time – incredibly enough – as a beatnik.)[12] By contrast, in the early 1980s no secret was made of the travels of Richard Stone, United States Special Envoy to Central America.

Special missions of high-powered officials seem valuable where deeply suspicious enemies need to be convinced of each other's good faith in seeking an accommodation. Nevertheless, they are fraught with peril. Such missions may seriously damage a state's prestige if they are made with public knowledge, especially if they fail to produce results. This is even more likely if they are made to the home territories of other parties rather than to arranged meetings on neutral ground, since the states launching the missions are placed in the position of supplicant. Besides, public missions invite sabotage of the policy initiatives which are behind them. For these reasons they are usually secret. However, if they are made in secret the high rank of the envoy means that there are formidable obstacles to be overcome in order to ensure that they remain secret. And, if caution dictates a secret meeting on neutral ground, the host government will normally have to be told a good deal of what is going on. The French government seemed to know a lot more about Kissinger's secret talks with the Chinese and the North Vietnamese in Paris in the early 1970s than most administration officials in Washington. Finally, the contact provided by special missions is, by definition, spasmodic. They can, therefore, never be the only form of contact between states seeking to repair long-embittered relations.

Joint commissions

Finally, when diplomatic breakthroughs are made between hostile states on a narrow but important front, which is nevertheless insufficient to support a full normalisation of relations, it is now common for existing channels of communication to be supplemented by one or more 'joint commissions'. These bodies are standing committees composed of representatives of the hostile states and also, quite often, third-party 'observers'. Important examples in the period since 1945 include the Military Armistice Commission set up following the Korean War at the beginning of the 1950s, and the Iran–United States Claims Tribunal established in The Hague in 1981 following settlement of the hostages crisis. A joint commission was created immediately following the American-brokered ceasefire in Bosnia in October 1995. The main purpose of joint commissions is to consolidate a specific diplomatic breakthrough, but they can obviously be exploited for communication on other matters as well.

Mediation

There is thus a variety of methods whereby hostile states may make direct diplomatic contact. But in addition to these there are, of course, various *indirect* ones. When mediation is employed, hostile states vest in a third party more or less limited powers to help them achieve a settlement, ranging from acting simply as a bearer of messages to being in the chair of the talks and an active supporter of a specific solution. The mediator is normally a state, or a body such as the UN or the EU (these two have acted jointly in the Bosnia crisis). However, non-governmental organisations such as the International Committee of the Red Cross (ICRC), together with pressure groups and private individuals, may also be employed in order either to stimulate or supplement mediation in the first track. Now known appropriately enough as 'track two diplomacy', its practitioners also include journalists and business-men, whose work provides them with legitimate reasons for foreign travel and contact with governments. During the Cuban missile crisis the Soviet Union used both to convey messages to Washington.

The hostile states themselves may or may not be prepared to negotiate face to face following the intervention of the third party. If 'recognition' of one or more of the states is an issue this will certainly not take place. In such circum-stances 'proximity talks' are employed, that is, negotiations in which a mediator carries messages between hostile delegations, usually located in separate rooms in the same building. An example is provided by the UN-mediated talks on the conflict in Afghanistan between Pakistan and the Soviet-backed regime in Ka-bul, which started in 1981 and finally reached agreement in April 1988.

What are the qualities (other than those required in any diplomacy) of the ideal mediator? Impartiality in the specific dispute is normally important, though this should not be taken to imply that the mediator needs to be indifferent to the nature of the solution. Power, whether military or economic, is also a very important asset if the mediation involves active chairmanship. This argues for mediation by a major power (though a small state, Algeria, achieved a reputation for modest success in mediation efforts in the 1970s and early 1980s). A considerable part of Jimmy Carter's achievement at Camp David is explained by his ability to offer both the Egyptians and the Israelis large amounts of money – 'side payments'. A decade later, in 1988, the pres-sure which the United States was able to bring to bear on both the Angolans and the South Africans was also an important ingredient in the success of the mediation efforts in south-western Africa of US Assistant Secretary of State for African Affairs, Chester Crocker. The mediator also requires staying power, because if the conflicts were not intractable they would not have required mediation in the first place. This argues for mediation by interna-tional organisations or stable autocracies, rather than by democratic regimes subject to periodic changes in direction after elections. This is where the United States falls down, as witness the essentially episodic nature of its efforts in the Arab–Israeli conflict, which eventually required track two diplo-macy in the early 1990s to bring them to a successful conclusion.

States which assume the role of mediator rarely do so out of high-mindedness but because they expect some benefit. They may hope that by helping to defuse a conflict they will remove the risk of being dragged into a dangerous military intervention in it themselves. They may anticipate an increase in their international prestige. Or they may be looking for a quid pro quo of one sort or another from either or both parties. All of these considerations influenced the American diplomatic intervention in the Angola/ Namibia negotiations, while Yahya Khan's good offices in the early stages of America's *rapprochement* with China were repaid by President Nixon's 'tilt to Pakistan' (relative to its long-standing differences with India) in 1971. It is because mediation by a state usually requires payment of some kind that mediation by the UN or a regional organisation or the Vatican, each of which – under different charters – has an obligation to engage in mediation, may be advisable. Besides, agencies such as these can bring *continuous engagement* to mediation – and sometimes more power, too, than is commonly supposed. The importance of continuity is borne out strikingly by the achievements finally won by UN mediation in the Iran–Iraq conflict and in Afghanistan in the second half of the 1980s.

The survival of the resident embassy

Despite the fact that modern diplomacy has witnessed substantial changes in both its personnel and the contexts in which it occurs, it remains obvious that the announcements of the 'death' of the permanent ambassador which were confidently made in the 1960s were decidedly premature. The bilateral diplomacy of the kind described by Harold Nicolson in his famous lectures as 'the French system of diplomacy'[13] is alive and well: its servants are still to be found in every national capital in the world, as well as at the UN and elsewhere. Some of them, such as Anatoly Dobrynin (Soviet ambassador in Washington from 1962 until 1986) and Sir Anthony Parsons (British ambassador in Tehran from 1974 until 1979), were figures of considerable influence in the relations between their own governments and those to which they were accredited.

Most of the central functions of diplomacy cannot usually be performed adequately by anyone other than the permanent ambassador and the embassy's increasingly expert staff. This does not apply, it is true, to negotiation, in which – especially in fairly well 'integrated' regions such as Western Europe – embassies have been substantially replaced by politicians and home-based experts. Nevertheless, if the latter were to be called on to negotiate on every matter which cropped up in bilateral relations, their mental and physical resources would soon be exhausted. Hence embassy staff are still frequently employed to negotiate on matters of lesser importance even in regions where direct government contacts are highly developed. Where this is not so, embassies still commonly play an important role in high-level negotiations as well. Dobrynin's role in Soviet–American negotiations, at least during the Nixon years, was clearly pivotal.

For political reporting to the sending government, the resident embassy is indispensable. Provided its senior staff have been carefully selected, it will have a better understanding of local realities than the foreign ministry at home, easier access to high government officials (including heads of government) than either secret intelligence agents or the media, and obviously a greater inclination than the latter to ask the questions in which its government is interested. The embassy's local knowledge plus its privileged access in turn place it in a better position than anyone else to *lobby* on behalf of its government, and, while others – for example, sportsmen – may be 'great ambassadors for their country' in the creation of goodwill abroad, only the embassy can be relied on to make this a continuous priority. Finally, though many governments may find this a dispensable function, the resident embassy is a permanent reminder of the fact that beyond the state there is a states-system, a political order to which all states owe some allegiance.

Notes

1. Kissinger, *The White House Years*, p. 803.
2. *Diplomacy*, p. 60.
3. Bull, *The Anarchical Society*, p. 166.
4. Quoted in Uldricks, *Diplomacy and Ideology*, p. 17.
5. *The Times*, 3 July 1981.
6. *Diplomacy for a Crowded World*, p. 34.
7. R. D. Putnam, 'The lessons of western summitry', in S. P. Huntington and J. S. Nye, Jr (eds), *Global Dilemmas* (University Press of America: Boston, 1985), p. 18.
8. O'Brien, *The United Nations*, p. 15.
9. 'The role of the United Nations in maintaining and improving international security', *Survival*, vol. 28, no. 5, 1986, p. 390.
10. The excellent phrase of K. T. Young, *Negotiating with the Chinese Communists, 1953–1967* (McGraw-Hill: New York, 1968), p. 303.
11. John Carlin, *The Independent*, 22 March 1990.
12. Nobody will believe *this* without a source! Here it is: Moshe Dayan, *Breakthrough: A personal account of the Egypt–Israel peace negotiations* (Weidenfeld & Nicolson: London, 1981), p. 38.
13. *The Evolution of Diplomatic Method*, ch. 3.

Further reading

General

Anderson, M. S., *The Rise of Modern Diplomacy* (Longman: London and New York, 1993).
Ball, G., *Diplomacy for a Crowded World* (Little, Brown: Boston, and Bodley Head: London, 1976).
Berridge, G. R., *Talking to the Enemy: How states without 'diplomatic relations' communicate* (Macmillan: London, 1994).

Berridge, G. R., *Diplomacy: Theory and practice* (Prentice Hall/Harvester Wheatsheaf: Hemel Hempstead, 1995).

Binnendijk, H. (ed.), *National Negotiating Styles* (Center for the Study of Foreign Affairs, Foreign Service Institute, US Department of State: Washington, 1987).

Bozeman, A. B., *Politics and Culture in International History* 2nd edn (Transaction: New Brunswick and London, 1994), pp. 457–89.

Bull, H., *The Anarchical Society: A study of order in world politics* (Macmillan: London, and Columbia University Press: New York, 1977), ch. 7.

Cohen, R., *Theatre of Power: The art of diplomatic signalling* (Longman: London and New York, 1987).

Cohen, R., *Negotiating across Cultures: Communication obstacles in international diplomacy* (US Institute of Peace Press: Washington, DC, 1991).

Craig, G. A. and F. Gilbert (eds), *The Diplomats, 1919–1939* (Princeton University Press: Princeton, NJ, 1953).

Craig, G. A. and F. L. Loewenheim (eds), *The Diplomats, 1939–1979* (Princeton University Press: Princeton, NJ, 1995).

De Callières, F., *The Art of Diplomacy*, ed. H. M. A. Keens-Soper and K.W. Schweizer (Leicester University Press: Leicester, 1983).

Eban, A., *The New Diplomacy: International affairs in the modern age* (Weidenfeld & Nicolson: London, 1983).

Edwards, R. D., *True Brits: Inside the Foreign Office* (BBC Books: London, 1994).

Haass, R. N., 'Ripeness and the settlement of international disputes', *Survival*, May/June 1988.

Hamilton, K. and R. Langhorne, *The Practice of Diplomacy: Its evolution, theory and administration* (Routledge: London, 1995).

Heinrichs, W. H., Jr, *American Ambassador: Joseph C. Grew and the development of the United States diplomatic tradition* (Oxford University Press: New York, 1986).

James, A., 'Diplomacy and international society', *International Relations*, vol. 6, no. 6, 1980.

James, A., 'Diplomatic relations and contacts', *The British Yearbook of International Law 1991* (Clarendon Press: Oxford, 1992).

Keens-Soper, H. M. A., 'The liberal disposition of diplomacy', *International Relations*, vol. 5, November 1975, pp. 908–16.

Kissinger, H. A., *The White House Years* (Little, Brown: Boston, and Weidenfeld & Nicolson and Michael Joseph: London, 1979), esp. ch. 11, pp. 112–14, 138–43, 436–7, 722–5, 762–3, 802–6, 816–22 and 1,020–1.

Mattingly, G., *Renaissance Diplomacy* (Penguin: Harmondsworth, 1965).

Mayers, D., *The Ambassadors and America's Soviet Policy* (Oxford University Press: New York and Oxford, 1995).

Newsom, D. D. (ed.), *Diplomacy under a Foreign Flag: When nations break relations* (Hurst: London, and St Martin's Press: New York, 1990).

Nicolson, H., *The Evolution of Diplomatic Method* (Constable: London, and Macmillan: New York, 1954).

Nicolson, H., *Diplomacy*, 3rd edn (Oxford University Press: London, Oxford and New York, 1954).

Parsons, Sir A., *The Pride and the Fall: Iran, 1974–1979* (Cape: London, 1984).

Peyrefitte, A., *The Collision of Two Civilisations: The British expedition to China in 1792–4*, trans. J. Rothschild (Harvill: London, 1993).

Queller, D. E., *The Office of Ambassador in the Middle Ages* (Princeton University Press: Princeton, NJ, 1967).

Russell, J. G., *Peacemaking in the Renaissance* (Duckworth: London, 1986), ch. 3.

Sofer, S., 'Old and new diplomacy: a debate revisited', *Review of International Studies*, vol. 14, 1988.

Sullivan, W. H., *Mission to Iran* (Norton: New York, 1981).

Touval, S., *The Peace Brokers: Mediators in the Arab–Israeli conflict, 1948–79* (Princeton University Press: Princeton, NJ, 1982).

Uldricks, T. J., *Diplomacy and Ideology: The origins of Soviet foreign relations, 1917–1930* (Sage: Beverly Hills and London, 1979).

Zartman, I. W. and M. R. Berman, *The Practical Negotiator* (Yale University Press: New Haven and London, 1982).

Summit diplomacy

Ball, G., *Diplomacy for a Crowded World* (Bodley Head: London, 1976), ch. 3.

Bulmer, S. and W. Wessels, *The European Council* (Macmillan: London, 1987).

DeMenil, G. and A. M. Solomon, *Economic Summitry* (Council on Foreign Relations: New York, 1983).

Dunn, David H. (ed), *Diplomacy at the Highest Level* (Macmillan: London, 1996).

Kissinger, H. A., *The Necessity for Choice: Prospects of American foreign policy* (Harper & Row: New York, 1960), pp. 180–91.

Kissinger, H. A., *The White House Years*, pp. 769, 781 and 919–21.

Merlini, C. (ed.), *Economic Summits and Western Diplomacy* (Croom Helm: London, 1984).

Nixon, R. M., 'Superpower summitry', *Foreign Affairs*, vol. 64, no. 1, 1985.

Putnam, R. D. and N. Bayne, *Hanging Together: Cooperation and conflict in the seven power summits*, 2nd edn (Sage: London, 1988).

Rusk, D., 'The president', *Foreign Affairs*, April 1960.

Schaetzel, J. R. and H. B. Malmgren, 'Talking heads', *Foreign Policy*, no. 39, 1980.

Weihmiller, G. R. and D. Doder, *US–Soviet Summits: An account of East–West diplomacy at the top, 1955–1985* (University Press of America: Lanham, New York and London, 1986).

Diplomacy at the United Nations

Bailey, S. D., *The Procedure of the UN Security Council*, 2nd edn (The Clarendon Press: Oxford, 1988).

Berridge, G. R., *Return to the UN: UN diplomacy in regional conflicts* (Macmillan: London, 1991).

Berridge, G. R. and A. Jennings (eds), *Diplomacy at the UN* (Macmillan: London, and St Martin's Press: New York, 1985).

Bourantonis, D. and M. Evriviades (eds), *A United Nations for the Twenty-First Century: Peace, security and development* (Kluwer: The Hague, 1996), ch. by Berridge.

Finger, S. M., *American Ambassadors at the UN* (Holmes & Meier: New York and London, 1988).

Franck, T. M., *Nation Against Nation: What happened to the UN dream and what the US can do about it* (Oxford University Press: Oxford and New York, 1985).

O'Brien, C. C. and F. Topolski, *The United Nations: Sacred drama* (Hutchinson: London, and Simon & Schuster: New York, 1968).

Roberts, A. and B. Kingsbury (eds), *United Nations, Divided World: The UN's roles in international relations*, 2nd edn (The Clarendon Press: Oxford, 1993).

Thompson, K. W., 'The new diplomacy and the quest for peace', *International Organization*, vol. 19, pp. 394–409.

Urquhart, B., *A Life in Peace and War* (Harper & Row: New York, and Weidenfeld & Nicolson: London, 1987).

Yesselson, A. and A. Gaglione, *A Dangerous Place: The United Nations as a weapon in world politics* (Grossman: New York, 1974).

12

Peacekeeping

'Peacekeeping', an important adjunct of diplomacy, predated the creation of the United Nations, and the UN is still not the only body by which it may be authorised. Nevertheless, peacekeeping under UN authority is now the principal species of this important but fragile institution.

Ceasefire observation groups were sent by the UN to Palestine and Kashmir in the late 1940s but UN peacekeeping did not develop fully until the United Nations Emergency Force (UNEF) was hurriedly created and dispatched to Egypt during the Suez crisis in 1956. It is true that only a small number of additional forces (of greatly varying sizes) were created over the following three decades, but with the euphoria over the potential of the UN created by the end of the cold war and the successful action against Iraq in 1991, the period since the late 1980s has seen a veritable explosion in the dispatch of UN peacekeeping forces and military observer missions all over the world (see Boxes 12.1 and 12.2). What are the purposes of such forces? How are they made up? Under what rules do they operate? What conditions must obtain for them to be launched? How useful are they? Are they likely to be more effective than the non-UN, 'multinational' forces which were introduced into the Middle East in the 1980s? These are the questions which this chapter will consider.

Peacekeeping and collective security

The first and most essential points to grasp about UN peacekeeping, however, are that it has got very little in common with 'collective security' as envisaged in Chapter VII of the UN Charter, and that it emerged in response to the latter's failure. The doctrine of collective security assumes that insecurity is the principal cause of war (the 'structural' theory of conflict, discussed in Chapter 4). As a result, it concludes that the best way to stop wars is for each state to provide to *all* other states (irrespective of their importance, ideology, remoteness, and so on) a legal guarantee of swift assistance in the event that they are attacked. The 'police action' thus triggered will be orchestrated by a permanent international body set up for the purpose. Thus relieved of anxiety about their security, states will have no need to take the unilateral steps to increase their military strength that initiate the spiral of fear which culminates in war. Alliances can be forgone and armaments reduced to a level merely commensurate with the responsibilities of members to the international body.

Box 12.1   UN peacekeeping forces

In contrast to observer missions (see Box 12.2), UN peacekeeping forces are generally larger and have broader mandates. They are also armed, albeit lightly.

- *UN Emergency Force (UNEF)*: Egypt, 1956–67; maximum strength, 6,073.
- *Opération des Nations Unies au Congo (ONUC)*: Congo Republic (ex-Belgian Congo), 1960–4; maximum strength, 19,828.
- *UN Force in Cyprus (UNFICYP)*: 1964–; maximum strength, 6,411.
- *UN Emergency Force II (UNEF II)*: Suez Canal sector and Sinai, 1973–9; maximum strength, 6,973.
- *UN Interim Force in Lebanon (UNIFIL)*: 1978–; maximum strength, 5,827.
- *UN Transition Assistance Group (UNTAG)*: Namibia, 1989–90; military component, 4,650.
- *UN Protection Force (UNPROFOR)*: Bosnia, Croatia, and Macedonia, 1992–; maximum strength, 40,000.
- *UN Transitional Authority in Cambodia (UNTAC)*: 1992–3; maximum strength, 22,000 military and civilian personnel.
- *UN Operation in Mozambique (ONUMOZ)*: 1992–4; maximum strength, 7,000–8,000 military and civilian personnel.
- *UN Operation in Somalia (UNOSOM)*: 1992–3; maximum strength, 4,000.
- *Unified Task Force (UNITAF)*: Somalia, December 1992–3; maximum strength, 37,000.
- *UN Operation in Somalia II (UNOSOM II)*: 1993–5; maximum strength, 28,000 military personnel and 2,800 civilian staff; the first 'peacekeeping' force authorised to use force under Chapter VII of the UN Charter.
- *UN Assistance Mission to Rwanda (UNAMIR)*: 1993–; prescribed maximum strength, 2,548.
- *UN Mission in Haiti (UNMIH)*: 1995–; prescribed maximum strength, 6,000 troops, 900 civilian police.
- *UN Angola Verification Mission (UNAVEM III)*: 1995–; prescribed maximum strength, 7,000 military personnel plus 350 military and 260 police observers.

Unfortunately, conditions for the greater part of the period since the end of the Second World War have been extremely unfavourable to the operation of collective security. Among other factors, the division of the world into ideological, religious and regional camps made it inevitable that any 'aggression' would have significant support. The notion of the universally condemned

---

Box 12.2 Major UN observer missions*

- *UN Truce Supervision Organisation (UNTSO)*: Middle East, 1948–; maximum strength, 572.
- *UN Military Observer Group in India and Pakistan (UNMOGIP)*: 1948–; strength, 38.
- *UN Observation Group in Lebanon (UNOGIL)*: 1958; maximum strength, 598.
- *UN Yemen Observation Mission (UNYOM)*: 1963–4; maximum strength, approximately 150.
- *UN India–Pakistan Observation Mission (UNIPOM)*: 1965–6; strength, 90.
- *UN Disengagement Observer Force (UNDOF)*: Golan Heights (Syria), 1974–; maximum strength, 1,317.
- *UN Iran–Iraq Military Observer Group (UNIIMOG)*: 1988–; strength, 400.
- *UN Angola Verification Mission (UNAVEM)*: 1988–91; strength, 60.
- *UN Angola Verification Mission (UNAVEM II)*: 1991–5; strength, 103.
- *UN Good Offices Mission in Afghanistan and Pakistan (UN-GOMAP)*: 1988–90; maximum strength, 50.
- *UN Observer Mission in El Salvador (ONUSAL)*: 1991–5; strength, 380.
- *UN Iraq–Kuwait Observation Mission (UNIKOM)*: 1991–; strength, 320.
- *UN Mission for the Referendum in Western Sahara (MINURSO)*: 1991–; strength, 325.
- *UN Observer Mission Uganda–Rwanda (UNOMUR)*: 1993; strength, 81.
- *UN Observer Mission in Georgia (UNOMIG)*: 1993–; strength, 88.

*Figures exclude civilian staff.

'lone aggressor', in other words, was simply unreal. In such circumstances a general hue and cry is impossible and a partial one highly dangerous. Britain found this to its chagrin after Argentina launched its 'aggression' on the Falkland Islands in 1982 and received considerable sympathy throughout Latin America. Even when Saddam Hussein launched his spectacular invasion of Kuwait in August 1990, he was supported by the PLO, while Jordan, Libya and Iran remained effectively neutral, and some key states (Syria, Egypt, Algeria and Morocco) were under strong popular pressure to throw in their lot with him. On the Security Council itself two members (Cuba and Yemen) voted against the resolution authorising the use of force, and China abstained. In the Bosnian crisis in the first half of the 1990s firm international action against the Serbs (see Box 6.3) was long delayed not only by the complexity of the conflict but also by sympathy for the Serbian position in Russia and Greece. Most acts of 'aggression' today are in any case much more ambiguous than these, often involving, as was noted in Chapters 5 and 6, covert support for the internal enemies of a regime. In such circumstances, 'aggression' is seldom easy to substantiate.

The enormous discrepancy in power between states is also a serious obstacle to collective security. Thus, while a collective response to an aggression by a small, non-nuclear (and non-aligned) state may not be completely unrealistic, a similar response to a limited aggression by a major nuclear power (say, the invasion of Afghanistan by the Soviet Union in 1979) certainly is. This is because it would probably prove fatal to the whole world if tried. (It is for this reason that the framers of the UN Charter provided the great powers with the right to veto any proposal which they considered inconsistent with their interests. Of course, should a great power launch a *major* war, there may well be no alternative to a collective response, whatever the risks.)

Finally, the speed and destructive capacity of modern weapons are such that states can hardly be blamed for taking little comfort from promises of assistance *after* an attack. Though Kuwait was rescued from the Iraqis, this did not occur until early 1991 (nearly six months after the initial occupation), and the blazing oil fields left behind by Saddam's retreating army were only the most eloquent evidence of the consequences of this delayed deliverance.

In response to the failure of collective security to take root in these unpropitious circumstances, in the mid-1950s Dag Hammarskjöld, the most assertive of the UN's secretaries-general, came up with a pragmatic, alternative solution not *explicitly* recognised in the Charter at all: peacekeeping. In marked contrast to collective security, this is not predicated on the strong distinction between 'aggressor' and 'victim' but rather on the relativistic concept of a 'conflict' in which *all* are victims. Into such situations UN forces are injected not in order to give battle to the 'aggressor' but with strict instructions to maintain complete impartiality between the combatants and, most strikingly, to *use force only in self-defence*. In what sense, then, do UN peacekeepers purport to 'keep the peace'?

The mandates which have been given by the Security Council to the various peacekeeping forces that it has authorised have varied both in detail and (notoriously) in clarity, and have typically included the monitoring of a ceasefire or truce. Behind all of the major ones, however, has been the idea that their chief purpose was to interpose – upon, and only upon, invitation to do so from the lawful government of the territory in question – a neutral buffer between warring parties. Such a response, according to the theory, should at least contribute to the *containment* of the conflict (on the assumption that this is better than the complete defeat of one side) and prevent the intervention of the great powers; at most, it should allow time for a diplomatic settlement which the peacekeepers themselves might help to implement. (The UN operation in the early 1960s to end the secession of the Katanga province of the former Belgian Congo, which was ultimately successful, does not fit this theory, which is why it was so controversial.)

Unlike a collective security operation, therefore, a UN peacekeeping operation is not conceived principally as a military mission at all, but rather as a *diplomatic* one. Like the priest who intervenes in a bar-room brawl, its hope is that, by moral authority, minimal physical obstruction, and the provision of a face-saving excuse for the cessation of hostilities ('OK – if *you* ask us to'), it will have a calming influence and thus create an interval in which saner – or at any rate more pacific – voices might prevail.[1] It is for this reason that Hammarskjöld preferred to regard the activity as part of what he called 'preventive diplomacy' and Michael Harbottle, who was chief of staff to the UN Force in Cyprus (UNFICYP) from 1966 until 1968, insists that it is best thought of as 'peaceable intervention'.[2]

The character of peacekeeping operations

Most of the distinguishing characteristics of UN peacekeeping operations flow from the lack of explicit reference to them in the UN Charter and their generally limited roles. First, they are created on an entirely *ad hoc* basis, any genuine intelligence, planning or operations staff in the UN Secretariat being likely to arouse suspicions on the part of some member states that the UN is getting too big for its boots. (Extensive planning would also be likely to prove a waste of time since the UN never knows for certain where it will have to go or what resources it will be volunteered.) Second, since the crisis provoked in the first half of the 1960s by the refusal of certain member states, in particular France and the Soviet Union, to make financial contributions to the Congo force (ONUC), the financing of peacekeeping has had a large voluntary element. Third, while the commanders of both UN forces and their constituent units are subject to the formal authority of the UN, the units remain to a great extent under the effective control of their national governments. Fourth, not being fighting formations, UN peacekeeping forces have until recently been small (see Box 12.1) and only lightly equipped. (ONUC was more than twice the size of any other force because of its exceptional task of ending the secession of Moise Tshombe in Katanga.) Finally, at least during the cold war, contingents from the permanent members of the Security Council were generally excluded from peacekeeping forces in order to minimise internal tensions and make impartiality more likely. Instead, the forces have been composed of units from small and medium powers, especially those which – like India, Austria, Ireland and the Nordic countries – have traditions of neutrality. Having said this, even during the cold war the United States often provided back-up assistance, typically in the form of transport, while British forces in Cyprus (on hand in the 'sovereign base areas')[3] have always played an important role in UNFICYP, and troops from France – which has historical connections with Lebanon – have served in the UN Interim Force in Lebanon (UNIFIL). Soviet bloc troops were employed for the first time in UN peacekeeping when in 1973 Poland contributed a contingent to UNEF II.

With the end of the cold war and the (short-lived) enthusiasm for the 'new world order' produced by the apparent success of the Kuwait operation in 1991, however, the characteristics of UN peacekeeping operations have changed somewhat. The operations have been larger (see Box 12.1), troops from the Security Council's permanent members have been much more in evidence, and heavier equipment has been employed.

Conditions required for launching peacekeeping operations

UN peacekeepers can only be introduced when invited, and no side winning a war is likely to do this. Hence only when there is either a stalemate or total confusion – as in the Congo after the precipitate withdrawal of the Belgians and the mutiny of the *Force Publique* or in Somalia after the collapse of that state into interclan warfare in 1991 – is it possible for the creation of a UN force to be considered. Then the great powers have to conclude that their own interests are better served by deference to the UN, a conclusion at which they do not instinctively arrive and which they will not normally be encouraged to draw by the parties themselves – consider, for instance, the Angolan civil war, and Israel's repeatedly expressed preference for American rather than UN intervention in the Middle East. The combatants, together with the members of the Security Council or the General Assembly (depending on which has authorised the operation), also have to agree on the size, composition, mandate and commanding officer of the peacekeeping force. Finally, voluntary force contributions from member states have to be forthcoming, a requirement which cannot be taken for granted in view of their cost, the exceptional vexations of the duties which they may be called on to perform, and the political problems which tend to come in their train. (Ireland's relations with Israel were not under strain until Israeli-backed militia started murdering Irish members of UNIFIL.)

These are exacting conditions, and it is thus not surprising that, despite the great number of armed conflicts which have occurred since the creation of the United Nations and are still occurring, only a handful of them have witnessed the intervention of the 'Blue Berets'. But this, of course, is no argument against UN peacekeeping when the conditions are right, and after the mid-1980s this fortunate conjuncture occurred on an increasing number of occasions. The main reasons for this, of course, were the increasing anxiety displayed by the Soviet Union for face-saving exits from the intractable regional conflicts which were draining its diminishing resources, its mounting preoccupation with domestic reform and its desire to use the UN to place a curb on American 'adventurism' of the kind displayed by the Reagan administration in Libya, Lebanon and the Gulf. With Mr Gorbachev paying off Soviet debts to UN peacekeeping operations, urging their wider use and generally cooperating to an unprecedented degree with the United States in various attempts to settle regional conflicts, from Afghanistan to Angola, it is not surprising that UN peacekeeping operations were multiplying even before the idea of a 'new world order' was encouraged by the victory over Saddam Hussein in 1991.

How effective is UN peacekeeping?

There is a view that, owing to the legacy of Hammarskjöld's more or less pacifist conception of UN peacekeeping and the great practical difficulties under which its soldiers labour, UN peacekeeping is completely ineffective. With one hand tied behind its back, this argument goes, it only 'works' when it is not needed. When the chips are really down, as on the eve of the Middle East war in 1967, in Cyprus on the occasion of the Turkish invasion in 1974, Lebanon at the time of the second Israeli invasion in 1982, Somalia in 1994–5, and Bosnia-Herzegovina in early 1995, UN forces either withdraw or are contemptuously brushed aside. But apart from ignoring, for example, the invaluable work which UN forces had already done in reducing the mayhem caused by armed bands (especially in Cyprus, Lebanon, and – for a time – in Somalia) and mutinous troops (the Congo), and the protection which they have given to relief convoys in Bosnia, this criticism mistakes the principal function of UN peacekeeping altogether. This, it is worth re-emphasising, is not so much to prevent or stop wars between states as *to consolidate peace achieved by other means*. Without the face-saving facility of UN troops it would have been less easy to end the Suez war in 1956, or to separate the Israelis from the Egyptians in Sinai and from the Syrians on the Golan Heights in 1974. Though there was a subsequent increase in general Israeli hostility to the UN and a refusal to believe in UNIFIL's ability to prevent Palestinian infiltration into southern Lebanon and northern Israel, it would be surprising if the first Israeli withdrawal from Lebanon had not been made easier by the presence of UN forces. And the UN Transition Assistance Group (UNTAG), after a difficult start, was clearly central to the peaceful transition of Namibia to independence in 1989–90.

One reason why the 'Blue Berets' sometimes prove effective even when obviously outgunned by local forces temporarily disaffected with them, is that while the latter may have no fear of 'the UN', they may be apprehensive of the diplomatic consequences of killing, say, French, Irish, or Indian troops. Another reason is that, as the years have passed, a more muscular interpretation has been given by the UN to the rule that its soldiers will only use force in 'self-defence'. In September 1964 this was broadened to include attempts to disarm them or to remove them from positions which they occupied, and in March 1978 it was made even more permissive. On this occasion, the secretary-general, Kurt Waldheim, announced that as far as UNIFIL was concerned, 'self-defence would include resistance to attempts by forceful means to prevent it from discharging its duties under the mandate of the Security Council'.[4] As Verrier remarks, the vagueness of this formulation 'in effect [gave] a pretty wide latitude to the men on the spot to decide what their duties were'.[5] Both of the above points were well illustrated by an incident in early 1985 involving the Israelis and the French contingent in UNIFIL, which flew over each of its barracks in southern Lebanon a large *drapeau tricolore* alongside a handkerchief-size UN flag. On direct orders from Paris, the French informed the Israelis that they would not be permitted to conduct a punitive raid on the village of Marrake, which the Israelis believed housed PLO sympathisers. When this advice was ignored, the French laid their flag across the road outside the village and announced that they would kill the first Israelis to drive over it. The Israelis retreated.[6] (After violent exchanges with Lebanese militia, the French battalion in UNIFIL was subsequently withdrawn.) In June 1993 UNPROFOR was authorised to use force in Bosnia in response to bombardments or attacks against 'safe areas' or deliberate attempts to destroy humanitarian convoys.

A further criticism of peacekeeping is that by 'containing' conflicts UN peacekeepers take the pressure off the parties (and, in some cases, their external backers) to find a political settlement. But this assumes that a political settlement is always obtainable. In fact, in some conflicts the issues are so intractable and the resolve of the parties to hold to their positions so great that, at least in the foreseeable future, there is no 'problem' capable of a *political* 'solution' at all. Instead there is a *dilemma*, and with a dilemma all that one can do is try to contain it and thereby reduce the grief which it causes. Until recently the Arab–Israeli conflict was the paradigm dilemma of this kind. Ultimately, however, the balance of forces may change, weariness set in, memories of wrong grow dimmer, and more important things to worry about appear on the horizon – and time may throw up a solution. It is precisely to buy time that we have UN soldiers. Besides, many intractable conflicts have ramifications which are wider than their local borders. Thus, leaving the parties to their own devices could well produce a quicker (though not necessarily durable) 'solution' but in the process entail fighting which might well risk dragging in other states. Here a case in point, where UN forces have been successfully operating for nearly three decades, is the Cyprus conflict, one of the main issues in the perennially tense relations between Turkey and Greece. A parallel case is Bosnia, which as it happens has exacerbated regional divisions along almost identical lines.

With the development in the late 1980s of an unprecedented big power consensus behind the need for more – and more varied – peacekeeping operations, attention has naturally focused on how their effectiveness might be increased. Stress has been placed on the need for more money (including a general fund to give the secretary-general the ability to react quickly in emergencies), a bigger staff at UN headquarters, a better logistical network, the addition to operations of aerial surveillance, and better stand-by and training provision. However, most interest has concentrated on the suggestion, strongly supported before its collapse by the Soviet Union, that peacekeeping forces should now contain contingents from the P5 countries themselves; and, as noted above, this has already happened.

There are some advantages to this idea. Peacekeeping forces including soldiers from the P5 would be likely to retain enthusiastic Security Council support. Financing would also be much less of a problem. On the other hand, apart from being more attractive targets for hostage-taking, such forces might be more inclined to throw their weight around. The problem with this (which is the general problem of whether or not 'peacekeeping' forces should be allowed to become more aggressive) is that they may then become part of the problem rather than part of the solution. As Brian Urquhart has rightly observed, it is the non-threatening character of UN peacekeepers which enables those wishing to stop fighting to defer to them without loss of face: 'The use of force, unless very carefully considered, will tend to destroy this characteristic and, along with it, the necessary co-operation of at least one of the parties to the conflict.'[7] This lesson was unmistakably underlined by the UN operation in Somalia, which was composed largely of American troops with heavy equipment and was wound up in orderly but nevertheless humiliating circumstances in early 1995.[8] If, nevertheless, there remain conditions in which it is appropriate for peacekeeping forces to be marginally more assertive (without becoming collective security operations on the model of action against Iraq, Somalia, or latterly Bosnia), it is perhaps as well that they should contain contingents from the P5. In this eventuality, the *show* of force would probably be adequate, though it would be likely to prove even more so if the membership of the Security Council itself was felt to be more representative.

Non-UN peacekeeping

Peacekeeping – even of the armed, large-scale variety – is not an activity carried out by the UN alone and predates its creation. As for small observer missions, these are now quite often constituted on the authority of associations like the British Commonwealth and regional organisations such as the Organisation of American States (OAS) and the EU, the latter currently having a Monitoring Mission in the former Yugoslavia. The important point is simply that they be acceptable to the main parties to the conflict in question.

Perhaps the most famous of earlier examples of large-scale peacekeeping was the force put together in 1900 by the great powers in order to relieve the foreign diplomats besieged in the Legation Quarter of Peking during the Boxer rebellion. Since the founding of the UN, three non-UN forces have been created, each time because of local hostility (chiefly from Israel) to UN intervention. The 'Multinational Force and Observers' (MFO) operating in Sinai (see Box 12.3) has been very successful, and the 'Multinational Force' in Beirut (MNF I), a 2,000-strong force made up of troops from the United

---

Box 12.3   The Multinational Force and Observers (MFO)

In the Egypt–Israel Peace Treaty of 1979 it was assumed that UNEF II would oversee the implementation of the treaty's provisions on the Israeli withdrawal from Sinai and the substantial demilitarisation of the desert peninsula. However, as a result of Arab hostility to the Camp David 'peace process', this was blocked by the Soviet Union and in April 1982 MFO came into being as an American-sponsored substitute for the United Nations force. The United States, Colombia and Fiji each contributed an infantry battalion, and various kinds of small-scale support have been provided by the United Kingdom, France, Italy, the Netherlands, Norway, New Zealand, Canada, Australia and Uruguay. The United States has made the largest financial contribution to the MFO. The force was about 2,700 strong until 1988 but has declined somewhat since then.

States, France and Italy, fulfilled its own instructions (to cover the evacuation by sea of PLO 'fighters' under the guns of the Israel Defence Force in 1982) and was then wound up. Why, then, did the third non-UN peacekeeping force, MNF II, end in humiliating failure and call into question the very conception of this sort of operation?

MNF II, which had a maximum strength of 5,200 troops drawn from the United States, France, Italy and Britain, assembled in Beirut in the latter half of 1982 and early 1983. Its mandate was to interpose itself between the Israel Defence Force and the Muslim Lebanese militias in Beirut and assist the Lebanese government to restore its authority in the city. Unfortunately, after a smooth start, the operation fell to pieces during 1983 (with considerable loss of life on all sides) and in early 1984 the various contingents were withdrawn. The main reason for this was that the task of supporting the narrowly based (Christian-dominated) Lebanese government made MNF II a partisan in Lebanon's internal affairs in the eyes of the government's Muslim enemies and their friends abroad, a situation analogous to that in which ONUC had found itself in the Congo in the early 1960s. However, the situation in the Lebanon was compounded by the composition of MNF II, since France (the ex-colonial power) had long been associated with the protection of the Lebanese Christians, and the United States was aligned with Israel which was itself allied to the Lebanese Christians.

The experience of MNF II does not prove that peacekeeping forces should not be used on any 'law and order' missions, nor that non-UN forces engaged on such operations are always doomed to failure. However, it does suggest that the employment of peacekeeping forces constituted on *any* basis is inappropriate when the recognised government has a sectarian foundation. Having said this, it remains likely that a UN force would have had a slightly better chance than MNF II in holding the ring in Beirut.

Notes

1. The actual methods employed by UN forces depend on whether or not the emphasis of their missions is on containment or diplomatic settlement. The best analysis of UN peacekeeping methods is to be found in *The Politics of Peacekeeping* by Alan James.
2. *The Blue Berets*, p. 1.
3. Britain, along with Greece and Turkey, is also nominally a guarantor of the 1960 Cyprus constitution.
4. Quoted in Verrier, *International Peacekeeping*, p. 130.
5. *Ibid.*, pp. 130–1.
6. Robert Fisk, *The Times*, 28 February 1985.
7. 'Beyond the "sheriff's posse"', *Survival*, May/June 1990, p. 202.
8. Having been underlined, the lesson was also reportedly absorbed by the American military at this time and clearly stated in its new Army manual, *Peace Operations*. Previously the Pentagon had believed – astonishingly – that peacekeeping and peace enforcement were distinguished only by different levels of violence and that, as a result, a military unit could move freely from the one kind of activity to the other, *The Independent*, 29 March 1995.

Further reading

Berdal, M. R., 'Whither UN peacekeeping? An analysis of the changing military requirements of UN peacekeeping with proposals for its enhancement', Adelphi Paper No. 281, 1993 (International Institute of Strategic Studies, London).

Berridge, G. R., *Return to the UN: UN diplomacy in regional conflicts* (Macmillan: London, 1991), ch. 3.

Bourantonis, D. and J. Wiener (eds), *The United Nations in the New World Order* (Macmillan: London, 1995), ch. by James.

Bourantonis, D. and M. Evriviades (eds), *A United Nations for the Twenty-First Century: Peace, security and development* (Kluwer: The Hague, 1996), ch. by Grinberg.

Chopra, J., A. Eknes and T. Nordbo, *Fighting for Hope in Somalia* (Norwegian Institute of International Affairs: Oslo, 1995).

Claude, I. L., *Swords into Plowshares* (Random House: New York, 1964), ch. 14.

Durch, W. J. (ed.), *The Evolution of UN Peacekeeping* (St Martin's Press: New York, 1993).

A. Eknes, *Blue Helmets in a Blown Mission* [on Bosnia] (Norwegian Institute of International Affairs: Oslo, 1993).

Findlay, T., *Cambodia: The legacy and lessons of UNTAC* (Oxford University Press: Oxford, 1995).

Finkelstein, L. S. (ed.), *Politics in the United Nations System after Forty Years* (Duke University Press: Durham, NC, 1988), ch. by James.

Forsythe, D. P. (ed.), *The United Nations in the World Political Economy* (Macmillan: London, 1989), ch. by James.

Harbottle, M., *The Blue Berets*, rev. edn (Cooper: London, 1975).

Higgins, R., *United Nations Peacekeeping, 1946–67: Documents and commentary*, vol. i, *The Middle East* (Oxford University Press: New York and London, 1969).

Higgins, R., *United Nations Peacekeeping, 1946–67: Documents and commentary*, vol. ii, *Asia* (Oxford University Press: New York and London, 1970).

Higgins, R., *United Nations Peacekeeping, 1946–67: Documents and commentary*, vol. iii, *Africa* [i.e. The Congo] (Oxford University Press: New York and London, 1980).

Higgins, R., *United Nations Peacekeeping, 1946–67: Documents and commentary,* vol. iv, *Europe, 1946–1979* [incl. Cyprus] (Oxford University Press: New York and London, 1981).
International Journal, 'Peacekeeping's new look', special issue, Spring 1995.
James, A., *The Politics of Peace-Keeping* (Chatto & Windus: London, and Praeger: New York, 1969).
James, A., *Peacekeeping in International Politics* (Macmillan: London, 1990).
James, A., 'Internal peace-keeping: a dead end for the UN?', *Security Dialogue,* vol. 24, no. 4, Dec. 1993.
James, A., 'The history of peacekeeping. An analytical perspective', *Canadian Defence Quarterly,* vol. 23, no. 1, Sept. 1993.
Lash, J. P., *Dag Hammarskjöld* (Doubleday: Garden City, NY, 1961; Cassell: London, 1962).
Lefever, E. W., *Uncertain Mandate: Politics of the UN Congo operation* (Johns Hopkins Press: Baltimore, 1967; Oxford University Press: London, 1968).
McDermott, A. and K. Skjelsbaek (eds), *The Multinational Force in Beirut 1982–1984* (Florida International University: Miami, 1991).
Nelson, R. W., 'Multinational peacekeeping in the Middle East and the United Nations model', *International Affairs,* vol. 61, no. 1, 1984/5.
Norton, A. R. and T. G. Weiss, *Soldiers with a Difference: The rediscovery of UN peacekeeping* (Foreign Policy Association: New York, 1990).
O'Brien, C. C., *To Katanga and Back: A UN case history* (Grosset and Dunlop: New York, and Hutchinson: London, 1962).
Rikhye, I. J. and K. Skjelsbaek (eds), *The United Nations and Peacekeeping: The lessons of 40 years of experience* (Macmillan: London, 1990).
Siekmann, R. C. R., *National Contingents in United Nations Peacekeeping Forces* (Nijhoff: The Hague, 1991).
Smith, H. (ed.), *International Peacekeeping: Building on the Cambodian experience* (Australian Defence Studies Centre: Canberra, 1994).
Stoessinger, J. G., *The United Nations and the Superpowers: China, Russia and America,* 4th edn (Random House: New York, 1977), pt 2.
Survival, 'United Nations Peace-keeping', special issue, vol. 32, no. 3, 1990.
Tabory, M., *The Multinational Force and Observers in the Sinai* (Westview Press: Boulder, CO, 1986).
Thakur, R., *International Peacekeeping in Lebanon* (Westview Press: Boulder, CO, 1987).
United Nations, *The Blue Helmets: A review of United Nations peace-keeping* (UN: New York, 1986).
Urquhart, B., *Hammarskjöld: The diplomacy of crisis* (Knopf: New York, 1972; Bodley Head: London, 1973).
Urquhart, B., 'United Nations peacekeeping in the Middle East', *World Today,* March 1980.
Urquhart, B., *A Life in Peace and War* (Weidenfeld & Nicolson: London, and Harper & Row: New York, 1987).
Urquhart, B., 'A risky business . . . ', *UN Chronicle,* December 1988.
Verrier, A., *International Peacekeeping: United Nations forces in a troubled world* (Penguin: Harmondsworth, 1981).
Wiseman, H. (ed.), *Peacekeeping: Appraisals and proposals* (Pergamon: New York, 1983).

NB: Most general books on the United Nations include a chapter on peacekeeping.

13

The UN welfare network

When the United Nations was set up in the final months of the Second World War, its duty to preserve 'international peace and security' was naturally the focus of most attention and the Security Council, dominated by the five permanent members, held centre stage. Nevertheless, the new body did not prove particularly adept at preserving the peace and in any case this was not the only function given to it. It was also charged with helping to rebuild the world economic order (see Box 13.1) and, with the completion of reconstruction in Europe by the end of the 1950s, the UN came to be associated more and more with economic development and social work on behalf of the poorer countries. In this sphere the General Assembly, via its Economic and Social Council (ECOSOC), now nominally presides over much of a complex, far-flung and ever-expanding network[1] of what are in effect public services and social security agencies (see Figure 13.1). In UN parlance, most of these are known as 'specialised' agencies. (The network which embraces them is commonly described as the UN 'development' system but this designation is too narrow for the purposes of this chapter since disaster relief, help to refugees and various other activities undertaken by UN agencies operating in the economic and social fields do not fit comfortably beneath it.) Here, then, the UN is a 'doer' as well as a forum for negotiation, and it is in the former role that it will be discussed in this chapter. (The work of some of the key economic agencies is discussed in Chapter 2.)

Before proceeding, however, it should be noted that there is a certain awkwardness in treating the UN welfare network as an institution of the *states*-system, since its most enthusiastic supporters – the 'functionalists' – have usually seen it as the most effective way of undermining the sovereign state. According to functionalist theory, the most influential purveyor of which was the Romanian émigré, David Mitrany, international cooperation in performing technical, non-political *functions* erodes parochial loyalties to the state while simultaneously demonstrating the advantages which might be gained by extending such cooperation into more controversial areas. Gradually a sense of world community will develop alongside an expanding network of international functional agencies and the state will become obsolete. At this point, and only at this point, it should be possible to create some kind of world government along federal or confederal lines.

Nevertheless, the specialised agencies remain firmly under the policy direction of their member states rather than that of idealistic functionalists, and the idea of an independent international civil service can hardly be said to have taken firm root either. Furthermore, while 'one state, one vote' is still the

---

Box 13.1   The 'constitutional' origins of the UN welfare network

These are to be found in Chapter IX of the Charter of the United Nations:

International Economic and Social Cooperation:

ARTICLE 55

With a view to the creation of conditions of stability and well-being which are necessary for peaceful and friendly relations among nations based on respect for the principle of equal rights and self-determination of peoples, the United Nations shall promote:

(a) higher standards of living, full employment, and conditions of economic and social progress and development;
(b) solutions of international economic, social, health, and related problems; and international cultural and educational cooperation; and
(c) universal respect for, and observance of, human rights and fundamental freedoms for all without distinction as to race, sex, language, or religion.

ARTICLE 56

All Members pledge themselves to take joint and separate action in cooperation with the Organization for the achievement of the purposes set forth in Article 55.

---

constitutional norm in most of these organisations, the larger financial contributions, greater ability to supply expert staff, and general prestige of the bigger powers tend to give the latter disproportionate influence within them and the 'one state, one vote' rule has itself been heavily qualified in practice over the last decade. As a result, the functionalist inspiration behind the UN network need not after all prevent us from seeing it as an institution of the *states*-system.

What, then, of the range and style of activity in this final institution? What problems bedevil its work? And how effective is it? These are the main questions which this chapter will consider.

The work

There is a vast range of activity within the UN welfare network, as can be seen from Figure 13.1. However, this becomes more intelligible when it is understood that each of the specialised agencies normally fulfils three main functions, although the emphasis placed on these functions varies from agency to agency. In the first place, each is responsible for *research and information exchange* in its particular field. In the second, each is concerned with

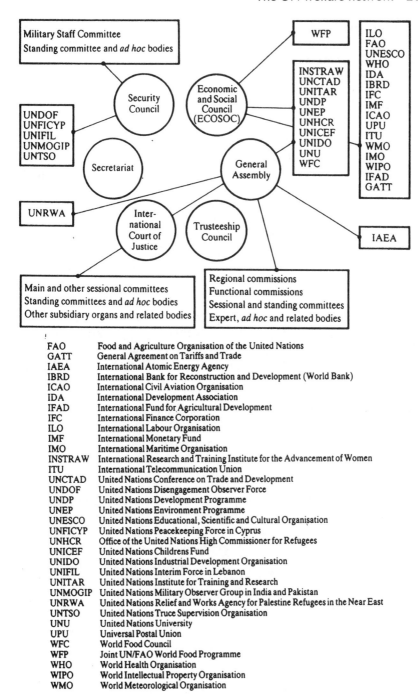

FAO	Food and Agriculture Organisation of the United Nations
GATT	General Agreement on Tariffs and Trade
IAEA	International Atomic Energy Agency
IBRD	International Bank for Reconstruction and Development (World Bank)
ICAO	International Civil Aviation Organisation
IDA	International Development Association
IFAD	International Fund for Agricultural Development
IFC	International Finance Corporation
ILO	International Labour Organisation
IMF	International Monetary Fund
IMO	International Maritime Organisation
INSTRAW	International Research and Training Institute for the Advancement of Women
ITU	International Telecommunication Union
UNCTAD	United Nations Conference on Trade and Development
UNDOF	United Nations Disengagement Observer Force
UNDP	United Nations Development Programme
UNEP	United Nations Environment Programme
UNESCO	United Nations Educational, Scientific and Cultural Organisation
UNFICYP	United Nations Peacekeeping Force in Cyprus
UNHCR	Office of the United Nations High Commissioner for Refugees
UNICEF	United Nations Childrens Fund
UNIDO	United Nations Industrial Development Organisation
UNIFIL	United Nations Interim Force in Lebanon
UNITAR	United Nations Institute for Training and Research
UNMOGIP	United Nations Military Observer Group in India and Pakistan
UNRWA	United Nations Relief and Works Agency for Palestine Refugees in the Near East
UNTSO	United Nations Truce Supervision Organisation
UNU	United Nations University
UPU	Universal Postal Union
WFC	World Food Council
WFP	Joint UN/FAO World Food Programme
WHO	World Health Organisation
WIPO	World Intellectual Property Organisation
WMO	World Meteorological Organisation

Figure 13.1 The UN welfare network

promoting agreement on *international regulations* and then with lobbying member governments to comply with them. (The work of GATT – now the WTO – on international trade rules has already been mentioned in Chapter 2. Another good example here is the UNCTAD liner code – see Box 13.2). And

---

Box 13.2   The UNCTAD Liner Code

Cargo liners (as opposed to tramps) follow established schedules and ply regular routes. They are thus of the first importance to world commerce. In the early 1960s the liner trades were dominated by the shipping companies of the developed world. Since most of these were also organised into hypersecretive cartels known as 'conferences' or 'shipping rings', the whole set-up of international shipping was regarded with intense suspicion by the newly independent countries of the Third World. Not only was it feared that existing arrangements posed insurmountable obstacles to entry into these trades by new Third World merchant marines but also that they enabled freight rates to be held at excessively high levels.

It was against this background that the UN Conference on Trade and Development (UNCTAD), which is technically an 'organ' of the UN rather than a 'specialised agency', created a permanent Committee on Shipping in 1965. Following intensive study of freight rates and shipping markets (and a lame attempt at voluntary regulation by the traditional maritime powers), the third session of UNCTAD (1972) called on the General Assembly to convene a special conference to draft a code of conduct for liner conferences. This met in 1973 and 1974 and the 'UNCTAD Convention on a Code of Conduct for Liner Conferences' was duly drawn up, though it did not become law until 1983. Among other things, it stipulates the following:

- That the national flag shipping of the countries at both ends of a trade are entitled to up to 40 per cent of the cargo carried by the conference controlling that trade, with only the 20 per cent remaining being available to 'cross-traders', i.e. shipping lines of third countries.
- That explanations of the need for general freight-rate increases must be given to all interested parties at least 150 days in advance of their introduction, and that the minimum time between such increases is fifteen months.
- That consultation with shippers on a range of vital matters (including freight-rate increases) is mandatory.
- That conference policy cannot be made without the consent of the national shipping lines of the countries at each end of the trade.
- That the traditionally secret conference 'agreements' must be disclosed to interested governments.

in the third place, the agencies provide *technical assistance* (including education and training) to those countries which require it; this is substantially a post-Second World War development. Williams groups together UNESCO, FAO, WHO, ILO and UNIDO[2] (see Figure 13.1) as the biggest and the most controversial – the 'Big Five'.[3] Industrial development in Africa is a priority for UNIDO, but it is also finding a role in the transitional economies of the former Soviet bloc, where it is helping to encourage small and medium-sized businesses.

The problems

The range of problems afflicting the UN welfare network is almost as extensive as the range of activities which it embraces, though most of them fall under the (related) headings of 'politicisation', poor coordination, bureaucratic incompetence and underfunding.

'Politicisation'

To the dismay of functionalists, bitter political disagreement within the network has been one of the most debilitating of its problems over much of the postwar period, though the attention devoted to certain cases may well have led to an exaggeration of its impact over the network as a whole. In any event, controversy reflected the intensely political nature of the agendas of some agencies (such as the ILO – workers' rights) together with the East–West and North–South conflicts which dominated these years, and the deep frustrations within the UN over Israel and South Africa. Indeed, the frustrations over some of these issues were so considerable that, for propaganda reasons, they were also raised in agencies with only the most marginal of constitutional responsibilities for dealing with them. This was encouraged by a feature of the specialised agencies borrowed from the UN's General Assembly: public debate in a large assembly, followed by voting on resolutions.

The paralysing acrimony which predictably afflicted the Human Rights Commission is notorious, while the United States absented itself from the ILO in the second half of the 1970s in response to the decision of that agency to interest itself in Israel's violation of trade union rights in the Occupied Territories. A decade later the transformation of some of UNESCO's work into anti-Western propaganda (for example, on the 'New World Information and Communications Order' and the 'Peace Education Programme') contributed to the loss of 30 per cent of its income when both the United States and Britain left in protest in 1984 and 1985 respectively. But not even the World Health Organisation has escaped political wrangling. For example, the Soviet Union sought to raise the Vietnam war in this organisation under the heading of 'the epidemiological situation in Vietnam in connection with US aggression in South East Asia',[4] while 'health conditions in the occupied territories of Israel' were also placed on its agenda. Subsequently the WHO became the scene of a long-running dispute between the United States and its Third World members over what the former regarded as the anti-free market impulses behind the agency's campaign against the drug multinationals.

With the ending of the cold war, the painful financial lessons inflicted on politically extravagant parts of the UN network by the United States, Britain and some others, the democratisation of South Africa, and the peace settlement between Israel and the PLO, politicisation has recently become less of a problem in the network. Nevertheless, the North–South split will not go away as readily as the East–West one did, and new conflicts are surfacing to bedevil the agendas of the specialised agencies.

Poor coordination

Extremely poor coordination between the specialised agencies, perhaps most visible in the area of disaster relief, is the problem plaguing the welfare network which the UN itself likes to talk about most of all, presumably because it is believed to be merely technical and thus in principle remediable. It means duplication of activities, the absence of standardisation in procedural matters such as personnel and financial policy, and confusion in the determination of priorities.

That the problem of coordination within the network should always have been serious is hardly surprising. The most important reason for this is that ECOSOC, nominally charged with prime responsibility for coordination under the Charter, merely has liaison agreements with, rather than formal authority over, the majority of its constituent units – the properly designated 'autonomous organisations' (see Figure 13.1); and it has little practical influence even over those where such authority ostensibly exists. This is compounded by the frequent weakness of coordination *within the governments of member states*. As Williams observes: 'It . . . is a common occurrence that the delegations of member states in the intergovernmental organs of the Specialized Agencies support policies or decisions that contradict the views expressed by the delegations of the same states at other Agencies of the United Nations.'[5] Besides, the network has always been fractured by considerable geographical distances. The main concentrations of agency headquarters are divided between New York, Geneva and Vienna, while UNESCO is based in Paris, the IMF and the World Bank in Washington, the FAO in Rome, and so on. The position also seems to have been made infinitely worse since the mid-1960s by four additional factors: the growing sprawl of UN welfare activities; the trend towards conducting more activities at the regional as opposed to the global level; the enormous growth in UN membership; and the tendency of the Afro–Asian 'bloc' to override ECOSOC in the General Assembly.

Varied and repeated attempts to improve coordination within the network have been made. New machinery has been designed to tackle the problem, beginning with the Administrative Committee on Coordination (composed of the secretary-general plus agency heads) which was set up in 1947. Broad plans for economic and social development, notably those for the three 'Development Decades' and the 'New International Economic Order', have been drawn up under the aegis of the General Assembly and the agencies exhorted to tailor their activities to them. And an attempt to enforce coordination by channelling all voluntary funds through one agency, the UN Development Programme, began in the late 1960s. But none of these efforts achieved much success. This was partly because of the size and complexity of the problem, but also because agency heads saw these moves as threats to their sovereignty, because their resistance was stiffened by the fact that the UN Secretariat itself had no great reputation for efficiency, and because a significant fall in United Nations Development Programme (UNDP) funds after 1977 seriously diminished the ability of the centre to employ financial pressure.

There is a view that the damaging consequences of poor coordination in the UN network have been assumed rather than proven, and that they are probably less severe than has been supposed. Some also point to the advantages of its polycentric arrangements, advantages which obtain in any decentralised, *laissez-faire* set-up, where the dead hand of a top-heavy system is avoided: speed of reaction to crises and scope for experimentation. Had coordination been better, 'politicisation' may also have been more extreme. These are, at any rate, consoling thoughts.

Bureaucratic incompetence

Though this was clearly unfair to some of its components, by the 1970s (if not before) the UN welfare network, including the Secretariat, had become a byword in the West for administrative slovenliness, employing staff of poor calibre and low morale. What were the reasons for this state of affairs? First, member states had from the beginning tended to keep their best people at home, a disposition which in the West at least can safely be assumed to have intensified with the long decline of UN prestige. Second, in making appointments, energy, ability and integrity were typically placed second to the political need to ensure 'fair geographical representation', with the result that staff of poor calibre were often appointed to positions above individuals with stronger claims, simply because their region was underrepresented. Third, efficiency was reduced by the great growth in cultural and linguistic diversity of the staff which was the corollary of the need for 'fair geographical representation' against the background of the vast post-decolonisation explosion in UN membership. And finally, some member governments (most notoriously the Soviet Union) prevented their own nationals from taking long-term contracts with the UN, thus impeding the development of loyalty to it.

There is as yet no clear evidence that the airing which was given to this particular problem during the 1980s has produced dramatic results. Nevertheless, the report of the 'Eighteen-member Group of High-Level Intergovernmental Experts', commissioned by the General Assembly in December 1985 and delivered the following year, made recommendations for reform in personnel procedure which were favourably received. Two years after this, in tune with its radically more positive approach to the United Nations in general, the Soviet Union agreed to allow long-term appointments of Soviet citizens to the organisation. Some of the agencies which had come in for particularly savage criticism, such as UNIDO, also made belated improvements in the early 1990s.

Underfunding

Last but not least, since the mid-1980s the UN has been afflicted by an acute cash crisis. Contributions to the UN regular budget are assessed roughly on the basis of members' wealth, though there is an arbitrary ceiling of 25 per cent of the budget above which no state can be obliged to pay and an arbitrary floor of 0.01 per cent below which the contribution of none can be permitted to fall. (In 1990 seventy-seven members were assessed for the minimum contribution of 0.01 per cent of the budget, while the Soviet Union – including Ukraine and Belorussia – was assessed at 11.57 per cent and the United States, as usual, was asked to pay the maximum of 25 per cent.) With only limited exceptions, however, voting in the UN network was not weighted according to the size of financial contributions: the principle, as already noted, was 'one state, one vote'. Despite their proportionately huge contributions, therefore, since the early 1960s the United States, Western Europe and Japan had been forced by the voting power of the Third World and the Soviet bloc to witness the spending of more and more money on UN programmes of which they strongly disapproved – because they were either impracticable, or irrelevant, or anti-Western in their thrust.

By 1985 the UN was already in financial difficulties as a result of inflated budgets on the one hand and defaults and dilatoriness on the part of some contributors on the other. However, the real crisis started in this year as a result of two decisions of the US Congress: first, the Kassebaum Amendment, which required the administration to reduce the US contribution from 25 to 20 per cent unless weighted voting on budgetary matters was introduced in the UN by October 1986; and second, the Gramm–Rudman–Hollings Deficit Reduction Act which ordered immediate across-the-board cuts in federal spending. By 1986 the United States was paying only half of its assessed contribution and, as the Secretary-General himself declared, the United Nations was 'on the brink of bankruptcy'. By early 1988 the position had become so desperate that Pérez de Cuéllar was considering private borrowing.

The UN weathered this storm, partly by reorganisation and retrenchments under the lash of the 'Group of Eighteen' report, partly by demonstrating its unique combination of diplomatic assets in the regional crises of the late 1980s – but perhaps above all by acceptance *in practice* on the part of the General Assembly that the biggest contributors must have the biggest say in budgetary allocations. This was the significance of the General Assembly's reluctant agreement in December 1986, in the course of debate on the Group of Eighteen's report, that more consensus-making machinery would have to be built into the budgetary process. Unfortunately, by 1995 – the year of the UN's half-centenary – the financial crisis had returned, a situation not helped by the fact that the United States, where the Republican-led Congress had once more turned hostile, remained in arrears to the tune of $1.18bn. Total arrears at the end of August stood at $3.7bn, and the Secretary-General was forced not only to impose savage spending restrictions but to draw on funds earmarked for peacekeeping operations on an unprecedented scale in order to pay salaries and keep his administration afloat.

Is the UN welfare network dispensable?

This is a question which was asked with increasing frequency in the 1980s, especially in the United States, which is not surprising since of all states in the world America needs the UN least. In the mid-1990s the question was being asked in that country again – and answered increasingly in the affirmative. Among the more moderate suggestions being made in the US Congress in 1995 was for the United States to pull out of UNIDO and for UNCTAD to be subsumed by the new World Trade Organisation. In light of America's continuing financial arrears, the UN Association of the United States actually warned earlier in that year that by the end of the decade Washington could have forfeited its vote in the General Assembly, dropped out of several more UN agencies, and begun the organisation's effective dismantlement. The question of dispensability itself breaks down into two parts. First, is the UN's welfare work effective? Second, whether it is or not, could it not be better carried out in other ways, for example by regional groupings or by universal organisations outside the UN in which weighted voting, as already occurs in the IMF and the World Bank, might be introduced?

Of course, the network is so enormous and so varied that no sensible generalisations about either its effectiveness or alternative forms of provision can be made with any confidence. Each part must be considered separately. The reputation of some of the organisations such as the WHO, the

International Atomic Energy Agency (IAEA) and the Vienna-based drug agencies, is high, even in the United States, while that of others, such as UNESCO and the Office of UN Disaster Relief Coordinator (UNDRO) – created after the occurrence of severe natural disasters in Peru and East Pakistan in 1970 – is very low indeed. As to alternatives, the idea of regional groupings overlooks the point that considerable regional *devolution* within global organisations is not only possible but already a feature of many of the agencies, including the World Health Organisation, and also that for certain welfare functions universal cooperation is clearly indispensable. This is the case, for example, with those which require uniform practice for success, as in the eradication of disease (see Box 13.3), and with those in which unambiguous political neutrality is of exceptional value, as with the provision of relief to refugees. For its part, the argument for more non-UN universal organisations ignores the fact that most of the UN's agencies are to all intents and purposes autonomous anyway, and is now weaker because since the mid-1980s the bigger UN contributors have begun to win more influence over budgetary allocations within the network, as noted above.

Box 13.3 'Rapid reaction force' against disease

According to the World Health Organisation (WHO), there is a growing threat from infectious diseases as a result of overcrowded cities and the dramatic increase in international travel. The problem was highlighted by the outbreak of plague in India in 1994 and Ebola in the Kikwit region of Zaire in 1995. At least twenty-nine new diseases have appeared during the past twenty years. Alarmed by these trends, in 1995 the WHO announced that it was setting up a global surveillance network of laboratories equipped to detect rare disease-causing bacteria and viruses and provide early warning of epidemics. On receipt of such warnings, rapid reaction teams of medical experts from the WHO headquarters in Geneva and the US Centres for Disease Control will fly out to tackle the outbreaks at less than 24 hours' notice.

The UN welfare network, then, with all its obvious blemishes, might as well be accepted. If it were to collapse, many of the activities which it currently undertakes would suffer, even if pursued to some degree by other means. And if this happened the 'political' work of the UN might also come under threat. If the first of these things were to happen what little restraint there is on the violence of the state, provided by the idea of a common humanity, would also suffer and hope would die a little – and not only in the Third World.

Notes

1. I have borrowed the concept of 'network' from A. Judge's 'International organisation networks: a complementary perspective', in Taylor and Groom (eds), *International Organisation*. This is the best label here because, unlike the term 'system' which is usually preferred in the UN context, and also unlike the term 'confederation' with which it is only roughly analogous, 'network' suggests some kind of liaison between parts but little in the way of overall authority – precisely the character of ECOSOC's relationship with the UN agencies and their relationships one with another.
2. UNIDO became a specialised agency in January 1986.
3. *The Specialized Agencies and the United Nations*, p. 29.
4. Quoted in Luard, *The United Nations*, p. 141.
5. *The Specialized Agencies and the United Nations*, p. 49.

Further reading

Alston, P. (ed.), *The United Nations and Human Rights: A critical appraisal* (Oxford University Press: Oxford, 1992).
Baehr, P. and L. Gordenker, *The United Nations in the 1990s* (St Martin's Press: New York, 1992).
Beigbeder, Y., *Management Problems in United Nations Organizations: Reform or decline?* (Pinter: London, 1987).
Berridge, G. R., *Return to the UN: UN diplomacy in regional conflicts* (Macmillan: London, 1991), chs 2–4.
Buckley, W. F., Jr, *United Nations Journal* (Putnam: New York, 1974; Michael Joseph: London, 1975).
Feld, W. J., R. S. Jordan and L. Hurwitz, *International Organisations: A comparative approach* (Greenwood: Westport, CT, 1994).
Hill, M., *The United Nations System: Coordinating its economic and social work* (Cambridge University Press: Cambridge, London and New York, 1978).
Hoggart, R., *An Idea and Its Servants: UNESCO from within* (Chatto & Windus: London, and Oxford University Press: New York, 1978).
Imber, M., *The USA, ILO, UNESCO, and IAEA: Politicisation and withdrawal in the specialised agencies* (Macmillan: London, 1989).
Kent, R. C., *The Anatomy of Disaster: The international relief network in action* (Pinter: London, 1987).
Luard, E., *International Agencies: The emerging framework of interdependence* (Macmillan: London, and Oceana: Dobbs Ferry, NY, 1977).
Luard, E., *The United Nations: How it works and what it does*, 2nd edn, rev. by D. Heater (Macmillan: London, 1994).
McLaren, R. I., 'The UN system and its quixotic quest for coordination', *International Organization*, vol. 34, no. 1, 1980.
Ogata, S., P. Volcker and others, *Financing an Effective United Nations: A report of the independent advisory group on UN financing* (Ford Foundation: New York, 1993).
Pines, B. Y. (ed.), *A World Without A UN: What would happen if the UN shut down* (The Heritage Foundation: Washington, DC, 1984).
Riggs, R. E. and J. C. Plano, *The United Nations: International organisation and world politics*, 2nd edn (Wadsworth: Belmont, CA, 1994).
Roberts, A. and B. Kingsbury (eds), *United Nations, Divided World*, 2nd edn (The Clarendon Press: Oxford, 1993).

Strange, S., *States and Markets: An introduction to international political economy* (Pinter: London, 1988), ch. 10.

Taylor, P., *International Organisation in the Modern World: The regional and the global process* (Pinter: London, 1993).

Taylor, P. and A. J. R. Groom (eds), *International Organisation: A conceptual approach* (Pinter: London, and Nichols: New York, 1978).

Van der Haag, E. and J. P. Conrad, *The UN: In or out?* (Plenum Press: New York, 1987).

Wells, C., *The UN, UNESCO and the Politics of Knowledge* (Macmillan: London, 1987).

Williams, D., *The Specialized Agencies and the United Nations: The system in crisis* (Hurst: London, 1987).

Williamson, R. S., 'The United Nations: some parts work', *Orbis*, vol. 32, no. 2, 1988.

14

Conclusion

In the course of this book it has been emphasised that international politics (and economics) is still principally the field of action of states, and is dominated by a relatively small number of them. It has also been noted that, while the cold war between the Communist states and the 'Free World' may be over (with the added benefit which this has had for the ending or subduing of a number of dangerous regional conflicts), the economic black hole in which Russia remains makes the future of this deeply unstable 'superpower', and thus of international relations in general, quite unpredictable. Moreover, the ending of this commanding conflict should not blind us to the fact that conflicts with incendiary potential still divide other states, as well as dividing national, ethnic and religious groups within them – notably in Bosnia–Herzegovina. It is also depressing that, as some of the factors which exacerbate these conflicts subside, others arise to take their place. Thus Islamic fundamentalism in the Middle East appears to be losing a little of its steam (or shifting its focus to North Africa and Turkey) just as Hindu nationalism begins to assume dangerous proportions in India. Events in the Gulf from August 1990 until February 1991 also showed only too clearly that states are still inclined to resort to the drastic use of military force in order to prosecute their conflicts. Whether famine in Africa, the AIDS epidemic still sweeping most of the Third World, and the environmental problems threatening the whole globe will exacerbate conflicts such as these or unite people against common enemies is difficult to say.

It is true that the UN 'worked' in Kuwait, which inspired the speech writers of US President, George Bush, to claim that the 'New World Order' replacing the cold war had 'passed its first real test'. However, the circumstances which allowed the Security Council to bless military action and which allowed that action to be successful were extraordinarily fortuitous and are unlikely to be often repeated. Most subsequent tests for the 'New World Order' were failed, notably in Somalia, which almost wrecked altogether the fragile edifice of peacekeeping. In 1995, the year of its half-centenary, the UN was once more on the verge of bankruptcy. Moreover, it should not be forgotten that the governments standing shoulder to shoulder in the Gulf crisis were simultaneously at daggers drawn in the Uruguay Round of trade negotiations, and while this Round was eventually concluded successfully its last years coincided with an unprecedented burst of regionalism. Nor should there be any illusions that Coalition action in the Gulf war provided sufficient incentives to bring the international arms trade under control. Not surprisingly, NATO, described by George Bush as 'history's most successful alliance', has become the pillar of the 'New World Order', as events in Bosnia in 1995 amply demonstrated.

Nevertheless, the international system survives and it survives through its institutions. Central here are the balance of power and the civilised and civilising activity of diplomacy which it engenders; and what has been impressive since 1945 is the inventiveness which has gone into sustaining diplomatic activity in the most unpropitious circumstances. A myriad of international organisations (notably the UN itself) together with, among other things, bilateral and multilateral summits, special envoys, interests sections, and increasingly rapid and sophisticated modes of telecommunication, now supplement the resident ambassador to provide a thick network of contacts between governments. This alleviates the ignorance which nurtures fear, cushions the collision of elephantine political egos, and – more often than not – eventually produces agreements where none was initially thought possible. Where there is diplomacy there is hope.

Appendix 1
Notes on reference books

In a subject in which the raw material of study is as rapidly expanding as in international relations, reference works – especially ones which are updated annually – are indispensable for student and teacher alike. The usefulness of those now appearing on CD-ROM with key-word search facility is even greater (see the *CD-ROM Directory* and *CD-Roms in Print*). Below are some notes on a selection of the more important reference books which have a world focus, listed alphabetically. Many works with a regional focus will also be of interest to students of international relations but these have been largely excluded from this list.

Brassey's Battles: 3,500 years of conflict, campaigns and wars from A–Z, John Laffin (Brassey's: London and Washington, 1995). First published in 1986, the 1995 edition contains an 'update supplement' dealing with 'conflicts since 1986'. This is a dictionary (prefaced with a chronology) which gives succinct accounts of more than 7,000 battles (broadly defined) going back to the Greco-Persian wars of the fifth century BC. Contains useful maps. Relatively inexpensive paperback edition available. Persuade someone to buy it for your birthday.

CIA World Factbook (CIA: Washington, DC, annually). This is a bald summary of what the CIA takes to be the key features of each country in the world, primarily intended for the use of US government officials but on sale to the public. Its greatest usefulness is probably as a primary source for the study of how the CIA itself sees the outside world; among other things, it classifies each government by political type. It is now complemented by the *KGB World Factbook*, which, according to *CD-Roms in Print*, is 'compiled from open Soviet literature and translated into English by A. Petrochenkov'.

The Dictionary of World Politics: A reference guide to concepts, ideas and institutions, by G. Evans and J. Newnham, 2nd edn (Harvester Wheatsheaf: Hemel Hempstead, 1992). This very useful dictionary has a cross-referencing facility.

The Europa World Yearbook, 2 vols (Europa Publications: London, 1926–). Volume I of this highly regarded annual publication deals with international organisations and countries from Afghanistan to Jordan, while Volume 2 covers the remaining states. Each entry includes an introductory survey, a statistical survey and a directory. Europa also publishes seven excellent annual regional surveys: *Africa south of the Sahara*; *The Middle East and North Africa*; *The Far East and Australasia*; *Eastern Europe and the Commonwealth of Independent States*; *South America, Central America and the Caribbean*; *Western Europe*; and *The USA and Canada*.

Facts on File, the Index of World Events (Facts on File: New York, 1940–). This is a weekly loose-leaf publication which presents succinct summaries of US and world affairs; very well indexed; available on CD-ROM from 1980.

International Relations Dictionary, 4th edn, by J. C. Plano and R. Olton (ABC-Clio: Santa Barbara, CA, 1988). This is not strictly a dictionary at all because the entries are grouped into sections, and an index (with cross-references) is provided. There are twelve main sequences, with headings such as 'Arms control and disarmament', 'Diplomacy' and 'American foreign policy'. The 'dictionary' is useful and clearly laid out.

The International Who's Who (Europa: London, 1935–). This well-established reference work now contains nearly 20,000 biographies of personalities of international standing in politics, diplomacy, business and finance, and other fields. It has a section devoted to reigning royal families and an obituary listing. It is especially useful for personalities whose own countries do not publish a biographical register.

Keesing's Record of World Events [formerly *Keesing's Contemporary Archives*] (Longman: London, July 1931–). Now a monthly publication, like *Facts on File* this is a press digest. Each issue begins with a comprehensive summary of the previous month's world news, and is completed by a 'reference section' presenting political and economic data by country, international organisation and theme. It is well indexed and cross-referenced, and very easy to use. If you want to check a date or find out the main points of agreement at a recent international conference, for example, this is the place to go. Widely regarded as the most comprehensive and authoritative news digest; available on CD-ROM from 1983.

The Major International Treaties since 1945: A history and guide with texts, by J. A. S. Grenville and B. Wasserstein (Methuen: London and New York, 1987). This extremely authoritative and well-organised work is the sequel to an earlier version published by Grenville which covered the 1914–73 period. Prefaced by an introduction on 'international treaties', it then deals with its subject under the following main headings: the foundations of postwar diplomacy; the US treaty system; the Soviet treaty system; the German question; Western European integration; South and East Asia and the Pacific; Africa; the Middle East and Eastern Mediterranean; Latin America and the South Atlantic; *détente* and arms control.

The Military Balance (International Institute for Strategic Studies: London, 1959–). This clearly presented and authoritative source presents an annual, *quantitative* assessment of the military power and defence expenditure of countries throughout the world. This will tell you, for example, how many and what type of tanks the Israelis have and what comparable fighting vehicles they face. It also contains 'analytical essays' on such related subjects as arms control, and always has useful appendices.

The Oxford Companion to Politics of the World, editor in chief, Joel Krieger (Oxford University Press: Oxford and New York, 1993). Described by the editor as 'a comprehensive guide to international relations and national domestic politics throughout the world', this work contains 650 individually authored (and signed) essays by eminent scholars from more than forty countries.

Political Handbook of the World (CSA Publications for Center for Education and Social Research, State University of New York: Binghampton, NY; previously published by Harper & Row for the Council on Foreign Relations, 1 January 1927–). This is another A-to-Z directory of world governments and politics but since 1977 has also been prefaced by a survey of regional and world issues.

The Statesman's Year-Book, Brian Hunter (ed.) (Macmillan: London, 1864–). The popularity of this work is testified to by its longevity. It is an annual A to Z of the states of the world, plus (at the beginning) the more important international organisations. Unfortunately, though, it no longer lists the states with which each state has accredited diplomatic representatives. Look for these in the Europa regional surveys, noted above.

The Strategic Survey (International Institute for Strategic Studies: London, 1967–). This is an annual survey of military developments which focuses both on general themes, such as arms control and the superpower relationship, and on the regions – Europe, the Middle East, and so on. It concludes with useful chronologies of the previous year, by region and with regard to East–West arms control developments.

Survey of International Affairs 1920/23–1963 (Oxford University Press, for the Royal Institute of International Affairs: London, 1925–1973). This well-known multivolumed and faintly intimidating work is only regarded as a reference work by virtue of its scope and its detail. In fact, it is a work of historical scholarship.

The Times Survey of Foreign Ministries of the World, by Z. Steiner (ed.) (Times Book: London, and Meckler: Westport, CT, 1982). This is also a very scholarly work. Zara Steiner is a well-known Cambridge historian of the British Foreign Office, and each chapter has been authored by an expert from the country in question. Twenty-four foreign ministries are covered, including those of China (three contributions here), the United States and the Soviet Union. Organisation charts and bibliographies are also included. Now dated but still useful for historical origins.

UN Monthly Chronicle (UN, May 1964–). This is a periodical produced by the UN to give an up-to-date record of the activities of the organisation and its related agencies.

World Armaments and Disarmament: SIPRI Yearbook (Oxford University Press: Oxford and New York, 1970–). This very substantial annual is produced by the Stockholm International Peace Research Institute, which is financed mainly by the Swedish parliament. Contributions are individually authored. All sections are supplemented by a great wealth of tables, documents and other appendices and the work has the great merit of being indexed. It has always been especially useful on the international arms trade.

The World Financial System, R. Fraser, 2nd edn (Longman: London, 1992). This volume outlines the way in which the world financial system has evolved, and deals in detail with the aims, structures, methods and operations of the major international and regional organisations with particular responsibilities in this field. Fraser now has a *World Trade System: A Comprehensive Reference Guide* (Longman: London, 1991) as well.

The World in Conflict. War annual: contemporary warfare described and analysed, by J. Laffin (Pergamon-Brassey's: London, 1987–). *War annual 3* has chapters on thirty-two major military conflicts. This is a clearly written and well-presented reference work, with many useful maps.

World Politics since 1945, by P. Calvocoressi, 6th edn (Longman: London and New York, 1991). This is a crisp, comprehensive and authoritative textbook not only of postwar diplomatic history but also of important internal political developments in all of the world's main regions. Its author wrote the RIIA's *Survey of International Affairs* (cited above) from 1947 until 1953.

Yearbook of International Organizations, 3 volumes, edited by the Union of International Associations (published intermittently since 1908; latest edition, 1995–96, K. G. Sauer: Munich, New Providence, London and Paris). This is a work of awesome detail, covering a vast number of 'international organisations': aims, structure, members, key events, addresses, etc. It is extremely useful.

Year Book of the United Nations (UN: New York, 1947–). This annual publication provides a full account of the issues debated in the UN and who voted which way on what. Important Resolutions, for example of the Security Council, are reproduced in full. In effect, it is a summary of the full published minutes of the General Assembly and Security Council which are not held by many college and university libraries. The volumes used to take a long time to appear but by 1995 the series had reached 1992.

Index

ABMs 107, 112 n. 12
Abyssinia 157
Afghanistan 90, 104, 125, 196, 199
agents in place 85, 86
agricultural interests 36, 37, 40
aid *see* foreign aid
Allende, Salvador *see* Chile
alliances 72, 82, 171–7
   see also grand alliance, NATO,
      Warsaw Treaty Organization
Ames, Aldrich 85
anarchy, international 72
Angola 56, 104–5, 136
Angola/Namibia negotiations 184,
   193, 199
appeasement 167, 187
Arab-Israeli conflict 71, 73
   and economic sanctions 125
   and nationalist ideology 65–6
   peace agreements in 74 n.11
   and wars 97, 98, 99
   see map 67
   see also Camp David (1978);
      peacekeeping, non-UN;
      peacekeeping, UN; *and*
      under individual wars
arms control 86, 177–80
   see also SALT I, SALT II
ARMSCOR 127
Asia-Pacific Economic Cooperation
   forum 41
'assured destruction' 100, 105, 108
   see also nuclear weapons

balance of power
   and arms control 177–80
   definition and 'objectives' of 166–7
   and diplomacy 167–71 *passim*,
     187, 188
   and European states-system
     169–70
   and First World War 167
   and global states-system 170–1
   and ideology 169, 170, 171
   and international law 157

and nuclear weapons 167, 170–1
   precepts of 167–9
'balance of terror' 105
balancer, role of 168–9
Ball, George 190
balloons 133, 145 n. 1
Bandung Conference (1955) 69
Barber, James 129 n. 7
Battleship Potemkin 143–4
'Bay of Pigs' invasion 90
BBC 139
Beaufre, General André 96, 104,
   112 n. 2
Berlin Wall 141
bilateral diplomacy *see* resident
   ambassador
bipolarity 170–1
Bosnia 110–12, 198, 199, 207, 212
Bretton Woods regime 24, 26–35
Britain
   and European balance of power
     168, 169
   and indirect approach 101
   and Indonesia 49
   and interests sections 195
   and nuclear weapons 9, 82
   rank of 10–17 *passim*
   secret intelligence of 83, 84,
     85
   and South Africa 54, 66, 177
   and world economy 24, 26, 28, 34
   see also Falklands crisis (1982),
     propaganda
British Council 139
brute force, definition of 95
Bull, Hedley
   and common interests of states
     162 n. 4
   and great powers 11–12
   and institutions of states-system
     162 n. 13

Cairns Group 40
Cairo Radio 132, 140, 143, 145
Callières, François de 184, 185